Cloud Penetration Testing

Learn how to effectively pentest AWS, Azure, and
GCP applications

Kim Crawley

Cloud Penetration Testing

Group Product Manager: Pavan Ramchandani

Publishing Product Manager: Neha Sharma

Book Project Manager: Uma Devi

Senior Editor: Sayali Pingale

Technical Editor: Arjun Varma

Copy Editor: Safis Editing

Proofreader: Safis Editing

Indexer: Subalakshmi Govindhan

Production Designer: Joshua Misquitta

Marketing Coordinators: Marylou De Mello and Shruthi Shetty

First published: November 2023

Production reference: 2211024

Published by Packt Publishing Ltd.

Grosvenor House

11 St Paul's Square

Birmingham

B3 1RB, UK

ISBN 978-1-80324-848-6

www.packtpub.com

To my romantic partner, Jason "Schizoid" Smith. Thank you for your loving encouragement of me and for allowing my star to shine alongside yours, albeit in a different medium. Your loving support has helped my professional focus.

To the Smith and Kowatsch families, thank you for accepting me.

To my late father, Michael Crawley, thank you for nurturing my writing talent and interest in computers when my age was in the single digits.

To Ossington, Amelia, Indie, Insfjull, Luci, Annie Aurora, Etoile, Bronto, Leonard, and the rest of my animal family, thank you for the naps and cuddles.

To all of my social media followers on BlueSky, LinkedIn, and Mastodon, thank you for reading what I write!

Contributors

About the author

Kim Crawley is a thought leader in cybersecurity, from pentesting to defensive security, and from policy to cyber threat research. For nearly a decade, she has contributed her research and writing to the official corporate blogs of AT&T Cybersecurity, BlackBerry, Venafi, Sophos, CloudDefense, and many others. She has been an internal employee of both Hack The Box and IOActive, a leading cybersecurity research firm.

With the hacker mindset, she hacked her way into various information security subject matters. She co-authored one of the most popular guides to pentester careers on Amazon, *The Pentester Blueprint*, with Philip Wylie for Wiley Tech. She wrote an introductory guide to cybersecurity for business, *8 Steps to Better Security*, which was also published by Wiley Tech. She also wrote *Hacker Culture: A to Z* for O'Reilly Media.

To demonstrate her knowledge of cybersecurity operations, she passed her CISSP exam in 2023. In her spare time, she loves playing Japanese RPGs and engaging in social justice advocacy. She's always open to new writing, research, and security practitioner opportunities.

About the reviewers

Johnny Justice is an army veteran and cybersecurity professional, with over 23 years of experience. He is CEO and co-founder of ./Security, LLC, specializing in network penetration testing, digital forensics, and management. He spent 14 years conducting offensive cyberspace operations for the National Security Agency and US Cyber Command. He has developed cybersecurity courses for Mile2. He holds an MS in computer science education and a BS in information technology management. He is pursuing a Doctor of Science degree in cybersecurity and holds **Offensive Security Certified Professional (OSCP)** and **GIAC Exploit Researcher and Advanced Penetration Tester (GXPN)** qualifications. Apart from this book, he has reviewed the first edition of *Hacker Culture: A to Z*.

I would like to thank Kim for giving me the chance to review this book. A heartfelt thank you to the publication team and everyone at Packt Publishing for giving me this opportunity. Collaborating with you was a delightful experience.

To my wife, Mary, and our daughters, Diana and Gemma – your unwavering support means the world to me. The successes I achieve mirror the abundant love and backing you've always given me – I love you guys very much.

Shahrukh Iqbal Mirza, a seasoned cybersecurity professional with five years of experience, specializes in offensive security, particularly red teaming and penetration testing. Transitioning from petroleum engineering to information security for his master's degree, Shahrukh discovered his passion. He's an avid hacker, CTF player, and bug bounty hunter, and maintains a technical blog on Medium.

I'd like to thank my family, who understand the time and commitment it takes to research and test data that is constantly changing. Working and growing in this field would not be possible without the constant support and motivation from them. A huge shoutout to my wife for tolerating and standing by my side, despite my messed-up and workaholic schedule!

Zoe Braiterman is an IT security consultant, researcher and writer. She is passionate about open source; open knowledge sharing; education as a driver of innovation; and diversity, equity, and inclusion.

Table of Contents

3

Key Concepts for Pentesting Today's Cloud Networks   37

Part 2: Pentesting AWS

4

Security Features in AWS   61

5

Pentesting AWS Features through Serverless Applications and Tools   79

6

Pentesting Containerized Applications in AWS   105

Part 3: Pentesting Microsoft Azure

7

Security Features in Azure   123

Part 4: Pentesting GCP

10

11

Pentesting GCP Features through Serverless Applications and Tools   199

12

Pentesting Containerized Applications in GCP   223

13

Best Practices and Summary   241

Index   261

Other Books You May Enjoy   276

Preface

Congratulations, dear reader! Over the past 15 years or so, there has been tremendous growth in the use of cloud platforms. Amazon's AWS formally launched in 2006, and Microsoft Azure and **Google Cloud Platform** (**GCP**) soon followed in 2008. There are many cloud platforms out there, but AWS, Azure, and GCP are the most popular. AWS, Azure, and GCP empower companies, organizations, and enterprises to deploy networks that are more powerful and scalable than what was possible to do on their own premises. Many organizations even have more than one cloud platform in their networks.

Cloud networks are connected to the public internet, so naturally, they're susceptible to a wide range of cyberattacks. With the growing popularity of cloud platforms and companies realizing that they need to secure their cloud networks for the sake of business success, people with cloud penetration testing skills are greatly needed in the international job market. By learning how to simulate cyberattacks in cloud platforms for the sake of security testing, your abilities will be desired, no matter where in the world you are.

Pentesting and red teaming in cloud platforms is fundamentally different from doing so in a company's on-premises networks because Amazon, Microsoft, and Google own the infrastructure. There are rules and policies that you must abide by as a pentester beyond your organization's own rules and policies. This book will teach you how to perform penetration tests and red team engagements in a cloud-native way.

Who this book is for

This book is for both experienced pentesters and people who are just starting to learn pentesting. If you have experience with traditional pentesting in on-premises networks, this book will teach you how pentesting with AWS, Azure, and GCP is a bit different. If you're just starting to learn pentesting in general, this book is a great starting point because the cloud is the future of pentesting. Either way, you should be comfortable with computer networking and eager to refine your skills.

What this book covers

Chapter 1, *How Do Enterprises Utilize and Implement Cloud Networks?*, introduces AWS, Azure, and GCP, the difference between hybrid cloud, all-cloud, and multi-cloud networks, software-as-a-service, platform-as-a-service, and infrastructure-as-a-service, and the shared cybersecurity responsibilities between organizations and their cloud providers. Before you start pentesting in AWS, Azure, and GCP, it's important to understand why and how enterprises use those cloud platforms.

Chapter 2, How Are Cloud Networks Cyber Attacked?, examines how cloud networks are susceptible to a wide range of cyberattacks. This chapter explains the various types of cyber attacks, both external and internal, and attacks that impact the confidentiality, integrity, and availability of computer data, based on the CIA Triad cybersecurity model. You will test the security of cloud networks, based on simulating some of the actions of cyber threat actors.

Chapter 3, Key Concepts for Pentesting Today's Cloud Networks, covers the core concepts and procedures that are applicable to all cloud pentests. Before a pentest or red team engagement is conducted, security professionals must understand the state and scope of their pentest target. You should conduct a vulnerability assessment to find exposed services and integrations, and once a pentest is done, you need to share your findings effectively so that your client's security posture can be improved accordingly.

Chapter 4, Security Features in AWS, explores the plethora of features, applications, and tools that are specific to AWS and their implications for pentesters. This chapter also covers AWS's own security policies and security tools.

Chapter 5, Pentesting AWS Features through Serverless Applications and Tools, discusses the most relevant and effective security features and tools to conduct the most successful AWS pentest possible. There are a number of security controls, security features, and pentesting tools that are specific to AWS, both first-party and third-party.

Chapter 6, Pentesting Containerized Applications in AWS, dives into the specific technicalities of how Docker and Kubernetes are deployed and managed in AWS. Enterprises are increasingly deploying containerized applications within AWS to fully leverage the scalability of containerization for virtualization. You will then learn pentesting techniques that are unique to how those containerization platforms run in AWS.

Chapter 7, Security Features in Azure, explores the plethora of features, applications, and tools that are specific to Azure and their implications for pentesters. The chapter also covers Azure's own security policies and security tools.

Chapter 8, Pentesting Azure Features through Serverless Applications and Tools, examines the most relevant and effective security features and tools to conduct the most successful Azure pentest possible. There are a number of security controls, security features, and pentesting tools that are specific to Azure, both first-party and third-party.

Chapter 9, Pentesting Containerized Applications in Azure, covers the specific technicalities of how Docker and Kubernetes are deployed and managed in Azure. Enterprises are increasingly deploying containerized applications within Azure to fully leverage the scalability of containerization for virtualization. You'll also learn pentesting techniques that are unique to how those containerization platforms run in Azure.

Chapter 10, Security Features in GCP, dives into the plethora of features, applications, and tools that are specific to GCP and their implications for pentesters. This chapter also covers GCP's own security policies and security tools.

Chapter 11, Pentesting GCP Features through Serverless Applications and Tools, examines the most relevant and effective security features and tools to conduct the most successful GCP pentest possible. There are a number of security controls, security features, and pentesting tools that are specific to GCP, both first-party and third-party.

Chapter 12, Pentesting Containerized Applications in GCP, covers the specific technicalities of how Docker and Kubernetes are deployed and managed in GCP. Enterprises are increasingly deploying containerized applications within GCP to fully leverage the scalability of containerization for virtualization. You'll also learn pentesting techniques that are unique to how those containerization platforms run in GCP.

Chapter 13, Best Practices and Summary, reviews what you've learned after performing pentesting exercises in AWS, Azure, and GCP. This chapter also explains the work that you need to do before and after your pentests and red team engagements. Most importantly, you'll need to define a scope for your engagements with the organization that you work for that abides by AWS, Azure, and GCP's policies, sign legal documents that formalize your scope and responsibilities, and write a pentest report that will help the business leaders and defensive security team in your organization improve their network's cybersecurity.

To get the most out of this book

You'll need the following:

Software/hardware covered in the book	Operating system requirements
AWS web console at `aws.amazon.com`	Windows 7, 8, 10, or 11, macOS 11–14, or currently supported Linux distributions, with currently supported versions of the Safari, Edge, Chrome, Firefox, or Opera web browser
Microsoft Azure web console at `azure.microsoft.com`	Windows 7, 8, 10, or 11, macOS 11–14, or currently supported Linux distributions, with currently supported versions of the Safari, Edge, Chrome, Firefox, or Opera web browser
Google Cloud Platform web console at `console.cloud.google.com`	Windows 7, 8, 10, or 11, macOS 11–14, or currently supported Linux distributions, with currently supported versions of the Safari, Edge, Chrome, Firefox, or Opera web browser
Prowler	Supported in AWS, Azure, and GCP; the endpoint operating system is irrelevant
Pacu	Supported in AWS, the endpoint operating system is irrelevant
Cred Scanner	Supported in AWS, the endpoint operating system is irrelevant

CloudFrunt	Supported in AWS, the endpoint operating system is irrelevant
Redboto Python scripts	Supported in AWS, the endpoint operating system is irrelevant
Docker Desktop	Windows 7, 8, 10, or 11, macOS 11–14, or currently supported Linux distributions
ScoutSuite	Supported in AWS, Azure, and GCP; the endpoint operating system is irrelevant
MFASweep	Supported in Azure, the endpoint operating system is irrelevant
kube-hunter	Supported in all current versions of Kubernetes; the endpoint operating system is irrelevant
kdigger	Supported in all current versions of Kubernetes; the endpoint operating system is irrelevant
GCPBucketBrute	Supported in GCP, the endpoint operating system is irrelevant
GCP Scanner	Supported in GCP, the endpoint operating system is irrelevant

Code in Action

The *Code in Action* videos for this book can be viewed at `https://bit.ly/3rWmFnS`.

Disclaimer

The information within this book is intended to be used only in an ethical manner. Do not use any information from the book if you do not have written permission from the owner of the equipment. If you perform illegal actions, you are likely to be arrested and prosecuted to the full extent of the law. Packt Publishing does not take any responsibility if you misuse any of the information contained within the book. The information herein must only be used while testing environments with proper written authorizations from appropriate persons responsible.

Conventions used

There are a number of text conventions used throughout this book.

`Code in text`: Indicates code words in text, database table names, folder names, filenames, file extensions, pathnames, dummy URLs, user input, and Twitter handles. Here is an example: "Mount the downloaded `WebStorm-10*.dmg` disk image file as another disk in your system."

Any command-line input or output is written as follows:

```
pip install --upgrade pip
pip install prowler
```

Bold: Indicates a new term, an important word, or words that you see on screen. For instance, words in menus or dialog boxes appear in **bold**. Here is an example: "Select **System info** from the **Administration** panel."

> **Tips or important notes**
> Appear like this.

Get in touch

Feedback from our readers is always welcome.

General feedback: If you have questions about any aspect of this book, email us at `customercare@packtpub.com` and mention the book title in the subject of your message.

Errata: Although we have taken every care to ensure the accuracy of our content, mistakes do happen. If you have found a mistake in this book, we would be grateful if you would report this to us. Please visit `www.packtpub.com/support/errata` and fill in the form.

Piracy: If you come across any illegal copies of our works in any form on the internet, we would be grateful if you would provide us with the location address or website name. Please contact us at `copyright@packt.com` with a link to the material.

If you are interested in becoming an author: If there is a topic that you have expertise in and you are interested in either writing or contributing to a book, please visit authors.packtpub.com.

Share your thoughts

Once you've read *Cloud Penetration Testing*, we'd love to hear your thoughts! Scan the QR code below to go straight to the Amazon review page for this book and share your feedback.

https://packt.link/r/1803248483

Your review is important to us and the tech community and will help us make sure we're delivering excellent quality content.

Download a free PDF copy of this book

Thanks for purchasing this book!

Do you like to read on the go but are unable to carry your print books everywhere?

Is your eBook purchase not compatible with the device of your choice?

Don't worry, now with every Packt book you get a DRM-free PDF version of that book at no cost.

Read anywhere, any place, on any device. Search, copy, and paste code from your favorite technical books directly into your application.

The perks don't stop there, you can get exclusive access to discounts, newsletters, and great free content in your inbox daily

Follow these simple steps to get the benefits:

1. Scan the QR code or visit the link below

https://packt.link/free-ebook/9781803248486

2. Submit your proof of purchase
3. That's it! We'll send your free PDF and other benefits to your email directly

Part 1:
Today's Cloud Networks and Their Security Implications

Pentesters and red teams test the security of computer systems. In this book, the types of computer systems you will learn how to pentest are cloud applications and networks. Before you start testing something, you should understand what it is that you're testing in the first place! So, in this part, we will learn all about the different types of cloud services and applications, why organizations use them, and how they're configured and deployed. We will also learn about the basics of pentesting and red teams. This knowledge will set a foundation for everything else that you'll learn in this book.

This section has the following chapters:

- *Chapter 1, How Do Enterprises Utilize and Implement Cloud Networks?*

- *Chapter 2, How Are Cloud Networks Cyber Attacked?*

- *Chapter 3, Key Concepts for Pentesting Today's Cloud Networks*

1

How Do Enterprises Utilize and Implement Cloud Networks?

Welcome, readers! Whether you're already an experienced penetration tester or you're new to cybersecurity, penetration testing cloud networks requires specialized knowledge. One of the key differences between penetration testing cloud networks and penetration testing on-premises networks and computer systems is that the organization you're working for doesn't own everything in its computing environment. When you conduct red team engagements in cloud networks, both the organization you work for and its cloud provider (whether that's **Amazon Web Services** (**AWS**), Azure, or **Google Cloud Platform** (**GCP**)) have needs that must be respected. The good news is if you master the skill of pentesting cloud networks, you may have a lucrative career ahead of you. Organizations use the cloud now more than ever, and demand for cloud services continues to grow.

Penetration testers simulate cyber attacks within a network with permission of its owner, in order to find security vulnerabilities that an attacker can discover. The company that hires you to **penetration test** (**pentest**) will have likely already performed vulnerability assessments and audits on their network. A lot of security vulnerabilities can be found through assessments and auditing. Pentesting is a hands-on review for finding additional security vulnerabilities that may have been missed.

A red team is a group within an organization that performs targeted pentests on a regular basis. Your company's cybersecurity team may become aware of new cyber threats and **advanced persistent threats** (**APTs**) from the **security operations center** (**SOC**) or the broader cybersecurity community. The red team will be informed of particular emerging threats and be asked to simulate them. By doing that, the red team will discover vulnerabilities that the emerging attackers may exploit. Those discoveries are shared with the defensive security team, who will security harden their network accordingly before the threat strikes their organization. For instance, a new ransomware group may make news headlines. It's the red team's job to research how the new ransomware group operates. Then, the next step is for them to pretend to be that new ransomware group in their next red team engagement. The red team, the offensive security specialists, will probably be kept pretty busy year-round, because lots of new cyber attack groups and cyber threats emerge every year, every month, every week, and every day!

In this chapter, we'll cover the following main topics:

- Cloud networks today

- Hybrid cloud, all-cloud, and multi-cloud networks

- Why an organization would have a multi-cloud network

- The cloud migration process

- Security responsibilities in the cloud

- The difference between **Infrastructure-as-a-Service (IaaS)**, **Platform-as-a-Service (PaaS)**, and **Software-as-a-Service (SaaS)**

Let's get started!

Cloud networks today

To be able to effectively test your pentest target, you must first understand it. Cloud networks have been popular with the enterprise market ever since AWS took its current form in 2006. Microsoft Azure and GCP have been around since 2008. These three cloud platforms are the most frequently used by businesses and enterprises of all kinds, all around the world. Most enterprises use at least one cloud platform in their networks these days. Some enterprises even use multiple cloud platforms. So, what are cloud platforms, and why are they so popular? How do cloud platforms improve how companies do business over the internet?

In the 1990s, enterprises had to host their own data centers on their premises. Web hosting providers started to operate that decade, but they only offered web servers and email servers. That's good for an organization's website and email, but not for anything else. If companies needed to run their own, more complex applications and digital services, they needed to have their own server rooms and equipment.

Any network administrator with years of experience understands that enterprises can have rapidly changing computer networking needs. Bandwidth and data storage usage may double in a couple of months, and then halve in another couple of months. If their capacity needs quickly grow in a short period of time, lots of new server machines and networking infrastructure would have to be procured, and they would need a lot more physical space for them to occupy. If their capacity needs shrank quite a bit, a lot of expensive server machines, networking infrastructure, and physical space would have to go to waste. There are a lot of inconveniences, inefficiencies, and financial waste that are inevitable when a company deploys a large network on-premises.

The 21st century so far has brought useful advancements in computer networking technology. Tech giants such as **Amazon**, **Microsoft**, and **Google** have massive data centers all around the world. They began to utilize their massive computer networking infrastructure by offering it to third-party businesses and other entities. AWS launched in 2006, then Microsoft Azure and GCP followed in 2008. They made it easier and more frictionless than ever for businesses to deploy networks on *their* infrastructure.

Containerization is a way to implement operating system and hardware virtualization with load balancing to deploy applications through networks in a scalable and dynamic way that uses server machines more efficiently. When an operating system is virtualized, it runs like an application within another operating system with simulated hardware specifications. Load balancing distributes network traffic across multiple server machines, and it prevents server overload by improving application availability and responsiveness. Each container has operating system components and is part of an application. Containers run within a containerization orchestration platform and a host operating system or direct hypervisor. Because containers are self-sufficient virtualized entities, an application might use a large number of them at any given time, and any individual container might only live for a few days. Containers can be quickly launched and terminated according to what a cloud application needs as it operates continuously.

Docker emerged in 2013, and Kubernetes started to become popular in 2015. There are other containerization orchestration platforms, but Docker and Kubernetes are the ones you'll see in cloud networks the most often. Those are the containerization orchestration platforms that are best supported by AWS, Azure, and GCP. As containerization became more common, it helped to encourage more enterprises to implement cloud platforms into their networks.

The DevOps approach has transformed the manner in which organizations roll out their applications. It's a predominant method for developing applications intended for cloud deployments. By merging the development and operations (IT) teams, DevOps fosters continuous collaboration. The teams patch applications and deploy new features in small pieces, and very frequently. Instead of releasing version 1.5 of an application one year and version 1.6 the next, applications can be updated several times per month. DevOps complements agile application development, so applications are deployed more efficiently and responsively. It's possible to use the DevOps methodology without the cloud, but the cloud makes it much more feasible. You will likely be pentesting DevOps applications at least at some point as a cloud pentester. And because of how frequently DevOps applications change, that'll keep you very busy. DevSecOps is when security is implemented into DevOps, and you'll quite possibly be a part of the Sec component of the process.

Ever since AWS, Azure, and GCP launched, they've constantly added new services and new features. If each cloud platform's service list were a restaurant menu, it'd have a handful of dishes in 2009 and multiple pages of *entrées* by 2023. All of these new services and features have empowered organizations to do a greater variety of things with cloud platforms.

Amazon, Microsoft, and Google are responsible for maintaining their infrastructure and **application programming interfaces (APIs)** for their services. They're responsible for running their data centers and managing the massive facilities all around the world in which they operate. That's a lot of burden that enterprises no longer have to deal with when they use a cloud platform.

If an organization needs to double its data storage capacity and network bandwidth all of a sudden, all it has to do is ask Amazon, Microsoft, or Google, pay their fees, and it'll have it almost immediately. If an organization's networking needs are reduced, decreasing its data storage and bandwidth is just as easy. That's what we call scalability. Cloud services dynamically and responsively scale according to an organization's computing needs at any given time.

Combine AWS, Azure, and GCP's massive infrastructure with containerization, and cloud networks can grow and evolve very quickly without an enterprise having to deal with the hassles of running their own data centers. Applications can grow, shrink, and rapidly change. The organization deploying an application has full control, while the cloud platform provider deals with all of the physical tedium.

Services such as Netflix, Steam, and Dropbox are responsive and powerful today because they leverage the potential of the cloud. And of course, lots of much smaller organizations in a wide variety of industries also use cloud platforms. The same AWS data center could have a famous video streaming service and a tax and accounting small business operating in the same facility, perhaps even on some of the same physical server machines.

So, that's why cloud platforms are so popular these days. Businesses are now deeply committed to using cloud platforms, so you'll be expected to understand them very well as a pentester on a red team. Cloud platforms are an essential business tool in the 21st century. Unfortunately, because cloud platforms operate through the internet, they're subject to a wide variety of terrible cyber threats. Organizations need your talent and skill to think like a cyber attacker. Find the vulnerabilities an attacker will exploit so that your blue team (defensive security specialists) can security harden your cloud networks effectively.

As a red teamer, cyber threats will always keep you on your toes. You'll always be busy. Heed the words of famous computer scientist and cybersecurity expert Bruce Schneier:

> *"Security is a process, not a product. Products provide some protection, but the only way to effectively do business in an insecure world is to put processes in place that recognize the inherent insecurity in the products."*

In the next section, we'll examine the different kinds of cloud networks. How you pentest your organization's cloud network will vary according to what sort of cloud network it is.

Hybrid cloud, all-cloud, and multi-cloud networks

Cloud networks can take a few different forms. Some organizations maintain their client machines (such as PCs and mobile devices) on their own premises and then run their backend servers completely on one particular cloud platform. It's an all-cloud network on one platform such as AWS, Azure, or GCP.

Some organizations run some server machines on their own premises and run the rest of their network on one or multiple cloud platforms. That's a hybrid cloud network—partly on-premises, partly in the cloud.

Some organizations deploy their networks through more than one cloud platform. They may have some parts of their network running on AWS and other parts on Azure, for example. That's a multi-cloud network.

Let's examine how these different ways to operate cloud networks work, and why organizations may choose one way over another.

All-cloud networks

An all-cloud network is when an enterprise only has client devices on its premises, and the rest of its network is all on cloud services. Call it entirely cloud, cloud-first, cloud-only, or something else. Whether termed as fully cloud-based, cloud-first, cloud-only, or any other name, this shift away from on-premises backend systems is an emerging industry trend. For the sake of clarity, the backend functions of a network are everything that has to run as a server. That includes databases, web servers, email servers, authentication system servers, and any computer networking function that would typically run in a data center rather than inside someone's office. Those sorts of needs can theoretically all be run from cloud services, whereas people's phones, tablets, and PCs (client devices) serve as frontend devices when they're connected to the network. If I had to physically enter a data center in order to check my email on my phone, I'd find that to be very inconvenient!

Research firm Gartner refers to a cloud-first strategy where enterprises prioritize using cloud platforms. A cloud-first strategy doesn't necessarily mean that an enterprise has an all-cloud network. An enterprise with a cloud-first strategy may have a lot of legacy technology, or services that otherwise predate the popularization of cloud services from the mid-2000s onward. However, any new function or service is deployed on the cloud, and older services and applications are migrated to the cloud as much as possible.

In November 2021, Gartner said that 85% of organizations will embrace a cloud-first principle by 2025. It also believes that 95% of new digital workloads will be deployed on cloud-native platforms (`https://www.gartner.com/en/newsroom/press-releases/2021-11-10-gartner-says-cloud-will-be-the-centerpiece-of-new-digital-experiences`). So, if you're learning to pentest cloud networks, you're getting into a lucrative line of work!

Hybrid cloud networks

A hybrid cloud network is partly on the cloud and partly on-premises. At least some actual backend server operations must be on the enterprise's premises and connected to a cloud network in order for it to be a hybrid cloud network. If an organization has an on-premises network and a cloud network that aren't connected in any way, the organization has two separate networks, not one hybrid network.

Why would an organization choose to have a hybrid cloud network? There can be multiple reasons.

They may have a legacy on-premises network, but they've needed to integrate some SaaS or PaaS components that are exclusive to AWS, Azure, or GCP. Maybe they need GCP for Looker business data analytics, Azure for Azure DevOps to support Microsoft ecosystem APIs, or AWS for AWS Lambda hassle-free code execution. All three cloud platforms have services that are unique to their ecosystems, and they may serve a specific business need.

Some other organizations believe that maintaining a hybrid cloud network is effective redundancy. Uptime is the most important metric when it comes to operating any sort of network. Redundancy is an effective way to reduce operational downtime. For instance, if a server has a technical problem that puts it out of service, an identical server elsewhere can ensure that its functions keep running. An enterprise may find that having some network infrastructure that it physically controls is good for redundancy. Of course, it cannot physically control cloud servers; it can only physically control the servers that are on its premises. The same applies to networking infrastructure. Cloud providers give organizations a lot of control over the parts of their networks that run on cloud infrastructure, but they cannot allow an organization's network administrators to walk into one of their cloud data centers and physically turn a server machine off and on again. Other reasons why an organization may prefer to maintain a hybrid network are **disaster recovery** (**DR**) or regulatory compliance. There may be details in its DR procedures or in the regulations it needs to comply with that require it to have physical access to some of its network.

Some organizations may have **service-level agreements** (**SLAs**) with vendors that predate their usage of cloud services. An SLA is a legal agreement between a vendor and a client that outlines the services the client expects to receive, the services the vendor agrees to deliver, and the metrics they'll use to measure performance. A vendor can be anything from a cloud platform (such as AWS) or any other sort of IT service (such as Slack or Cloudflare). Old SLAs can sometimes make cloud migration tricky. So, some enterprises may wait until their older contracts expire before going all-cloud. In the meantime, they may find a compromise where they maintain their on-premises infrastructure for a period of time while they implement cloud services into their network.

If an organization has a hybrid cloud, it'll likely keep its more sensitive or critical data operations on-premises. Sensitive data and systems can include things such as **public key infrastructure** (**PKI**), critical databases, and highly sensitive financial or medical data that organizations must keep on their premises in order to be regulatory compliant.

Multi-cloud networks

In a multi-cloud network, more than one cloud provider is implemented into an enterprise's network. For example, it could have AWS and GCP, or a combination of AWS and Azure, or AWS, Azure, and GCP combined. A multi-cloud network may also be a hybrid cloud network if the enterprise also has an on-premises component. Either way, the parts of their network on different cloud platforms have to be connected in some way. Otherwise, they have multiple networks. When you conduct red team engagements for your organization, the reasons for their cloud strategy matter. It'll help you understand how it uses its cloud network, which will help you understand how cyber threats may impact the organization. Those are the sort of cyber threats you should be simulating in your pentesting. So, let's examine why many organizations choose to have multi-cloud networks.

Why an organization would have a multi-cloud network

As I've mentioned, AWS, Azure, and GCP each have some services that are unique to each of them. A business may find that the combination of PaaS and SaaS applications that best serve its operational needs are all on different cloud platforms. An enterprise could have Azure OpenAI Service for automated customer service, Amazon GameLift to host its online video game servers, and a payment gateway on GCP to process customer credit card transactions.

Michael Warrilow, VP Analyst at Gartner, says this:

> *"Most organizations adopt a multi-cloud strategy out of a desire to avoid vendor lock-in or to take advantage of best-of-breed solutions. We expect that most large organizations will continue to willfully pursue this approach."*

According to a survey Gartner conducted in 2019, 81% of their respondents are working with two or more providers. That was at least a few years ago. Gartner foretasted an increase in worldwide end-user spending on public cloud services to grow from $490.3 billion in 2022 to $591.8 billion in 2023. Maybe multi-cloud networks are an even larger market segment now. This is important to acknowledge because you may be pentesting some of these services.

You should also understand the difference between public clouds and private clouds.

Up until this point, all of my mentions of the cloud have referred to public clouds. Using AWS, Azure, and GCP usually refers to public cloud usage. A public cloud is a cloud network that shares physical servers and other infrastructure with other users, customers, and clientele.

A lot of consumer internet services are driven by public clouds. Listening to Spotify, watching YouTube, uploading personal files to Dropbox, conducting meetings over Zoom, buying games from Steam, and engaging in multiplayer gameplay—these are all common ways that consumers use public cloud-driven applications. And they might not even know it! Businesses often use public cloud services in similar ways—collaborating on documents with Google Docs, conversations over Slack, and meetings through Microsoft Teams.

The majority of business usage of AWS, Azure, and GCP is also public cloud. Private cloud services on third-party infrastructure (AWS, Azure, GCP) are often more expensive. If a company signs up for services such as AWS CodeArtifact for package management, or Computer Vision on Azure for image and video analysis, those are public cloud services. Any service with a free trial period is probably a public cloud service.

Private cloud services can take two forms. They can be on a company's own premises. Some enterprises have replicated the cloud computing model on their own infrastructure. Alternatively, AWS, Azure, and GCP do offer some private cloud services. For example, AWS offers **Amazon Virtual Private Cloud (Amazon VPC)**.

There are advantages and use cases for both public cloud and private cloud services.

Public cloud services are often a great choice for enterprises because they don't require capital expenditures; their accountants can budget it as an operational expenditure. From the business end, they're not paying for products; they're paying for services. There can be taxation and legal benefits to making a service an operational expenditure rather than a capital expenditure. Public cloud services are usually more scalable because there are no dedicated physical or virtual server machines involved. Enterprises can efficiently use as much or as little space as they need at any given time as long as they're willing to pay the service fees. Public cloud services also involve less overhead for a business because a third party is responsible for maintaining the infrastructure.

One of the main reasons why an organization may require private cloud services is cybersecurity. As with having any other sort of on-premises component in other types of hybrid cloud networks, regulatory compliance may mandate private instead of public cloud usage. Because an enterprise has exclusive use of a private cloud, it can maintain more control and implement stricter security measures. The regulations it may need to comply with are even more likely to apply to sensitive financial or medical data. For instance, using a private cloud rather than a public cloud may be necessary for the **Health Insurance Portability and Accountability Act** (**HIPAA**) (a set of medical data regulations in the United States), or Sarbanes–Oxley (a set of financial data regulations in the United States) compliance in some situations. Also, as with non-cloud on-premises network usage, an organization may choose to deploy the cloud computing model on its own infrastructure for its DR needs.

A hybrid cloud network may have a non-cloud on-premises component, a cloud on-premises component, or a private cloud on a third-party infrastructure component. If a private cloud is on third-party infrastructure through AWS, Azure, or GCP, it'll need to connect to the client machines on an enterprise's premises through private networking—often through some sort of **virtual private network** (**VPN**).

The organization you work for may be in the cloud migration process. How your organization migrates to the cloud will impact its security posture! So, we need to better understand cloud migration and how complex it can be.

The cloud migration process

Cloud migration is when an organization moves its data and services from its on-premises infrastructure to a cloud provider. With the rapid growth of the cloud market over the past 15 or 20 years, a large number of enterprises have engaged in the cloud migration process. But cloud migration isn't simple, and it can be done incorrectly or ineffectively.

All enterprises must plan carefully in order to migrate to the cloud effectively. Depending on the situation and their needs, they may prefer to migrate to the cloud in stages over the course of months or years rather than do it all at once.

When planning a cloud migration strategy, organizations should understand the problems that can occur with cloud migration so that they can be avoided.

An enterprise's services may experience downtime during the cloud migration process. Depending on how it migrates to the cloud, some of its servers may have to go completely offline for a period of time. The enterprise's customers may be very unhappy if the services they receive are interrupted, especially if they spend a lot of money on them. In the cloud migration process, an enterprise's supply chain must be considered as well as its customer base. An enterprise may have to either plan and prepare for the consequences of downtime, or carefully fine-tune its cloud migration strategy so that there's no downtime at all.

Interoperability may be a problem. The enterprise's applications run on its own infrastructure and may not be fully compatible with its cloud service without some tweaks or adjustments. Interoperability is less likely to be a problem if the cloud service it's migrating to is IaaS. But some applications require implementation with PaaS or SaaS. Interoperability issues must be carefully accounted for when designing a cloud migration strategy.

Crucial data could be lost in the cloud migration process. It could become subject to a data breach or become unavailable. Privileged access management and encryption are security measures that can be used in the cloud migration process to avoid that problem. It's also important to completely inventory data, applications, and workloads that are being migrated to the cloud. You can't secure what you can't see!

Employees who are used to managing data and workloads on-premises may not be familiar with how the details of their tasks may change once they are migrated to the cloud. An enterprise may need to assign new roles in the organization according to the specifics of its cloud infrastructure and implementation. Employees also need training on all of the applicable new technologies they'll be working with during and after cloud migration.

So, those are some of the more common problems that can occur during the cloud migration process. Those problems are avoidable with careful preparation and planning. Enterprises migrate to the cloud for many good reasons. Let's examine why.

Cloud networks offer enterprises operational agility. They make it more feasible for employees to work from home and work while they're traveling. The COVID pandemic has sparked ongoing effects. Scientific research from various entities around the world has shown that many millions of people have left the workforce worldwide due to early death and long-term disability from long COVID. Employees have found better safety and productivity by working from home instead of having to work on-site. Smart employers want to keep their workers healthy and productive and understand the benefits of protecting them from airborne disease. Facilitating working from home with cloud migration is an effective strategy.

The major cloud platforms have security controls that, if used properly, can make remote access to corporate networks more secure from cyber attacks. Cloud adoption and supporting remote work is the 21st-century way of doing business, and companies that don't understand that are losing crucial talent.

Cloud migration can help reduce capital expenditures and related burdens. Companies don't have to pay for additional real estate to provide spaces to run their own massive data centers. Amazon, Google, and Microsoft have many of the largest data centers on Earth, on all populated continents. From India to Japan, from the United States to Indonesia, from France to South Africa, many people and employers work within 1,000 kilometers of an AWS, GCP, or Azure data center. But even employers who are 5,000 kilometers from their nearest cloud platform data center still enjoy fast data transfer and minimal latency. Plus, all three cloud providers add new data centers to more parts of the globe each and every year. For many companies, replacing their own on-premises data centers with the flexibility and agility of operating in the cloud is an obvious choice. The reduction in capital expenditures also measurably improves their bottom line.

Even though some companies want to keep some of their network on their premises to facilitate DR (because they'll have physical access to some of their infrastructure), other companies cite DR as a reason to migrate to the cloud. This shows how complex and nuanced many of these practicalities of operating enterprise networks can be in the real world. AWS, Azure, and GCP all have DR tools and advise companies on how to use them effectively. The massive capacity of their data centers makes it easier and more affordable for companies to maintain backups of petabytes' and exabytes' worth of data. The cloud platforms also offer useful tools for organizations to periodically test the viability of their backups, and also to store different types of snapshots. If an organization keeps none of its backend on its premises, its data can be kept safer if its premises are hit by a flood, fire, or earthquake. Amazon, Google, and Microsoft also build redundancy and resiliency into their own networks. They have systems in place for operation if a disaster strikes one of their international data centers. Plus, their physical security is hardened beyond what most organizations can afford to do themselves for their own premises.

So, let's look at the cloud migration process. It's a little bit different for each organization that does it because the nature of their data assets and business operations is unique. But here's where there's usually some commonality.

IBM recommends the following steps for every organization's cloud migration checklist:

1. First, organizations should inventory their workloads. A workload is any database, application, containerization system, or service that operates in their network. Determine each workload's size, complexity, and whether or not it's in production.

2. Research each cloud platform and its applications and services carefully. AWS, Azure, and GCP each offer hundreds of unique services. An organization may need different services on different platforms. The most suitable service should be selected for each workload, and that may result in a need for a multi-cloud network.

3. With services and cloud providers selected, the next step is to conduct a cost assessment.

4. Next, a team should be assigned to execute the migration. There should be people with advanced computer networking and network security skills on that team. The goals of migration should be communicated to the team.

5. Determine how much of the migration will be handled internally, and how much by the cloud provider. All three major cloud providers offer cloud migration services, and organizations should verify what they entail.

6. Prioritize which workloads should be migrated first. There will likely be a period when workloads are mirrored on the on-premises network so that the migration process incurs minimal network downtime.

7. A plan should be prepared that schedules the migration process and outlines the roadmap. The full migration process could take months or a couple of years according to each company's specific needs and realities.

8. Determine whether there are already cloud services in the enterprise network, and whether or not they should be substituted with other cloud services or augmented into larger cloud workloads. For instance, why should a company keep using Dropbox when their Azure services include Microsoft Teams support or their GCP services include Google Drive integration?

9. Company stakeholders should be informed of what to expect during and after the cloud migration process. The company's entire supply chain should be included if this impacts them in any way!

10. **Key performance indicators** (**KPIs**) should be established for the cloud migration process—for example, "*50% of our database traffic should occur in our Amazon EC2 instances.*"

11. Progress should be verified and accessed with the cloud migration team periodically. Finally, during and after the process—test, review, and make adjustments when needed.

As a cloud pentester, the few months after the cloud migration process has finished would be an excellent time for a pentest. The common wisdom in our industry is that pentests should be conducted when major changes are made to networks, as change can create new security vulnerabilities. That's not the only time that pentests and red team engagements should be conducted, but it's certainly a time when conducting a pentest is crucial.

Understanding security responsibilities in the cloud will directly affect your everyday work as a cloud pentester! You must understand what you're allowed to do, what you're forbidden to do, and why. Let's examine the security responsibilities and the shared responsibility model.

Security responsibilities in the cloud

As a cloud pentester, it's important for you to understand how the shared responsibility model works in the cloud. The two entities involved are the organization that's using cloud services, and the cloud provider. When you conduct red team engagements, the organization is the entity you report to, whether you're an employee or a third-party contractor.

Overall, the organization and the cloud provider have shared security responsibilities. This is often called the shared responsibility model. However, cloud security controls and responsibilities are divided between the two entities.

It's important for you to understand what the cloud provider is responsible for and what the organization you're working for is responsible for. At the beginning of each pentest or red team engagement, you will sign a contract that outlines the scope of the pentests and what you're allowed and not allowed to do. You absolutely must abide by the contract and only pentest within your assigned scope. When you pentest a cloud network, you're not just simulating cyber attacks in your employer's environment. You're also simulating cyber attacks within AWS, Azure, or GCP's infrastructure. The cloud providers have their own rules for what you're allowed and not allowed to do. If you've pentested on-premises networks before, you may find that your scope and permissions are more limited when pentesting a cloud environment.

You must make absolutely certain that you understand each cloud provider's penetration testing policies. You should definitely read the contracts you sign with your employer very carefully, but you should also do your own research to verify what each cloud platform allows you to do. It's possible that the organization you're working for might ask you to perform pentests in a way that the cloud provider's policies forbid. In these situations, abiding by the cloud provider's policies is the top priority. Explain to your employer when the pentests they ask for violate the cloud provider's policies. Then, you and the organization you work for can modify your pentesting plans so that they're compliant with the cloud provider's policies.

On all three major platforms—AWS, Azure, and GCP—the platform is responsible for the security "*of the cloud*," while your organization is responsible for security "*in the cloud*."

The cloud platforms are always responsible for the security of their physical infrastructure and facilities. For instance, if a malicious attacker is able to enter a data center while pretending to be their employee and steals a bunch of data storage devices, the cloud provider is completely liable for that. How could your organization possibly be responsible for that attack? No one in your organization physically visits the cloud provider's data centers in the first place.

Your organization is always responsible for the security of the software your organization develops and maintains. Your organization is also responsible for the security of any software that the cloud provider doesn't give you. For instance, if you use a cloud service where AWS, Azure, or GCP provide you with their own **virtual machines** (**VMs**), then the security of the operating systems in those VMs is the cloud provider's responsibility. But if your organization installs its own VMs within the cloud provider's infrastructure, then the security of those VMs belongs completely to your organization. If I don't have root or administrator access to the host, I cannot be responsible for keeping the VM up to date; that would be on the cloud provider. If the cloud provider gave me a VM and root or administrator access, I would be responsible for keeping it up to date. There are cloud-specific deployments of VMs that are fully supported to update by the cloud provider, but that's not always the case. If your organization uses the cloud platform's APIs, the applications that your organization uses are its responsibility, but the cloud platform's software and services that the APIs connect to are the cloud platform's responsibility.

Generally speaking, the division of the shared responsibility model correlates with whether the service your organization is using is IaaS, PaaS, or SaaS. If AWS, Azure, or GCP are offering your organization a SaaS, the cloud provider has most of the responsibility, and what you're allowed to do as a pentester is the most limited. If AWS, Azure, or GCP are offering your organization an IaaS, your organization has most of the responsibility and you'll be allowed to do a lot more when you simulate cyber attacks as a pentester. And PaaS is somewhere in the middle.

According to AWS's shared responsibility model, your organization is responsible for the security of customer data, your organization's own platforms, applications, and **identity and access management (IAM)** systems, your organization's own operating systems, network and firewall configurations, client-side data, encryption, data integrity authentication, server-side encryption, and networking traffic protection. AWS is responsible for its compute, storage, database, and networking software and all of its hardware and global infrastructure.

According to Azure's shared responsibility model, your organization is always responsible for its information and data, its PC and mobile devices, and its accounts and identities. Azure is always responsible for its physical hosts, physical network, and physical data center. Depending on whether your Azure service is SaaS, PaaS, or IaaS, responsibilities for identity and directory infrastructure, applications, network controls, and operating systems can vary.

According to GCP's shared responsibility model, your organization is always responsible for its content and access policies. That applies to SaaS, PaaS, and IaaS services alike. If your GCP service is PaaS, your organization is also responsible for usage, deployment, and web application security. If your GCP service is IaaS, your organization has all of the responsibilities of SaaS and PaaS, and your organization is also responsible for identity, operations, access and authentication, network security, guest operating systems, data, and content. GCP is always responsible for audit logging, its own network, storage and encryption, hardened kernels and IPC, the booting process, and its own hardware.

Let's briefly summarize each cloud provider's pentesting policies. Links to their pentesting policies on the web will also be provided in the *Further reading* section of *Chapter 13, Best Practices and Summary*. Be sure to verify their policies directly from their website in case their policies change.

AWS

AWS permits pentesting as long as you abide by its policies. Neither you nor the organization you're working for need to contact AWS about your pentest. As long as you abide by AWS's policies, you can conduct pentests and red team engagements as needed.

These are the AWS services you're *permitted* to pentest (provided you abide by AWS's policies) (https://aws.amazon.com/security/penetration-testing/):

- Amazon EC2 instances, WAF, NAT Gateways, and Elastic Load Balancers

- Amazon RDS

- Amazon CloudFront

- Amazon Aurora

- Amazon API Gateways

- AWS AppSync

- AWS Lambda and Lambda Edge functions

- Amazon Lightsail resources

- Amazon Elastic Beanstalk environments

- Amazon Elastic Container Service

- AWS Fargate

- Amazon Elasticsearch

- Amazon FSx

- Amazon Transit Gateway

- S3-hosted applications (but S3 buckets are strictly prohibited)

These are the pentest activities you and your organization are *forbidden* to conduct:

- DNS zone walking via Amazon Route 53 Hosted Zones

- DNS hijacking via Route 53

- DNS Pharming via Route 53

- **Denial of Service (DoS)**, **Distributed Denial of Service (DDoS)**, Simulated DoS, Simulated DDoS (these are subject to the *DDoS Simulation Testing* policy)

- Port flooding

- Protocol flooding

- Request flooding (login request flooding, API request flooding)

If you're pentesting as part of a red team, you're conducting adversarial security simulations. If you plan to conduct an adversarial security simulation within AWS, you must submit a Simulated Events form for AWS to decide whether or not to grant you and your organization permission. The Simulated Events form can be found within your AWS console. Please search for it there.

Network stress testing entails a performance test that sends a large volume of legitimate traffic in order to test how well your AWS services will function under those conditions. Amazon EC2 has a specific network stress test policy for those situations. You'll find a link to it in the *Further reading* section of *Chapter 13, Best Practices and Summary*.

DDoS attacks are when a cyber threat actor deliberately and maliciously overwhelms a network target with traffic in order to force it to go out of service. A DDoS attack simulation may be a part of your red team engagement. AWS has a specific DDoS attack simulation policy (`https://aws.amazon.com/security/ddos-simulation-testing/`).

Simulated phishing (social engineering attacks that try to obtain sensitive information from human users) and malware testing may also be parts of your red team engagement. In those situations, you must submit a Simulated Events form for AWS to decide whether or not to grant you and your organization permission.

Azure

Microsoft Cloud (including but not limited to Azure) permits pentesting as long as you abide by its policies. Neither you nor the organization you're working for needs to contact Microsoft about your pentest, as long as you abide by Microsoft Cloud's policies, conduct pentests, and red team engagements as needed. Microsoft Cloud includes Azure Active Directory (which is being renamed Microsoft Entra ID), Microsoft Intune, Microsoft Azure, Microsoft Dynamics 365, Microsoft Power Platform, Microsoft Account, Office 365, and Azure DevOps.

Microsoft Cloud *forbids* the following activities in pentests and red team engagements:

- Scanning or testing assets belonging to any other Microsoft Cloud customers.
- Gaining access to any data that is not completely of your organization.
- All DoS testing (which includes DDoS attack simulations).
- Conducting network-intensive fuzzing against any asset except your organization's own Azure VMs.
- Automated testing of services that generate significant amounts of traffic. (What's a significant amount of traffic isn't defined in Microsoft Cloud's *Rules of Engagement*. Use your judgment.)
- Deliberately accessing other customers' data. Customers means other organizations that use Microsoft Cloud services.
- Going beyond **proof of concept** (**PoC**) reproduction steps for infrastructure execution issues.
- Violating their policies in any way.
- Attempting phishing or other social engineering attacks against Microsoft employees.

Microsoft Cloud *encourages* the following activities:

- Creating a small number of test accounts or trial tenants for demonstrating cross-account or cross-tenant data access. But don't access accounts belonging to Microsoft Cloud's other customers.
- Fuzz, port scan, and use vulnerability assessment tools against your organization's own Azure VMs.
- Load test your organization's applications by generating traffic that is expected to be seen during the normal course of business, including surge capacity.
- Testing security monitoring and detections (such as from anomalous security logs).
- Try to break out of shared service containers (that is, Azure websites or Azure Functions). But if you're successful, you must both immediately report it to Microsoft and don't dig any deeper. Never access another Microsoft Cloud customer's data.

- Apply conditional access or **mobile application management** (**MAM**) policies within Microsoft Intune to test the enforcement of the restriction accordingly.

GCP

GCP permits pentesting as long as you abide by its policies. Neither you nor the organization you're working for need to contact GCP about your pentest. As long as you abide by GCP's policies, you can conduct pentests and red team engagements as needed. The policies you must refer to are the *Google Cloud Platform Acceptable Use Policy* and the *Google Cloud Platform Terms of Service*. You'll find links to them in the *Further reading* section of *Chapter 13, Best Practices and Summary*.

According to the *Acceptable Use Policy*, you and your organization are *forbidden* to do the following:

- Distribute malware of any kind, corrupted files, hoaxes, or other items of a destructive or deceptive nature

- Acquire unauthorized access to, disrupt, or impair the use of any Google services or the equipment used to provide the services, and any of GCP's other customers or resellers

- Disable, interfere with, or circumvent any aspect of Google's software, services, or Google's equipment

Each cloud provider offers a wide range of products and services. Whether a service is IaaS, PaaS, or SaaS, these categorizations affect how your organization uses them and what you may or may not do as a pentester. Let's explore the different types of cloud services.

The difference between IaaS, PaaS, and SaaS

All of the services provided by AWS, Azure, and GCP are either SaaS, PaaS, or IaaS. The classification of each of these cloud services will directly affect what you're allowed to do when you're pentesting, as I've explained. So, understanding the differences between these types of services is crucial!

SaaS means the cloud provider gives your organization lots of components—the infrastructure everything runs on, its software platform and related APIs, and the application-level functions of its software. For instance, when we use Gmail, we're using a fully SaaS application. AWS defines SaaS thus:

> *"SaaS is a business and software delivery model that enables organizations to offer their solution in a low-friction, service-centric approach."*

So, your organization is putting its data into the service, but it isn't doing much—or any—software application development. Your organization's security concerns with SaaS are mainly how your organization configures it and what data your organization decides to put into the service. As a pentester, you'll be limited in what you're allowed to do. But simulating cyber attacks that don't penetrate into the cloud provider's own platform is usually okay, as is testing different SaaS configurations.

PaaS essentially offers your organization the cloud provider's infrastructure and platform. You can think of the cloud provider's platform as being somewhat analogous to an operating system, but not exactly the same thing. This is how AWS defines PaaS:

> *"PaaS remove the need for organizations to manage the underlying infrastructure*
> *(usually hardware and operating systems) and allows you to focus on the*
> *deployment and management of your applications. This helps you be more efficient*
> *as you don't need to worry about resource procurement, capacity planning,*
> *software maintenance, patching, or any of the other undifferentiated heavy lifting*
> *involved in running your application."*

IaaS gives your organization the cloud provider's infrastructure, which includes its servers, networking devices, and physical networks. The vast majority of the software and data your organization uses belongs to your organization. As AWS explains:

> *"IaaS, sometimes abbreviated as IaaS, contains the basic building blocks for cloud*
> *IT and typically provide access to networking features, computers (virtual or on*
> *dedicated hardware), and data storage space."*

As a pentester, you'll be allowed to do more in your simulated cyber attacks within each cloud provider's IaaS services.

So, you now understand hybrid cloud, multi-cloud, all-cloud, IaaS, PaaS, SaaS, cloud migration, and many of the various different ways organizations use the sorts of cloud networks you will be pentesting.

Summary

So, with this chapter, you now understand the basic nature of your testing targets—cloud networks. Later on in this book, I'll explain more information you'll need to know as a red teamer that's specific to AWS, Azure, and GCP. But in the next chapter, we'll explore how cloud networks in general are cyber-attacked. In a cloud pentest, the cloud is the "what" and your simulated cyber attacks are the "how."

Further reading

To learn more on the topics covered in this chapter, you can visit the following links:

- *What is red teaming?*: `https://www.synopsys.com/glossary/what-is-red-teaming.html`

- *About AWS*: `https://aws.amazon.com/about-aws/`

- *The History of Google Cloud Platform*: `https://acloudguru.com/blog/engineering/history-google-cloud-platform`

- *The History of Microsoft Azure*: `https://techcommunity.microsoft.com/t5/educator-developer-blog/the-history-of-microsoft-azure/ba-p/3574204`

- *What are the benefits of cloud computing?* (IBM): `https://www.ibm.com/topics/cloud-computing-benefits`

- *What is cloud networking?*: `https://www.cisco.com/c/en/us/solutions/cloud/what-is-cloud-networking.html`

- *A Brief History of Containers*: `https://d2iq.com/blog/brief-history-containers`

- *What is DevSecOps? A guide from PortSwigger*: `https://portswigger.net/solutions/devsecops/guide-to-devsecops`

- *Multi-Cloud vs. Hybrid Cloud: 10 Key Comparisons*: `https://www.spiceworks.com/tech/cloud/articles/multi-cloud-vs-hybrid-cloud/`

- *Gartner Says Cloud Will Be the Centerpiece of New Digital Experiences*: `https://www.gartner.com/en/newsroom/press-releases/2021-11-10-gartner-says-cloud-will-be-the-centerpiece-of-new-digital-experiences`

- *What is cloud migration?* (IBM): `https://www.ibm.com/topics/cloud-migration`

2

How Are Cloud Networks Cyber Attacked?

When you begin your journey to becoming a cloud pentester, it helps to start with the basics.

Your job is to test cloud networks to see how they can be cyber attacked. The organization you work for can then use your discoveries to improve the cybersecurity of its cloud networks.

Because Amazon (AWS), Microsoft (Azure), and Google (GCP) own the infrastructure on which you'll be testing, you won't be allowed to do literally anything a cyber attacker may try to do in real life. But you need to understand all the kinds of cyberattacks that cloud networks deal with, even if you can't simulate all of them.

The best pentesters can think like real cyber attackers. This chapter will give you a better understanding of how cloud networks are cyber attacked in order to help you conduct more effective pentests.

In this chapter, we'll cover the following main topics:

- Understanding penetration testing
- External and internal attacks
- Attacks on the confidentiality, integrity, and availability of data
- Understanding lateral movement in the cloud
- Zero-trust networks

Let's get started!

Understanding penetration testing

Penetration tests (or **pentests** for short) are simulated cyberattacks that are designed to find vulnerabilities in computer networks and applications. The biggest difference between a pentest and an actual cyberattack is that the former is conducted with the full consent of the owner of the computer or network, whereas the latter isn't.

As a pentester or red team member, not only will you need consent from the owner of the target you're testing, but you'll also have to sign a legal agreement that explains in detail what you're allowed to do, what you're forbidden from doing, and the scope of your pentest. This applies whether you're an employee of the organization being pentested, a third-party contractor of the organization being pentested, someone who conducts simple one-off pentests, or a red team member who pentests as part of your red team engagements.

Whether or not an organization has a red team, it will commence pentesting after a history of vulnerability assessments. A vulnerability assessment is the first way to find security vulnerabilities. It analyzes the state of an application or network based on checklists of criteria. The criteria are most often based on a set security standard, such as the **OWASP Application Security Verification Standard** (`https://owasp.org/www-project-application-security-verification-standard/`) or the **PCI PTS POI Modular Security Requirements** (`https://www.pcisecuritystandards.org/wp-content/uploads/2023/01/PTS_POI_v6.2_Bulletin.pdf`). There are hundreds of different security standards that could apply to the organization you work for. Vulnerability assessments are appropriate for all businesses and enterprises, at all possible security maturity levels. Security maturity is a complex concept, but in a nutshell, it's about how well developed an organization's security policies and controls are.

Once an organization has done some vulnerability assessments, security-hardened its networks based on those findings, and assembled a team of cybersecurity professionals, then it may be ready for pentesting. Pentesting is supposed to discover security vulnerabilities that can only be discovered by simulating cyberattacks. Legally and procedure-wise, pentesting is a lot different from cyber attacking, but the computers and networks you pentest don't know the difference. Your pentests will break things, even if the effects are as temporary as taking a few computers offline for an hour in a **denial-of-service** (**DoS**) attack. That's why only organizations with some security maturity should be pentesting, and it's also why a specific scope is always agreed upon before starting a pentest. For instance, your organization may move its production from one network segment to another so you can pentest within a segment without interfering with its everyday operations.

A red team is a dedicated group of people within your organization who conduct frequent pentests according to patterns in the cyber threat landscape. As an example, if a new enterprise ransomware threat emerges, your red team may be tasked with simulating that particular new ransomware within your network and seeing what happens.

In order to pentest effectively, you absolutely must understand how cloud networks are cyber attacked. In this book, you will learn about a lot of tools that are often used to pentest in AWS, Azure, and GCP environments. Using these tools in the right way and in the right situations will help you pentest effectively, finding vulnerabilities that your organization must address. But the greatest tools in the world are only good if you know how to use them and why. You'll also sometimes conduct some activities without those tools. In all scenarios, you must understand how cloud networks are cyber attacked in order to be an effective cloud pentester. That's what this chapter is all about!

External and internal attacks

When your organization's defensive security team prepares for cyberattacks, it needs to understand each and every step that threat actors take when they try to maliciously interfere with your data. No cyber intrusion is a one-step process. Ransomware may have needed an employee to accidentally execute an email attachment before it spread between poorly configured cloud instances. A data breach may have required bribing an employee and giving them a USB stick with custom-designed spyware.

The MITRE ATT&CK database (`https://attack.mitre.org/`) is an excellent resource to help all kinds of cybersecurity professionals understand the various steps cyber threat actors take when they engage in their crimes. I will be citing it frequently in this chapter. Especially if you're pentesting as part of a red team, these may be the kinds of cyberattacks you'll be simulating in your engagements.

Some cyberattack chains can be simple, and others are relatively complex. But they all have an origin that's either external or internal to your organization. You will need to understand the differences between external and internal cyberattacks as a cloud pentester. You'll likely be pentesting both kinds of scenarios over the course of your career. Business and enterprise cloud networks are a prime target for many of the most devastating cyber exploits.

There was a time, perhaps in the 1990s and early 2000s, when consumers were very frequently targeted by cybercriminals. Ordinary people should still be careful about the security of their phones, tablets, and PCs. They sometimes get targeted by phishing scams, digital surveillance, and malware. An ordinary person may be exploited to pay a cyber attacker a few hundred dollars' worth of cryptocurrency in a ransomware attack. Even small businesses may have revenue in the millions of dollars, and they could be coerced into paying a cyber attacker a million-dollar cryptocurrency ransom. Also, other sorts of financially motivated cybercrime, such as data breaches, are much more profitable when businesses are targeted than when a senior citizen is targeted.

The companies you'll be working for as a pentester, both as an employee and as a third-party contractor, are lucrative targets for cybercrime. And that's why they're hiring you to simulate these cybercrimes, so they can learn how they can improve their defenses.

The classic kinds of cyberattacks you'll hear about most often in the news and in your favorite fictional entertainment media will usually be external in origin. For example, a hoodie-wearing cybercriminal working from their PC in their dark basement cracks an encrypted terminal on the network, then downloads all of the terminal's sensitive files! A skull-and-crossbones graphic blinks on the screen... "You've been hacked!" The victim organization never sees the attacker. It hires a top-notch cyber investigations team to follow the attacker around the world. Eventually, the cops identify the cybercriminal at a café on another continent. The criminal is handcuffed. Everyone applauds and the credits roll.

Real-world cybercrime can be just as devastating, but it can look much more benign in person. Investigating it isn't quite as quick or exciting, because you'll be helping the company you work for prepare for real cyberattacks and it won't follow a typical movie script. Now, let's understand the nature of these attacks and look at some real-life examples.

External cyberattacks

External cyberattacks originate from outside of the targeted organization. The attacker usually has to go through the internet to start the process of cyber attacking your organization's cloud servers.

An external cyber attacker has to break into the organization's network they're attacking. Then, they'll likely have to privilege escalate.

> **Privilege escalation**
>
> This is when an attacker begins with access to a user account with limited access control privileges and works their way up to using accounts with more access control privileges. Sometimes, they'll escalate all the way up to accessing an account with full administrative privileges in the network they're attacking... which is especially dangerous!

Now, let's examine some possible vectors for external cyberattacks on cloud networks.

Drive-by compromise

First, there's "*drive-by compromise.*" According to MITRE ATT&CK (`https://attack.mitre.org/techniques/T1189/`), drive-by compromise happens when a user visits a website through their usual web browsing activities. An attacker with control of the website uses it to attack the user through their web browser. Sometimes, attackers also use this technique for malicious actions that aren't exploits, such as acquiring application access tokens.

A lot of access to cloud networks is through the web, so this is a really pertinent attack vector.

Exploit public-facing application

Another external attack vector that's really relevant to cloud networks is "exploit public-facing application." MITRE ATT&CK (`https://attack.mitre.org/techniques/T1190/`) describes it as when adversaries take advantage of internet-connected computers or applications through their vulnerabilities. Frequent means of exploitation include SQL databases, standard internet services such as SSH or SMB, network management protocols, and applications with internet-accessible open sockets such as web browsers. But other internet-connected technologies can also be used in these exploits.

If these exploits involve cloud infrastructure or containerized applications (such as with Kubernetes or Docker), attackers can do really catastrophic damage. They could intercept other instances or containers, and quite often acquire access to their APIs too.

External remote services

The next entry point vector from MITRE ATT&CK that I'm going to cover is "external remote services." It's another common way in which external cyberattacks begin. MITRE ATT&CK (https://attack. mitre.org/techniques/T1133/) describes it as when attackers target external services to acquire malicious access or maintain persistence in a network. Commonly targeted remote services include VPNs, Citrix, or similar technologies that facilitate remote access. Attackers often need access to valid accounts for their targeted service in order for this exploit to work. Access to valid accounts can be acquired by stealing credentials through already compromised networks or means such as credential pharming. Of course, in external cyberattacks, access to a valid account may be acquired by phishing an employee. Phishing attacks take many forms, but they most often use fake websites, fake emails, fake text messages, or fake social media posts to imitate a trusted entity.

Valid accounts

This next MITRE ATT&CK vector category is a common entry point for most internal cyberattacks, known as "valid accounts." According to MITRE ATT&CK (https://attack.mitre.org/ techniques/T1078/), attackers can acquire malicious access to computer systems by compromising legitimate user accounts that have privileges within them. They may also compromise privileged accounts to establish persistence, for privilege escalation, or for defense evasion. Sometimes, inactive user accounts are also exploited. Network administrators should watch the behavior of the accounts in their system and deactivate user accounts of former employees and contractors as soon as possible.

Cloud accounts

I'm going to include one subcategory of attack vector here because it's specifically relevant to cloud pentesting; it is known as "valid accounts: cloud accounts" (https://attack.mitre.org/ techniques/T1078/004/). Go ahead and read about it on MITRE ATT&CK's website. Cloud networks have lots of working parts. They can have multiple SaaS applications, containers, servers within servers, virtual machines, and so on. They can get really complicated. So, there can be a lot more user accounts and machine identities that attackers can exploit.

Organizations not only have to watch internal cyber attackers with active accounts but also inactive accounts, which are a common attack vector. When you work as a cloud pentester, you may need to compromise an inactive account that an organization forgot to remove.

Internal cyberattacks

Internal cyberattacks originate from inside the targeted organization. Either a company employee, contractor, executive, or supply chain entity is the cyber attacker, or an external cyber attacker bribes or otherwise motivates an employee, contractor, executive, or supply chain entity to help them with their cyberattack.

An internal cyber attacker already has their foot in the door of your network. If they work for the organization, they have a user account in your network and applications that at least has some privileges, even if they're minimal. They very likely have physical access to the company's computers and on-premises network. That can make it a lot easier to attack the cloud network. A supply chain entity also already has privileged access to an organization that an outsider won't have. Your organization's supply chain consists of the other businesses that provide products and services to your organization – for instance, companies that make metal and sell it to car manufacturers. The metal manufacturer is part of the car manufacturer's supply chain. The web development firm that makes custom web applications for a school is a part of the school's supply chain.

The following are MITRE ATT&CK's "initial access" vectors that can pertain to an internal cyberattack.

Hardware additions

The first is "hardware additions." MITRE ATT&CK (`https://attack.mitre.org/techniques/T1200/`) defines this as when adversaries use computer hardware such as networking devices as a vector to acquire malicious access. This technique often uses "more robust hardware additions" than removable media (such as USB drives) to deploy new attack functionalities and features rather than simply distributing malicious payloads.

Your organization's cloud network could be attacked by a hardware device that a cybercriminal physically connects to your on-premises network.

Supply chain compromise

Another technique that can be used in an internal cyberattack is "supply chain compromise." MITRE ATT&CK (`https://attack.mitre.org/techniques/T1195/`) describes this as when attackers manipulate or intercept products or product delivery mechanisms to compromise the users and networks that are connected for data or system compromise. A company's supply chain can include other businesses they work with, companies that provide applications and network services, and so on. In these exploits, sometimes source code repositories, development tools, open source dependencies, or software updating mechanisms are manipulated.

For the purposes of this book, supply chain compromises are especially relevant because AWS, Azure, and GCP services and applications can be considered to be a part of a company's supply chain.

Supply chain entities often have connections to an organization's internal network, both on-premises and in the cloud. As a cloud pentester, you may sometimes be simulating supply chain attacks. At other times, you may have to cooperate with one of your organization's supply chain entities while pentesting.

Trusted relationship

This next vector applies to a lot of internal cyberattacks, and is known as "trusted relationship" (`https://attack.mitre.org/techniques/T1199/`). MITRE ATT&CK defines this as when attackers take advantage of individuals or organizations that the target trusts in order to conduct cyberattacks. They can include people and entities such as managed service providers, IT contractors, or building maintenance workers.

Here's a hypothetical scenario. The janitor asks for keys to the server room because they need to clean something in there. It's not someone else pretending to be the janitor, but the real janitor who has worked there for months. Once the janitor gets access to the server room, they plug a USB stick with executable malware into one of the main server machines on-premises in order to infect all the client computers that are managed through it.

Cyber attackers will find a wide variety of ways to exploit cloud networks and applications. To acquire access, they may find vulnerabilities in internet-facing parts of applications, such as web applications and open ports. They may hijack accounts with access privileges. They may even go so far as to bribe someone who works for the company to physically place a malicious device into their targeted network. As a pentester, you'll mainly be simulating exploits within applications and networks remotely. But it's good to keep in mind the many other techniques that cyber attackers use when you conduct your red team engagements, even if they're difficult to simulate.

Attacks on the confidentiality, integrity, and availability of cloud data

So, we've looked at the difference between internal cyberattacks and external cyberattacks, and some of the different entry point attack vectors they can use. There's another way for you to categorize the cyberattacks you'll be simulating as a pentester.

We must look at the **CIA (confidentiality, integrity, and availability) Triad** of cybersecurity. It's one of the most important concepts in our area of study.

All cyberattacks impact one, two, or all three components of the CIA Triad:

- **Confidentiality** is all about making sure that your organization's data is only readable to the entities that are allowed to access it. A data breach is an example of a type of cyberattack that impacts confidentiality.

- **Integrity** is all about making sure that only authorized entities can alter or modify your organization's data. If a cyber attacker replaces a legitimate component of your organization's cloud application with malware, that's an example of a cyberattack that impacts integrity.

- **Availability** is all about making sure that your organization's data, servers, and applications are available whenever authorized entities need it. If a cyber attacker performs a **distributed denial-of-service (DDoS)** attack on your organization's cloud web servers and customers cannot use your web application, that's an example of a cyberattack that impacts availability.

Some cyberattacks impact more than one component of the CIA Triad. For example, enterprise ransomware these days often not only maliciously encrypts your organization's data with a decryption key you cannot access without paying a ransom, but also often breaches your organization's data. So, that's availability and confidentiality harmed in one malware attack. If the ransomware infection establishes persistence by altering some of the data on your cloud servers, that's integrity harmed too!

Confidentiality

Let's look at a cyberattack from the news that impacted the confidentiality of data in cloud networks.

DC Health Link tweeted in March 2023 that sensitive data from its system was data breached. DC Health Link helps to provide health insurance to many people who work for the American government. It definitely has at least a large component of its network hosted by a cloud provider. The tweet (`https://twitter.com/DCHealthLink/status/1634342617235312640`) said the following:

> *"The DC Health Benefit Exchange Authority takes the data breach of enrollee information very seriously. On Monday, March 6, 2023, upon becoming aware of the incident, we immediately launched an investigation, began working with law enforcement, and engaged a third-party forensics firm-Mandiant. While our investigation is ongoing, we'd like to provide an update on the current situation. There are 56,415 customers impacted. The data fields include the following, although not all data fields were necessarily included for each enrollee: name, Social Security number, date of birth, gender, health plan information (e.g. plan name, carrier name, premium amounts, employer contribution, and coverage dates), employer information, enrollee information (e.g. address, email, phone number, race, ethnicity, and citizenship status)."*

Just because the breach was reported in March 2023, that doesn't mean that it occurred in March 2023! Data breaches often go months without being reported. Either the organization knew about the breach much earlier and only publicized the information months later, or it took months for the organization to discover it in the first place.

What we do know is that 56,415 customers were impacted, and it can be safely assumed that much of the network is on the cloud. We don't know how the data breach occurred, but we can make educated guesses. "Data from cloud storage" is a recognized attack vector in the MITRE ATT&CK database (`https://attack.mitre.org/techniques/T1530/`). It says the following:

> *"Many cloud service providers offer solutions for online data object storage such as Amazon S3, Azure Storage, and Google Cloud Storage. These solutions differ from other storage solutions (such as SQL or Elasticsearch) in that there is no overarching application. Data from these solutions can be retrieved directly using the cloud provider's APIs. In other cases, SaaS application providers such as Slack, Confluence, and Salesforce also provide cloud storage solutions as a peripheral use case of their platform. These cloud objects can be extracted directly from their associated application. Adversaries may collect sensitive data from these cloud storage solutions. Providers typically offer security guides to help end users configure systems, though misconfigurations are a common problem. There have been numerous incidents where cloud storage has been improperly secured, typically by unintentionally allowing public access to unauthenticated users, overly-broad access by all users, or even access for any anonymous person outside the control of the Identity Access Management system without even needing basic user permissions."*

Later in this book, I will show you how to use tools and techniques to conduct pentests that involve unauthorized access to cloud storage.

Integrity

Let's look at cyberattacks on the integrity of cloud data. The following is a story that *Ravie Lakshmanan* of *The Hacker News* (`https://thehackernews.com/2023/03/large-scale-cyber-attack-hijacks-east.html`) reported regarding the targeting of adult entertainment websites:

> *"A widespread malicious cyber operation has hijacked thousands of websites aimed at East Asian audiences to redirect visitors to adult-themed content since early September 2022. The ongoing campaign entails injecting malicious JavaScript code to the hacked websites, often connecting to the target web server using legitimate FTP credentials the threat actor previously obtained via an unknown method. 'In many cases, these were highly secure auto-generated FTP credentials which the attacker was somehow able to acquire and leverage for website hijacking,' Wiz said in a report published this month. The fact that the breached websites – owned by both small firms and multinational corporations – utilize different tech stacks and hosting service providers has made it difficult to trace a common attack vector, the cloud security company noted."*

As a cloud pentester, you may have to conduct a pentest that involves injecting malicious code into a web application that's run from a multi-cloud environment. This is the sort of attack that very clever attackers may succeed at, and takes very skilled cloud pentesters to simulate.

Integrity attacks can involve malicious code injection, man-in-the-middle attacks, or maliciously acquiring user and machine identities, such as **Transport Layer Security** (**TLS**) certificates.

> TLS
>
> TLS certificates are used to grant users and machines access to services that are encrypted with TLS, such as encrypted web applications deployed through the HTTPS protocol.

Availability

Finally, there are attacks on the availability of cloud data.

In August 2022, the official Google Cloud blog reported one of the biggest DDoS attacks they've ever detected on one of their GCP services.

The corporate customer was using **Google Cloud Armor**. Google Cloud Armor is a cybersecurity service that GCP customers (such as enterprises) can use to protect GCP-hosted applications and networks from a few common sorts of security exploits. Some of the common attacks Google Cloud Armor is designed to detect and prevent include DDoS attacks, **cross-site scripting** (**XSS**) attacks, and SQL injection attacks.

We'll get into XSS and SQL injection later in this book, but we'll cover DDoS attacks here.

> What's a DDoS attack?
>
> A DDoS attack is when a cyber attacker uses a distributed collection of computers to overwhelm a network target with more data than it can handle. Overwhelming a target with data can cause it to shut down or go offline temporarily. Web servers and cloud instances are some of the most common targets of DDoS attacks.

Most DDoS attacks are conducted with a botnet. A botnet is a network of computers that a cyber attacker controls through a command-and-control server in order to execute cyberattacks. Computers get infected with zombie malware that makes them controllable by the attacker and part of the botnet. PCs, mobile devices, servers, and networking devices such as routers are often infected with zombie malware and used in a botnet. An ordinary person's phone could be part of a botnet and they don't even know it!

When an attacker can use a little bit of the computing power of a large collection of devices in their botnet, they can execute more destructive cyberattacks. In a botnet-driven DDoS attack, thousands of devices can be synchronized to overwhelm one network cyberattack target with an immense amount of data packets.

The DDoS attack didn't target Google Cloud Armor directly. Rather, Google Cloud Armor was able to detect the DDoS attack. It was reported on the official Google Cloud blog (`https://cloud.google.com/blog/products/identity-security/how-google-cloud-blocked-largest-layer-7-ddos-attack-at-46-million-rps`) as follows:

> *"On June 1 (2022), a Google Cloud Armor customer was targeted with a series of HTTPS DDoS attacks which peaked at 46 million requests per second. This is the largest Layer 7 DDoS reported to date—at least 76% larger than the previously reported record. To give a sense of the scale of the attack, that is like receiving all the daily requests to Wikipedia (one of the top 10 trafficked websites in the world) in just 10 seconds.*
>
> *Cloud Armor Adaptive Protection was able to detect and analyze the traffic early in the attack lifecycle. Cloud Armor alerted the customer with a recommended protective rule which was then deployed before the attack ramped up to its full magnitude. Cloud Armor blocked the attack ensuring the customer's service stayed online and continued serving their end-users."*

It's great that Google Cloud Armor was able to mitigate such a massive DDoS attack on a customer's GCP-hosted servers. As a cloud pentester, you might be challenged to find a way around Google Cloud Armor!

All cyberattacks impact at least one part of the CIA Triad – confidentiality, integrity, or availability. Confidentiality is about protecting data from unpermitted access. Integrity is about making sure that only authorized users and entities can make changes to data. And availability is about making sure that data can be accessed by authorized users when they need it. Some attacks may impact more than one part of the CIA Triad, such as ransomware (availability) that also breaches the public's data (confidentiality).

Understanding lateral movement in the cloud

Cyberattacks on cloud applications can be external or internal. They can impact the confidentiality, integrity, and availability of data. Here are some more cloud cyberattack concepts to understand.

Cyberattacks against complicated enterprise systems such as cloud networks are seldom simple. Attacks don't just break in, enter, and leave. Many attacks strike one part of a complex system and then move on to other parts of a complex system.

A cloud network can include multiple cloud platforms (AWS, Azure, and GCP) with several different services and applications on each platform. They can also contain multiple containerization systems through orchestration platforms such as Docker and Kubernetes, integrating numerous services and applications within each one. All of the components of cloud networks can communicate with each other through shared credentials such as cryptography keys and machine identities (such as TLS certificates).

As a cloud pentester, you may be asked to simulate these more complex lateral exploit techniques.

MITRE ATT&CK has a whole category for lateral movement exploits. It's all about when an attacker moves within a computer system. The attacker could be moving between different entities within your organization's cloud instance on one cloud platform. They could be moving between different instances or services on the same cloud platform. They could even be moving from your organization's services on one cloud platform to another if you have a multi-cloud network.

Here's MITRE ATT&CK's list of lateral movement exploits.

Exploitation of remote services

As cloud networks often contain entities in multiple geographic locations, this can be a common cloud cyberattack technique. When it comes to networks, "internal" and "external" pertain to access control, not to physical location per se. If a hybrid multi-cloud network has one on-premises location and components in AWS, Azure, and GCP data centers in different parts of the world, it's all a part of an internal network if the access control is configured so that the public is forbidden access.

MITRE ATT&CK defines the exploitation of remote services (`https://attack.mitre.org/tactics/TA0008/`) as follows:

> *"Adversaries may exploit remote services to gain unauthorized access to internal systems once inside of a network. Exploitation of a software vulnerability occurs when an adversary takes advantage of a programming error in a program, service, or within the operating system software or kernel itself to execute adversary-controlled code."*

Internal spearphishing

In a phishing attack, adversaries pose as trustworthy entities by replicating their websites, emails, text messages, or social media communications. Phishing attacks can be random. For example, I've received phishing text messages from an attacker pretending to be from a major Canadian bank that I don't have an account with. The attacker only knew that I was in Canada, and Canada only has a handful of major banks, each of them having 5 million customers or more. I wasn't specifically targeted; the attacker sent massive amounts of phishing text messages to Canadians, hoping that some who have accounts with that bank would fall for the scam.

Spearphishing is different. Spearphishing targets a specific individual or entity. For instance, there could be a particular individual who works for the company the attacker is trying to break into. They could look up information about the individual on LinkedIn, and then pretend to be one of the individual's LinkedIn contacts.

MITRE ATT&CK defines internal spearphishing (`https://attack.mitre.org/tactics/TA0008/`) as follows:

> *"Adversaries may use internal spearphishing to gain access to additional information or exploit other users within the same organization after they already have access to accounts or systems within the environment. Internal spearphishing is multi-staged campaign where an email account is owned either by controlling the user's device with previously installed malware or by compromising the account credentials of the user. Adversaries attempt to take advantage of a trusted internal account to increase the likelihood of tricking the target into falling for the phish attempt."*

Lateral tool transfer

Within a cloud network, various applications and services can be interconnected. These applications inherently possess privileged access to one another. An attacker can exploit these interconnections and privileges for lateral movement within the network.

MITRE ATT&CK defines lateral tool transfer (`https://attack.mitre.org/techniques/T1570/`) as follows:

> *"Adversaries may transfer tools or other files between systems in a compromised environment. Once brought into the victim environment (i.e. Ingress Tool Transfer) files may then be copied from one system to another to stage adversary tools or other files over the course of an operation. Adversaries may copy files between internal victim systems to support lateral movement using inherent file sharing protocols such as file sharing over SMB/Windows Admin Shares to connected network shares or with authenticated connections via Remote Desktop Protocol."*

Remote service session hijacking

Cloud networks and applications are full of services that are designed to be remotely accessed. Remote service session hijacking can help an attacker move between different nodes in a containerization orchestration, between different sessions within the same cloud service, and also between different cloud services that share credentials – even if they use different cloud platforms! For example, remote sessions can be hijacked between App Engine in GCP, App Service in Azure, and Amazon EC2 in AWS. Of course, this sort of exploit can be prevented by proper security configuration between the applications and platforms.

MITRE ATT&CK defines remote service session hijacking (`https://attack.mitre.org/tactics/TA0008/`) as follows:

> *"Adversaries may take control of preexisting sessions with remote services to move laterally in an environment. Users may use valid credentials to log into a service specifically designed to accept remote connections, such as telnet, SSH, and RDP."*

Software deployment tools

This is similar to remote service session hijacking, but instead of remote sessions being targeted, trusted third-party administrative tools are targeted. As a cloud pentester, you will likely need to simulate a lot of different types of hijacking techniques.

MITRE ATT&CK defines software deployment tools (`https://attack.mitre.org/techniques/T1195/001/`) as follows:

> *"Adversaries may gain access to and use third-party software suites installed within an enterprise network, such as administration, monitoring, and deployment systems, to move laterally through the network."*

Tainted shared content

Think of how much shared storage cloud applications constantly use! When securing a cloud network, every single data asset must be carefully monitored and guarded.

MITRE ATT&CK defines tainted shared content (`https://attack.mitre.org/tactics/TA0008/`) as follows:

> *"Adversaries may deliver payloads to remote systems by adding content to shared storage locations, such as network drives or internal code repositories. Content stored on network drives or in other shared locations may be tainted by adding malicious programs, scripts, or exploit code to otherwise valid files."*

Cloud applications and networks can get a lot more complicated than traditional applications and networks. There's your organization, then a cloud platform, or multiple cloud platforms. There can be several different services implemented per cloud platform. There can be an on-premises network component. A containerized application can have many virtualized containers that can each live and die within days. There can be hundreds of user accounts and many more machine identities. There are so many different attack vectors for threat actors. You may need to simulate attacks on many of these complex vectors during your red team engagements.

Zero-trust networks

Back in the days before cloud services were commonly used, enterprises only had networks on their own premises. Back in the 1990s and early 2000s, the network security paradigm was all about perimeters.

Different network segments could have different levels of security, but the internal network and all of its segments were contained within a heavily guarded perimeter. Sometimes, external traffic would be allowed into the internal network, but it'd have to pass a vector for authentication and authorization. But once that perimeter was cleared, the user could travel within the internal network without having their credentials checked again. All users were either trusted or distrusted, and existing inside the perimeter meant automatic trust. Think of a country with a heavily guarded border, but little police presence inside of the country.

The old perimeter model of network security has been obsolete for many years now. There are multiple reasons why.

First of all, the perimeter security model isn't very resilient or robust. Cyber attackers do sometimes breach authentication barriers. So, if they breach the perimeter, there are usually no other authentication barriers that they have to breach. It's like the way a bank robber might taunt a bank: "Your security has to succeed every single time, but I only have to succeed once!"

Secondly, the perimeter security model is totally incompatible with today's more complex cloud networks. The perimeter security model couldn't be applied to a cloud network even if someone wanted to try. The simplest possible enterprise cloud network has a few PC endpoints on-premises and connects to one cloud service on one cloud platform through the internet. The most complex hybrid multi-cloud networks entail on-premises networks and endpoints in multiple company-owned locations, remote employees and contractors working from their homes, multiple cloud services (AWS, Azure, and GCP), and several different SaaS, PaaS, and IaaS services and applications on each of the cloud platforms. Either way, users have to go through the internet to connect to their internal corporate networks.

Zero-trust security means that no user or machine is ever trusted automatically. A perimeter security network automatically trusts users inside of the perimeter. But in cloud networks and over the internet, there is no perimeter. So, authentication and authorization vectors and checks are implemented in as many places in the network as possible. It doesn't matter where you come from, you must show your identification to access this component!

An attacker would need to compromise several authentication points to navigate within the enterprise cloud network. Having numerous authentication points can significantly reduce the likelihood of a successful cyberattack. However, if an attacker manages to capture credentials, navigating within the cloud network might become effortless for them. Grasping these nuances is essential for anyone involved in cloud penetration testing.

Later in this book, we'll explore some of the most popular AWS, Azure, and GCP applications and services. We'll get into how virtualization and containerization are implemented in cloud networks. We'll also explore the various tools, techniques, and strategies you'll use on your cloud red team engagements.

Summary

The reason why we conduct pentesting is to learn about security vulnerabilities in computer systems by simulating cyberattacks.

There are possibly hundreds or thousands of potential cyberattack vectors in a cloud network, both internal and external. Users, user accounts, machine identities, and vulnerabilities in internet-facing applications are just some of the many possibilities.

You may not be able to simulate all of the possible types of exploits. For instance, cloud providers often prohibit simulating DDoS attacks, and you also won't be allowed to physically visit the cloud provider's data centers to plant test devices. But it's important to understand all the different things an attacker could do and keep them in mind when you're conducting your red team engagements.

Attacks can originate internally or externally from your organization. The CIA Triad of cybersecurity is a concept to explain how cyberattacks can impact your organization's data in terms of confidentiality, integrity, and availability.

As cloud networks have become a lot more common and networking technology has advanced, we now secure computer networks with zero-trust security. That means users and applications are authenticated at as many points of the network as possible, regardless of the user's origin being either internal or external to the network.

In the next chapter, we'll explore the key concepts for pentesting cloud networks.

Further reading

To learn more about the topics covered in this chapter, you can visit the following links:

- *MITRE ATT&CK*: `https://attack.mitre.org/`

- *DDoS botnets*: `https://www.cloudflare.com/learning/ddos/what-is-a-ddos-botnet/`

- *Zero-trust security and the cloud*: `https://www.paloaltonetworks.com/cyberpedia/what-is-a-zero-trust-for-the-cloud`

3

Key Concepts for Pentesting Today's Cloud Networks

Before you perform your first cloud pentest or red team engagement, there are some concepts you need to learn.

Cloud platforms have policies for pentesting that you and your organization must abide by. It's also important to understand and verify network performance with benchmark checks. Services enumeration is a way an attacker can learn things about your organization's public cloud services that can help them cyber-attack it.

Assure that your organization's public cloud has performed vulnerability assessments and that common cloud misconfigurations are addressed before you pentest.

Resources provided by MITRE's **Common Vulnerabilities and Exposures** (**CVE**) database, the **National Institute of Standards and Technology's (NIST's) National Vulnerability Database** (**NVD**) database, and the **Forum of Incident Response and Security Teams' (FIRST's) Exploit Prediction Scoring System** (**EPSS**) database help pentesters and red teamers define and understand specific known vulnerabilities.

You also must understand how to communicate and cooperate with your organization's defensive security specialists effectively.

In this chapter, we'll cover the following main topics:

- Cloud platform policies, benchmark checks, and services enumeration
- Exposed services, permissions, and integrations
- CVE, the **Common Vulnerability Scoring System** (**CVSS**), and vulnerabilities
- Purple teaming and writing pentest reports

Let's get started!

Cloud platform policies, benchmark checks, and services enumeration

Pentesting cloud networks on public cloud platforms is fundamentally different from pentesting on your organization's own premises and its own infrastructure.

If your organization owns the premises and infrastructure, it has the legal right to determine everything you're allowed and forbidden to do to its network for your pentest. If I buy a house, as long as the laws in my municipality and country don't forbid it, I could allow building contractors to replace walls, redo my roof, install new doors, and so on.

If I rent my house from a landlord, I don't own my house. I would need my landlord's permission if I wanted to pay building contractors to make those sorts of modifications to my house.

On **Amazon Web Services** (**AWS**), Azure, and **Google Cloud Platform** (**GCP**), your organization is "renting its house" from its "landlord"—Amazon, Microsoft, or Google. Amazon, Microsoft, and Google make the rules for what you're allowed to do as a pentester.

If the organization you work for asks you to do something in its AWS-, Azure-, and GCP-hosted networks that Amazon, Microsoft, and Google forbid in their policies, you absolutely shouldn't do it. It is important to locate the penetration testing policies for cloud providers on their respective websites and share them with your employer to clarify any restrictions or limitations on conducting penetration testing. We list them here:

- *AWS Customer Support Policy for Penetration Testing*: `https://aws.amazon.com/security/penetration-testing/`

- *Amazon EC2 Testing Policy*: `https://aws.amazon.com/ec2/testing/`

- *AWS DDoS Simulation Testing Policy*: `https://aws.amazon.com/security/ddos-simulation-testing/`

- *Microsoft Online Subscription Agreement*: `https://azure.microsoft.com/en-us/support/legal/subscription-agreement/`

- *Microsoft Cloud Penetration Testing Rules of Engagement*: `https://www.microsoft.com/en-us/msrc/pentest-rules-of-engagement`

- *Google Cloud Platform Terms of Service*: `https://cloud.google.com/terms/`

- *Google Cloud Platform Acceptable Use Policy*: `https://cloud.google.com/terms/aup`

I recommend reading the cloud provider's policies carefully before your organization proposes a pentest or red team engagement of its public cloud networks. Then, read your organization's proposal and pentesting scope to verify that what you are being asked to do is compliant with Amazon's, Microsoft's, or Google's policies. Depending on what your organization is asking you to do, you might only have to make minor modifications to your scope and simulated cyber attacks in order to be policy-compliant.

I mentioned AWS, Azure, and GCP pentesting policies in *Chapter 1*. But for your reference, here are links to official policies and a brief summary of each. That's how important it is!

- **AWS**: General pentesting is permitted on most AWS services. DNS zone walking, DNS hijacking, and DNS pharming are forbidden on Route 53. Most **Denial-of-Service (DoS)** and **Distributed Denial-of-Service (DDoS)** simulations are forbidden. Protocol flooding and request flooding are forbidden. Pentesting with **Command and Control (C2)** servers requires direct approval from Amazon. You must also ask Amazon for approval for network stress testing, using the iPerf tool, simulated phishing, and using malware in your pentesting. See `https://aws.amazon.com/security/penetration-testing/`.

- **Azure and Microsoft Cloud in general**: Most pentesting without prior authorization is permitted. However, scanning and testing other customers' assets and accessing their data is forbidden. Automated testing that generates too much traffic is forbidden. All DoS and DDoS simulations are forbidden. Network-intensive fuzzing against anything but your organization's own Azure Virtual Machines is forbidden. Moving beyond **proof-of-concept (PoC)** reproduction steps for infrastructure execution issues is forbidden. Attempting social engineering against Microsoft employees is forbidden.

- **GCP**: Pentesting the GCP infrastructure your organization uses is subject to Google's Acceptable Use Policy (`https://cloud.google.com/terms/aup` and `https://cloud.google.com/terms/`).

Now, let's get into benchmark checks!

A benchmark is defined as a standard with which to measure performance. Your organization may have certain expectations for how its public cloud networks perform on a day-to-day or hour-to-hour basis. In the cloud, benchmarks are often based on application and server availability defined as uptime, responsiveness from application slowdowns, and how long it may take to remediate network functionality problems.

If your organization wants to conduct benchmark checks on its public cloud networks, I recommend basing them on AWS, Azure, or GCP's **service-level agreements (SLAs)**. Those are the network and infrastructure-related performance standards that the cloud providers guaranteed your organization when you signed up for their services.

For AWS services, Amazon guarantees a certain amount of monthly uptime. If these benchmarks aren't met, your organization may be entitled to a 10%, 25%, or 100% Service Credit.

For Azure and Microsoft Online Services in general, their SLAs are conceptually similar to AWS. If certain monthly uptime benchmarks aren't met, your organization may be entitled to a 10%, 25%, or 100% Service Credit. Microsoft's SLAs are updated at least a couple of times per year.

For GCP services, their SLAs are also similar. But they generally offer a 10%, 25%, or 50% Service Credit for uptime benchmarks not met.

Beyond benchmarking for uptime, your organization may also want to benchmark its public cloud networks for security. The **Center for Internet Security** (**CIS**) offers a set of cybersecurity benchmarks for AWS, Azure, and GCP, as follows:

- `https://www.cisecurity.org/benchmark/amazon_web_services`

- `https://www.cisecurity.org/benchmark/azure`

- `https://www.cisecurity.org/benchmark/google_cloud_computing_platform`

Enumerating cloud services is a way for an outsider to determine which cloud services your organization has, how they're used, their permissions, and which access tokens are for which service.

MITRE ATT&CK defines cloud enumeration as follows (`https://attack.mitre.org/techniques/T1526/`):

> *"An adversary may attempt to enumerate the cloud services running on a system after gaining access. These methods can differ from platform-as-a-service (PaaS), to infrastructure-as-a-service (IaaS), or software-as-a-service (SaaS). Many services exist throughout the various cloud providers and can include Continuous Integration and Continuous Delivery (CI/CD), Lambda Functions, Azure AD, etc.*
>
> *Adversaries may attempt to discover information about the services enabled throughout the environment. Azure tools and APIs, such as the Azure AD Graph API and Azure Resource Manager API, can enumerate resources and services, including applications, management groups, resources, and policy definitions, and their relationships that are accessible by an identity."*

Now, let's look at some of the more common security problems public cloud services can have.

Exposed services, permissions, and integrations

Every network should undergo vulnerability assessments before they're pentested. Make sure the organization whose cloud network you're pentesting has had some vulnerability assessments conducted recently.

A vulnerability assessment (sometimes called a vulnerability audit) is a systematic process where a checklist is used to identify common security weaknesses, misconfigurations, and other vulnerabilities pertaining to a type of computer system. A vulnerability assessment is a systematic process of identifying, analyzing, and prioritizing vulnerabilities in a system, network, or application. It involves scanning the system to identify existing weaknesses, flaws, or vulnerabilities that could be exploited by attackers. An old-fashioned vulnerability assessment may have a human network security specialist use a manual list of common vulnerabilities in a particular operating system or application and look through the software, hardware, and networking settings and configurations to make sure none of them makes the computer system more susceptible to cyber attacks. That can be tedious work, but relatively practical in a 20th-century on-premises network that doesn't change very often.

But 21st-century cloud networks change very frequently. This especially pertains to containerization through platforms such as Kubernetes and Docker where a single container (virtualized application or operating system) might only live for a few days. Modern cloud networks can also be a lot more complicated, with a lot greater variety of applications and services to be concerned about. Multi-cloud, hybrid cloud, and hybrid multi-cloud environments can be especially diverse and complex.

So, it's usually impractical to conduct old-fashioned manual vulnerability assessments in cloud networks. There's no way a few human beings would be able to keep up with everything proper cloud vulnerability assessments entail. That's why we use automated vulnerability scanners in the cloud.

There are a variety of different cloud vulnerability scanners that you can use.

AWS has its own Amazon Inspector (`https://aws.amazon.com/inspector/`). Microsoft recommends Microsoft Defender for Cloud (`https://www.microsoft.com/en-ca/security/business/cloud-security/microsoft-defender-cloud`) (a component of Microsoft Defender for Servers) for Azure. Google recommends Rapid Vulnerability Detection (`https://cloud.google.com/security-command-center/docs/concepts-rapid-vulnerability-detection-overview`), and for GCP, it depends on what kinds of service tiers your organization is subscribed to and which GCP services your organization uses.

There are also some third-party vulnerability scanners you could use if they suit your needs. Some of the most popular ones are Astra Pentest, Qualys Cloud Platform, and Aqua Security.

> **Information**
>
> Astra Pentest automates vulnerability scanning and has tools to automate some of your pentesting work, but it shouldn't replace your job as a cloud pentester.

Before you start your first cloud pentest, make sure your organization has used some cloud vulnerability scanners recently. Make sure it has fixed or remediated the problems the scanners detected, and make sure you can see the results of recent vulnerability scans. The reason for doing this is if your organization's cloud networks have a lot of common vulnerabilities that can be detected by vulnerability scanners, then your pentest will probably be wasteful.

This section is about some of the most common types of cloud security problems—exposed services, permissions problems (ineffective **identity and access management**, or **IAM**), and poorly configured cloud integrations. These issues should be remediated as much as possible before you pentest!

First, let's examine exposed services.

Exposed services

An exposed service is a service in your cloud network that's unguarded from unauthorized access. Think of all of the various types of services and protocols you can find in the cloud and on the internet—HTTPS web servers, FTP file servers, SSH-encrypted remote access servers, RDP Windows remote access services, SMB services such as Samba—the list goes on. All of these potential vectors in your cloud network should have strong authentication protection, and they should also be well monitored through your cloud network's logs. It's all too common for these connections from your cloud network to the public internet to be easy ways for a cyber attacker to break in.

Cloud vulnerability scanners are often very good at finding whichever exposed services your cloud network may have, so you can remediate the problem by either improving the encryption and authentication access on the service or disabling the service altogether if your organization doesn't use it.

Another way to find exposed services is to use Shodan. Shodan offers service plans with monthly fees to continuously monitor and scan your cloud network's IP addresses for exposed services.

Security researchers have studied the immense problem of exposed services in cloud networks. In 2021, Palo Alto Networks' Unit 42 conducted a research study. It deployed 320 honeypots into a cloud network. A honeypot is a computer or server that's made to be deliberately insecure in order to tempt cyber threat actors to attack it. The purpose of using honeypots is usually to distract attackers away from the servers an organization must keep secure and to monitor cyber-attack activity in order to better understand it.

The 320 honeypots Unit 42 deployed used a combination of SSH, Samba, Postgres, and RDP. It set up each honeypot with very weak credentials such as "`username: admin, password: admin`" and monitored the honeypots to see how often they'd be attacked. All of the honeypots were attacked in less than two days. Some of the honeypots were attacked within 30 seconds of deployment! Most of the honeypots were attacked multiple times per day; the most frequently attacked honeypot was compromised 169 times in a single day.

This is why your organization must be very careful to avoid having any exposed services in your cloud network. One of the many kinds of cyber attacks exposed services can make your cloud network susceptible to is data breaches. According to IBM's 2023 Cost of a Data Breach Report (`https://www.ibm.com/reports/data-breach`), data breaches cost an organization an average of $4.35 million per incident! And that's just one of the kinds of cyber attacks that exposed services are vulnerable to.

Now let's explore permissions and IAM in the cloud.

Permissions

In a secure computer system, all data assets are only accessible to authorized users and entities. According to Gartner (`https://www.gartner.com/en/information-technology/glossary/identity-and-access-management-iam`), IAM is a *"security and business discipline that includes multiple technologies and business processes to help the right people or machines to access the right assets at the right times for the right reasons."* Each entity that's allowed at least some access to a computer system requires an identity and means of authentication such as passwords, biometrics, and access tokens.

Permissions are what users are allowed to do within a computer system. For instance, on my own personal laptop, I have full administrative access in my Windows 11 installation. I can install, uninstall, and configure all of my applications. I can create as many new user accounts as I want and give them whichever permissions I want. I can alter the Windows Registry. I can change all of the Windows settings. I can read, write, and access absolutely everything in my filesystem on my data storage. But when I log in to my employer's cloud network, my permissions are a lot more limited. I can only access the applications that I need to use for my job. I cannot create new user accounts. I can only access data that I need to have in my role in the company. That's because I own my laptop, but I don't own my employer's cloud network. As with many networks with good cybersecurity, my employer's cloud network uses a **role-based access control** (**RBAC**) system.

In RBAC, permissions are assigned to user groups within a filesystem. The groups correlate with a user's role in a company. There might be a payroll department group that has access to the company's payroll servers and applications, a research and development group that has access to the company's research and development data, a web administrators group that can make changes to the company's web servers, and so on. Permissions aren't directly assigned to users; permissions are assigned to groups. It's a more streamlined access control system that avoids the tedium of managing permissions user by user.

Mandatory Access Control (**MAC**) is the strictest access control model. Resource objects in a system can be assigned a confidentiality level such as high, medium, low, and categories according to departments and specific projects. Then, permissions to those objects are very carefully configured for each user. It can be a tedious sort of access control model to maintain, which is why MAC is most often seen in use cases with highly classified data such as government agencies.

In **Discretionary Access Control** (**DAC**), users assign permissions to the data objects they create. It's the default access control system in the Windows operating system and other local operating systems on computers that people own themselves.

The major cloud providers have their own tools your organization can use to improve your IAM.

Amazon recommends its own AWS Identity and Access Management for AWS. You can use it to manage **attribute-based access control** (**ABAC**), which is similar to RBAC. You can also use it to implement guardrails to prevent privilege escalation attacks and unauthorized access to user accounts. You can also manage user and machine identities across single or multiple AWS accounts.

Microsoft recommends its own Microsoft Entra ID (formerly known as Azure Active Directory) for Azure, which is similar to Active Directory in Windows Server. Azure Active Directory has the advantage of also being able to control IAM in multi-cloud and hybrid-cloud environments. So, for instance, if your organization has a hybrid cloud with some Windows Server machines in your on-premises network, all of your IAM from your premises to your public cloud can be harmonized through the same Active Directory system.

Google also has its own GCP IAM. Some of its key features include automated access control recommendations, flexible roles, and context-aware access.

Penetration testing can be used to ensure that the IAM in your organization's cloud network is properly configured. That includes only assigning necessary permissions to each user (the **principle of least privilege**, or **PoLP**) and making sure users have strong passwords and multiple factors of authentication (such as one-time password multiple-factor authentication applications, biometrics, and access tokens).

Now, let's look at cloud integrations. It's essential that cloud integrations are configured and deployed securely because insecure integrations are a common cloud security problem.

Cloud integration

Cloud integration is all about connecting multiple cloud networks together. In a hybrid cloud network, integration also means connecting your on-premises servers to your cloud network. Unless your organization only has endpoints on-premises and a single public cloud, cloud integration is inevitable.

Security problems with cloud integration occur when there's poor network visibility, when security solutions are incompatible between cloud platforms, and when APIs between cloud applications are poorly secured.

Your organization cannot secure what it cannot see. So, poor network visibility means parts of your hybrid-cloud or multi-cloud network could have vulnerabilities your organization is unaware of. To address this problem, it's vital that as many applications and services are logged as possible and that security monitoring solutions are compatible and deployed throughout your integrated cloud environment.

Poorly secured APIs between integrated cloud applications and services are especially susceptible to code injection (SQL injection, command injection) and query injection attacks, as well as malicious requests that exploit poor access control and outdated components. Just as it's prudent to eliminate exposed services in general, it's also prudent to eliminate exposed APIs.

Vulnerability scanners may not detect visibility problems, but some vulnerability scanners are good at detecting insecure APIs.

Visibility problems can be mitigated by using data mapping solutions to maintain a thorough data asset inventory. It's also crucial to have robust logging throughout your multi-cloud or hybrid cloud and to feed those logs into security monitoring applications.

Now, let's get into what your work as a cloud pentester is supposed to find—security vulnerabilities!

CVE, CVSS, and vulnerabilities

In cybersecurity, we have formal systems for classifying security vulnerabilities in networks and applications. Known vulnerabilities are recorded in MITRE's Common Vulnerabilities and Exposures database, or CVE for short (`https://www.cve.org/`). CVE records are classified according to MITRE's CVSS (`https://nvd.nist.gov/vuln-metrics/cvss`). Also, known exploits are classified with EPSS (`https://www.first.org/epss/`). MITRE ATT&CK is a database for classifying known exploits to computer systems and networks (`https://attack.mitre.org/`).

So, MITRE is the organization that helps cybersecurity professionals of all kinds understand vulnerabilities and exploits. The knowledge in MITRE's databases grows constantly, every day. MITRE's databases are on the web, freely available for anyone to use as a reference. As a cloud pentester, your job is to discover vulnerabilities and exploits in the cloud networks you test so that the organization you work for can better understand how to improve the security of its networks and applications. Let's explore MITRE and how it maintains knowledge that's useful for pentesters and red teamers.

Vulnerabilities

A vulnerability is a bug, flaw, or mistake in a computer system that cyber attackers can exploit to harm your organization's data. For example, if someone from the general public can access customers' credit card numbers through your organization's cloud platform-hosted e-commerce web application by clicking on a button, that's definitely a major security vulnerability. That would be a vulnerability to the confidentiality of sensitive data, according to the CIA Triad of cybersecurity.

If no one in the cybersecurity community knows about a vulnerability and a cyber criminal exploits it in a cyber attack, we call it a zero-day vulnerability. If we're lucky, a security researcher or bug bounty hunter discovers a previously unknown vulnerability before a cyber attacker gets to exploit it. That's a zero-day vulnerability as well. If a vulnerability is recorded in MITRE's CVE database, it's not a zero-day vulnerability; it's a known vulnerability.

An exploit is a method or technique used to conduct a cyber attack. For example, here's a description of an FTP exploit in MITRE's ATT&CK database (`https://attack.mitre.org/techniques/T1071/002/`):

"*Adversaries may communicate using application layer protocols associated with transferring files to avoid detection/network filtering by blending in with existing traffic. Commands to the remote system, and often the results of those commands, will be embedded within the protocol traffic between the client and server.*

Protocols such as FTP, FTPS, and TFTP that transfer files may be very common in environments. Packets produced from these protocols may have many fields and headers in which data can be concealed."

When you conduct cloud pentests for your organization, you may find many vulnerabilities in its cloud network that are in MITRE's CVE database. You might possibly discover a zero-day vulnerability, but that's rare! Usually, zero-day vulnerabilities are discovered by bug bounty hunters, or by defensive security specialists once a cyber attacker has exploited it. Don't be hard on yourself if you never discover a zero-day vulnerability as a red teamer or pentester. Your job is to find vulnerabilities in your organization's computer systems, and those vulnerabilities will be known to the cybersecurity community most of the time.

And as a red teamer especially, you may be simulating cyber exploits according to what's in MITRE ATT&CK.

So, looking stuff up in MITRE's databases will certainly be a part of your job you'll do quite frequently.

Let's understand MITRE as an organization and how it maintains cybersecurity information for the public.

The MITRE database

MITRE was founded in 1958 as a private, not-for-profit organization to work with the US Air Force. Decades before cloud networks and before the internet became a part of our everyday lives, MITRE collaborated with the US government through departments such as the **Federal Aviation Administration** (**FAA**) to develop air traffic control systems and conduct research and development in areas including computer programming and data processing. In the 1990s, MITRE helped the US government prepare for the "Y2K bug." The "Y2K bug" was a problem many computer systems around the world had. Many databases, applications, and operating systems only had two characters for the year in computer timestamps and time-keeping. So, when the year 2000 came, those systems might think it was the year 1900, therefore causing serious operational problems. Many organizations, MITRE included, worked very hard in the 1990s to fix the "Y2K bug." And that's why there weren't many problems when the year 2000 finally happened.

MITRE started its CVE database in 1999. In that year, only 321 vulnerabilities were recorded. However, the CVE database steadily grew, not only by adding more vulnerability records each year but also in terms of the rate at which vulnerabilities were recorded. The year 2003 added 1,223 records. The year 2008 added 5,673 records. 14,645 records were added in 2017. And a whopping 25,059 records were added in 2022. Applications might not be less secure these days. Maybe applications have gotten more complex and the routines the cybersecurity community engages in to find vulnerabilities have improved.

In 2013, MITRE launched ATT&CK, their database for exploits that they describe as *"globally-accessible knowledge base of adversary tactics and techniques based on real-world observations"*(https://attack.mitre.org/).

Let's examine the CVE database.

How do vulnerabilities get recorded in the CVE database?

MITRE works with a large number of **CVE Numbering Authorities (CNAs)**. As of April 2023, there are 285 CNAs. The vast majority of CNAs are tech companies that produce software, hardware, and infrastructure that could have security vulnerabilities. Some examples of CNAs are Qualcomm (a producer of semiconductor chips), Airbus (an aircraft manufacturer), and FreeBSD (an operating system developer). Also, many of the big names most people are familiar with are CNAs: Microsoft, Apple, and Google, for example.

Some large tech companies have bug bounty programs. A bug bounty program lets members of the general public (outsiders who don't work for the tech company) report security vulnerabilities they've discovered. They must abide by the company's responsible disclosure policies, which generally means they report their vulnerability discovery to a certain individual or department within the company, and they're not supposed to make their discovery public knowledge. This gives the company an opportunity to fix the vulnerability without cybercriminals finding out and using that knowledge to conduct a cyber attack.

If the bug bounty hunter abides by the rules of the company's bug bounty program and the company considers the bug bounty hunter's discovery to be legitimate and useful, they may pay the bug bounty hunter anywhere from a few hundred dollars to over $100,000. The payout depends on how much the company has decided to reward for vulnerabilities and how important they consider the vulnerability to be. *HackerOne* maintains a database of most of the bug bounty programs out there (`https://hackerone.com/bug-bounty-programs`).

Being a bug bounty hunter is very different from being a pentester or a red teamer. Pentesters and red teamers are given specific pentesting assignments with well-defined scopes. Bug bounty hunters are outsiders who may find whatever kind of vulnerabilities they're interested in or good at finding, as long as they work according to the rules of a company's bug bounty program and don't engage in any cyber attacks. Pentesting and red teaming is like being a chef in a restaurant; being a bug bounty hunter is like donating food to a food bank. And only bug bounty hunters have to find zero-day vulnerabilities, whereas pentesters and red teamers have to find whichever vulnerabilities they discover within the scope the organization they work for assigns them by simulating cyber attacks.

Quite often, records enter the CVE database through bug bounty programs. If, for example, a bug bounty hunter finds a vulnerability in Windows 11, the bug bounty hunter must abide by Microsoft's bug bounty program. Then, Microsoft enters the vulnerability into the CVE database in its role as the CNA.

Sometimes, employees and contractors for particular tech companies that are CNAs discover zero-day vulnerabilities. The tech company as a CNA will record the vulnerability in the CVE in the same way as if it came from a bug bounty hunter.

It's the responsibility of the CNAs to make sure the vulnerabilities they discover in their products and services or the vulnerabilities in their products and services that are reported to them are recorded in the CVE database. CNAs usually won't record vulnerabilities that don't pertain to their own products and services. For instance, it's not Apple's responsibility to record vulnerabilities in the Android version of Mozilla Firefox, but it may be Apple's responsibility to record vulnerabilities in the iOS version of Firefox. Or, it might be Mozilla's responsibility. Or, it might be both Apple's and Mozilla's responsibility, depending on which parts of their products are affected.

CVE records usually aren't made as soon as a CNA discovers a vulnerability. CVE records are public knowledge, and a tech company might need a few months or a year to address the vulnerability privately. When it's safe to make the vulnerability public knowledge, that's often when a CVE record is published.

Quite often as a pentester, you might find that your organization's network has vulnerabilities that are a few years old. For instance, you might find a vulnerability that has a CVE record from 2018. The CNA may have a security patch for the vulnerability, but your organization hasn't installed it, or the vulnerability might be public knowledge but very difficult to patch or mitigate. As a pentester, finding zero-day vulnerabilities isn't really your job, and many of the vulnerabilities you discover may have been known by the technology vendor for years!

Here's an example of a real-life CVE record.

CVE-2022-3349 is a vulnerability in Sony's PS4 and PS5 video game consoles. That's the format each CVE record uses for identification: CVE, then a four-digit year, then a four-digit number that's unique to the year.

The record contains a basic description of the vulnerability:

> *"A vulnerability was found in Sony PS4 and PS5. It has been classified as critical. This affects the function* UVFAT_readupcasetable *of the component* exFAT *Handler. The manipulation of the argument* dataLength *leads to heap-based buffer overflow. It is possible to launch the attack on the physical device. It is recommended to upgrade the affected component. The associated identifier of this vulnerability is VDB-209679."*

Then, a list of references to the vulnerability is shown, usually as web hyperlinks to published reports external to the CVE database.

Next, the assigning CNA is named. In this record, it's VulDB. VulDB is a third-party vulnerability database. For whatever reason, Sony isn't a CNA. So, third-party Sony trusts handle the responsibility of adding vulnerabilities in Sony products and services to the CVE database.

Next, the date the record was created is shown. In this record, it's 20220928. That means September 28th, 2022. This disclaimer is mentioned: *"The record creation date may reflect when the CVE ID was allocated or reserved, and does not necessarily indicate when this vulnerability was discovered, shared with the affected vendor, publicly disclosed, or updated in CVE."* As I mentioned, there may be a few months or a year or so between when the vulnerability was discovered and when it was added to the

CVE database. That's usually to give the vendor (the tech company the vulnerability impacts) time to address the vulnerability before it becomes public knowledge, in order to prevent cyber attacks.

For more information about *CVE-2022-3349* (and other CVE records), you need to go to NIST's NVD. The NVD has web pages for most of CVE's records. See `https://cve.mitre.org/cgi-bin/cvename.cgi?name=CVE-2022-3349` and `https://nvd.nist.gov/vuln/detail/CVE-2022-3349`.

Here's the information NVD has about CVE-2022-3349 (`https://cve.mitre.org/cgi-bin/cvename.cgi?name=CVE-2022-3349`). There's a CVSS score. CVSS rates vulnerabilities between 0.0 and 10.0. Lower numbers are less critical, which means the vulnerabilities are less dangerous if a cyber attacker exploits them. Higher numbers are more critical and more dangerous if a cyber attacker exploits them! *CVE-2022-3349* is rated 6.8 (medium) under the CVSS version 3.X rating scale.

Then, NVD lists *"References to Advisories, Solutions, and Tools."* This is similar to the web hyperlink references in CVE's own database. In fact, CVE and NVD often cross-reference the references—they might be the same hyperlinks in both versions of the record.

Finally, the NVD lists *"Weakness Enumeration."* Those are links to MITRE's **Common Weakness Enumeration (CWE)** database, what MITRE calls *"a community-developed list of software and hardware weakness types."* Weaknesses are the types of flaws a vulnerability may have. NVD's record for *CVE-2022-3349* lists these CWEs:

- CWE-787, Out-of-bounds Write

- CWE-122, Heap-based Buffer Overflow

- CWE-119, Improper Restriction of Operations within the Bounds of a Memory Buffer

Let's look at the two frequently used CVSS scoring scales.

CVSS v2.0 is the older scale. Vulnerabilities scored 0.0 to 3.9 are classified as "low," 4.0 to 6.9 are classified as "medium," and 7.0 to 10.0 are classified as "high." The newer CVSS v3.0 has more categories. 0.0 always means that a vulnerability isn't at all dangerous. I don't think any vulnerabilities have a CVSS v3.0 score of 0.0; the number just exists as a concept to help quantify the rest of the scale. Vulnerabilities rated 0.1 to 3.9 are "low," 4.0 to 6.9 are "medium." 7.0 to 8.9 are "high," and 9.0 to 10.0 are "critical." Whichever CVSS version is used, higher numbers are more dangerous vulnerabilities and lower numbers are less dangerous vulnerabilities. You will be expected to help write pentest reports as a pentester or red teamer. You should mention CVSS scores in your report, and the CVSS scores will help your organization determine which vulnerabilities are most important to address first.

Finally, there's EPSS. The EPSS is maintained by FIRST. In its words, FIRST *"aspires to bring together incident response and security teams from every country across the world to ensure a safe internet for all."*

FIRST uses EPSS to describe the likelihood or probability that a vulnerability will be exploited by cyber attackers. FIRST recognizes that there are too many vulnerabilities to fix immediately, and vulnerabilities are often recorded in the CVE database before a vulnerability is completely addressed.

Some vulnerabilities are extremely difficult to fix completely. So, FIRST uses EPSS to determine whether a known vulnerability is likely to be exploited, and how likely it will be exploited. FIRST says that only 2% to 7% of known vulnerabilities are *"exploited in the wild."*

EPSS scores are given a percentage number, from 0% to 100%. 0% is a vulnerability that will never be exploited, and 100% is a vulnerability that will definitely be exploited and probably has been exploited lots of times already. According to FIRST, the vast majority of vulnerabilities score below 25%, and many below 10%.

FIRST recommends that pentesters and defensive security specialists triage vulnerabilities according to both CVSS and EPSS. So, a vulnerability with a CVSS score of 9.8 and EPSS score of 97% should definitely be addressed right away, as soon as possible, and given the absolute top priority. If a vulnerability has a CVSS score of 9.9 but an EPSS score of 2%, you may want to wait until vulnerabilities with higher EPSS scores are addressed first, even though exploiting the vulnerability would be very dangerous.

So, now that we know how information about vulnerabilities and exploits is recorded in public databases, we're ready to understand how to write effective pentest reports and how to engage in purple teaming. Purple teaming is when the red team works with the blue team—the defensive security specialists.

Purple teaming and writing pentest reports

As a cloud pentester, you will spend anywhere from a few days to multiple months on a single engagement, whether you're a third-party contractor to the organization you're working for or a part of the organization's internal red team. Your objective is to work within your organization's contractually defined scope to find as many security vulnerabilities as you can while performing simulated cyber attacks your organization and the cloud providers (AWS, Azure, GCP) permit you to do.

So, over the course of those days, weeks, or months, you may have found several vulnerabilities. Most of them are vulnerabilities that the cybersecurity community is familiar with, with extensive records in the CVE database, NIST's NVD, and in the security alerts and patch notes of the vendors (tech companies that provide products and services to your organization) to which the vulnerabilities you've found pertain. Maybe some of the vulnerabilities you've discovered are simply common examples of poor security configuration, such as leaving Windows' RDP enabled when it's never used. That should have been found in a vulnerability assessment. But at least you were able to catch it! Or, maybe you've found a number of other commonly found cybersecurity problems in the enterprise.

That's great! You've worked very hard over a period of time, and you and your team have found a bunch of terrible cybersecurity problems that can only be found by performing effective and appropriate penetration tests. (Well, except for the unnecessarily enabled RDP. Why didn't your organization find that in a vulnerability assessment?)

Now, you can go back home, play some video games, or treat your romantic partner to a delicious gourmet meal to celebrate your accomplishments at work.

Hey, wait a second. What was the point of all that pentesting? Was it to show off your clever hacking skills? That's great, and the company you work for was very impressed. You simulated cyber attacks that it thought only an APT could pull off. (**APT** stands for **advanced persistent threat**. It refers to a cybercrime group that can attack their targets for an extended period of time. They're the most advanced type of cyber attackers, and they are persistent!)

But ultimately, the real reason why organizations hire pentesters and assemble red teams is that they need to find security vulnerabilities that a vulnerability assessment might miss so that they can *improve the security posture of their networks*.

In order for them to be able to use the information you've found to improve the security posture of their networks, you'll need to be able to communicate the information you've found effectively. That means engaging in purple teaming and writing a pentest report that's easy for the defensive security specialists in your organization to understand.

Chances are that at some point in your life, you've seen a brilliant person trying to communicate their genius ideas in a way that no one around them could understand.

In order for your pentest to benefit the organization you work for, your goal should be to avoid being like that brilliant person who couldn't communicate properly. You need to help the organization you work for understand the security problems that you've found, and perhaps even suggest some tips on how to fix them.

I've worked with many other pentesters over the years. There are a lot of very knowledgeable and highly skilled professional hackers out there. But only a minority of those people can purple team effectively and write good quality pentest reports. Anecdotally, I've found that the pentesters who are effective communicators have had successful careers for decades, whereas the pentesters who were ineffective communicators were more likely to lose their jobs.

If you can show your organization that you've found information about the security vulnerabilities in their network that they can use to measurably improve their security posture, you will be highly valued by them and you'll probably have a successful career.

This book has lots of knowledge about pentesting tools and techniques that are effective for pentesting AWS, Azure, and GCP, and being familiar with those tools and techniques is crucial to being a successful cloud pentester in your red team. But well-written pentest reports and effective purple teaming are just as important.

First, let's learn about purple teaming and why it's a practice that your organization will require.

Purple teaming

Purple teaming is a relatively recent concept in cybersecurity.

The red team is a group of *offensive* security specialists. Their job is to replicate the particular tools and techniques that specific threat actors may engage in, which they may use to attack your organization.

Their engagements may last months at a time. They are engaging in offensive cybersecurity, playing the simulated cyber attacker role for the benefit of your organization. Unlike an ordinary pentest, they have to be particular to mimic a specific attacker, such as a recognized APT group.

The blue team is a group of *defensive* security specialists. Their job is to look for new ways to improve the security posture of their organization, each and every day that they work. **Security operations center** (**SOC**) analysts, digital forensics specialists, and the **incident response** (**IR**) group in general all work in areas of defensive cybersecurity. But a proper blue team is always curious about the latest cyber threats and techniques, and it designs its security hardening work according to what it learns that way.

If you've ever had fun with mixing paint and color theory, you know that mixing red and blue pigment makes purple. So, purple teaming is a combination of what the red team does and what the blue team does.

My friend Daniel Miessler is one of the top thought leaders in the area of purple teaming, and a pioneer of the concept. According to Miessler, a purple team is created when red team members and blue team members collaborate with each other effectively. Some organizations might consider creating a dedicated purple team as an alternative to encouraging their red teams and blue teams to communicate and cooperate better. That probably wouldn't work very well.

Miessler's analogies for why dedicated purple teams are a bad idea are based on a professional restaurant kitchen. If a restaurant finds its waitstaff has trouble getting food from the kitchen to its diners, the solution isn't to hire a new team of "kitchen-to-table coordinators." The solution is to find ways to get the waitstaff to serve food effectively. If a restaurant has an elite chef who thinks their meal creations are too exquisite for diners to appreciate, no amount of culinary skill will make the restaurant popular. The chef may keep their dishes in the kitchen, and restaurants fail if diners aren't served. So, if you're a red team member who doesn't value cooperating with the blue team, your skill and talent will benefit no one.

So, the craft of purple teaming is all about effective teamwork and communication skills. These aren't really technical skills; they're people skills. It's also crucial to be humble as a red team member and be willing to listen and learn from your blue team. I've seen a lot of huge egos in this industry—don't become one of them!

GitLab conducts a lot of purple teaming engagements. Their workflow goes like this.

First, there's the attack planning phase, in which both the red team and the blue team have equal ownership. They have a brainstorming session where they propose and discuss a possible cyber threat, perhaps using **threat intelligence** (**TI**) or new threat detection capabilities for inspiration. Next, they'll discuss the logistics of the operation (responsibilities, timelines, and so on) and profile the attacker they plan to replicate. What sort of C2 servers might they have? Which tactics and techniques might they use? What are the attacker's goals? Then, they'll conduct a tabletop scenario, which is a popular activity for defensive security specialists. It's kind of like playing a tabletop roleplaying game, except they'll use it to review real-world threat actor **tactics, techniques, and procedures** (**TTPs**). If the attacker uses those TTPs, how would the blue team react in IR? How could those TTPs harm their organization's network and data?

The attack emulation phase is where the red teams and blue teams focus on their duties separately. The red team will test the infrastructure and tooling required to execute its TTPs. The red team will then simulate cyber attacks using those TTPs, like a targeted pentest. While the red team simulates attacks, the blue team will validate the expected outcomes of those (simulated) attacks.

The final phase is the conclusion of the operation. The red team prepares and shares its pentest report. And then, the red team and blue team come together to discuss the details of what happened. What worked? What could've been done better?

There are many ways to conduct purple teaming. GitLab's workflow is one model. SCYTHE has publicly shared its own model, the **Purple Team Exercise Framework** (PTEF).

The workflow of SCYTHE's framework goes like this. Under the direction of an exercise coordinator, the red team and blue team come together to discuss a particular threat actor, the threat actor's TTPs, and the associated technical details. Then, the red team and the blue team are equal collaborators in a tabletop simulation or discussion of the TTPs and your organization's security controls. If the offensive side does something specific, how would the defensive side respond? Then, the red team simulates the attacker's TTP while the blue team watches carefully. The blue team probably should be taking notes. Then, the blue team detects and responds to the red team's TTP simulations; everything it's doing should be viewable by the red team. The detection engineering step has the blue team tweaking its security controls and improving its network security event logging to increase its visibility of the simulated attack from the red team. Finally, the red team and blue team come together to repeat their procedure, record their results, and then move on to the next TTP simulation—a new purple team exercise.

If you're simply working for your organization in the capacity of being a pentester, purple teaming workflows aren't really relevant to you. However, you must still be mindful of respecting the needs of your organization's defensive security specialists and communicating effectively with them.

If you are a part of a proper red team, those examples of how purple teaming is done in organizations can serve as a model for your work. If your company doesn't already have purple teaming procedures in place and agreed upon with the blue team, encourage purple teaming procedures to become established. If you can explain the importance of effective collaboration with the defensive security group with the leaders of your security team, your efforts will be well worth it. You may need to make a strong case about the importance of proper purple teaming to your supervisors, but your initiative will probably be rewarded.

Now, on to something you'll probably be expected to do, whether or not you're part of a red team. Let's learn about writing effective pentest reports!

Writing pentest reports

If you're not good at creative writing, your pentesting team will be okay if at least one of your pentesting colleagues is good at it. As long as everyone in your pentesting team can communicate with each other effectively in other ways, you can simply delegate the task of writing the pentest report to the best writer on your team. Of course, if you're pentesting as a team, your pentest report is a group effort. Findings from everyone should be included in the report. The writer of your pentest report will need all of your findings, and you'll need to be able to explain what you did and what happened when the writer asks you about it. You should also take good care of the logs from whatever tools you used during your pentest because you'll need to use them as a reference in your report.

But if you're a solo pentester, then the responsibility for writing the pentest report is entirely yours! This is an example of how pentesters need more than technical skills; they also need creative and communications skills.

So, let's examine what your organization will expect from your pentest report.

All good pentest reports must include the following:

- An executive summary at the beginning of the report.

- A definition of the scope of your pentest. This is the "what" of your test. What exactly was the subject of your test?

- A thorough and detailed explanation of the methodology of your pentest. This is the "how" of your test.

- A list of the vulnerabilities your pentest discovered. These should probably be triaged with the most critical vulnerabilities at the beginning and the least critical vulnerabilities at the end.

- An analysis of the impact the vulnerabilities you discovered could have on your organization if they're exploited. This part is absolutely crucial, because if your organization doesn't understand the harm that could occur if the vulnerabilities aren't addressed, then why should they care?

- Advice for how to remediate the specific vulnerabilities your pentest discovered. Go one by one, vulnerability by vulnerability.

Recommend how your organization's security strategies can be improved. This goes beyond remediating specific vulnerabilities. You need to make recommendations for how your organization can improve its security posture as a whole. For instance, if most of the vulnerabilities you successfully exploited have been in the CVE database for more than a decade, you could recommend that it improves its patch management and works on replacing legacy tech with more modern hardware and software.

There's a good reason why the executive summary should be at the beginning of your report rather than the end. The executive summary is for the *executives*. They're usually people with a lot of power and influence in your organization, but they aren't particularly technical.

They're also very busy people. On their list of priorities, reading your pentest report is probably number 27 for the day. They're not going to spend hours reading your report. If you're lucky, they'll give it 5 minutes. Therefore, the executive summary needs to be at the beginning, and it needs to be concise. The executive summary should be a page or two, and that's it. If you go by word count, aim for 300 to 600 words. It's unlikely the executives will read more than that.

In your executive summary, just explain what you pentested and what patterns you found in the results of your pentest or what the most significant problems you discovered were. Here's an example:

"*We tried to see if we could access the organization's microservices that are hosted on Amazon EC2 instances through code injection exploits in the e-commerce web interface. It worked and we acquired unauthorized access through these APIs and we were able to access sensitive data. This is how those vulnerabilities could harm the company if they're exploited. And this is how much money the company could lose in a successful real-world cyber attack.*"

Replace each instance of "*this*" with some of your actual pentest findings. And I'm a strong believer in mentioning estimated dollar figures of the harm those cyber attacks could do to the company. That's what your executives care about the most—money. Getting credible financial risk data is easier than you might think. For instance, if the likely impact of vulnerability exploitation is data breaches, you can get approximate dollar figures from IBM's *Cost of a Data Breach Report* (`https://www.ibm.com/reports/data-breach`). For ransomware, you could cite the following report: `https://www.cybereason.com/ransomware-the-true-cost-to-business-2022`.

The rest of your report is for the cybersecurity specialists in your organization to read. As long as the executive summary is short, the rest of your report can be however long it needs to be in order to include all of the important technical details. The length of your report will vary depending on how much you did during your pentest. But pentest reports are rarely over 100 pages. Most are between 20 and 70 pages.

Explain the scope of your pentest. "*We tested this particular DevOps network.*" "*We tested this particular web application.*" "*We tested this particular network segment.*" But of course, you'll need to provide more detail for the scope of your test. Cite network addresses, IP addresses, or whichever identifiers are applicable so that the security team knows exactly what you tested.

The methodology section also should be detailed and specific. You should explain step by step the exact actions you conducted in your test in chronological order. Name the tools you used, the exploits you simulated, and the techniques you attempted. When in doubt, err on the side of being more detailed rather than less. You may want to cite MITRE's ATT&CK database (`https://attack.mitre.org/`) to name specific exploitation techniques. It's a freely and publicly available resource on the web.

Next, you need to present the vulnerabilities your pentest discovered. Every single vulnerability you discovered must be included. Cite specific CVEs wherever they're applicable. I recommend presenting the vulnerabilities in order from most critical to least critical. Mention both CVSS scores and EPSS scores. Weigh the criticality of each vulnerability according to a combination of both CVSS and EPSS. For instance, if there are several vulnerabilities with CVSS scores of 7.0 to 9.0, the ones with an EPSS of 30% should go first, and the ones with an EPSS of 10% should go after. MITRE's CVE database (`https://cve.org`), NIST's NVD database (`https://nvd.nist.gov/`), and FIRST's EPSS database (`https://www.first.org/epss/`) are all freely and publicly available on the web for you to find CVE numbers, CVSS scores, and EPSS scores.

Next, you need to provide remediation advice. Be specific. Mention patches that need to be installed, configurations and settings that need to be changed, and so on. This will vary according to the nature of the vulnerabilities.

You know the phrase "can't see the forest for the trees"? It means someone is too focused on the details of a situation that they lose sight of the "big picture." But in the case of your pentest report, your organization will have to see both the forest *and* the trees. The remediation advice section is the "trees," and the security strategy improvement advice section is the "forest." "*Upgrade and replace legacy tech.*" "*Hire a security operations center team.*" "*Improve your incident response plan.*" Those are the sorts of things that pertain to security strategy, but use details that apply to your particular organization and your particular pentest.

I recommend looking at some publicly available real-world pentest reports before you write one for the first time. Check out the collection of real pentest reports juliocesarfort maintains on GitHub (`https://github.com/juliocesarfort/public-pentesting-reports`). There's also a large collection on the pentestreports.com website (`https://pentestreports.com/reports/`). If you want to go further than that, I gave a talk about writing effective pentest reports for *SANS Pen Test HackFest Summit 2021* titled *Writing Reports: The Overlooked Pen Testing Skill*. You can watch it on YouTube (`https://www.youtube.com/watch?v=r-6LBjlM14Y`).

And there you have it. That's why your pentest is conducted in the first place. You do it to find security vulnerability information, recommend a course of action, and help the defensive security team improve your organization's security posture.

Summary

AWS, Azure, and GCP have pentesting policies that you and your organization must abide by. Benchmark checks verify the performance of your organization's cloud services. Cloud provider SLAs are a good source of general benchmarks. CIS also has specific benchmarks for cybersecurity. Cloud service enumeration is a way that an attacker can find out information about how your organization uses cloud services. There are scripts you can execute to test your organization's susceptibility to vulnerabilities.

Vulnerability assessments can be performed by vulnerability scanning applications. Before pentesting, it's important to have a recent history of vulnerability assessments and mitigation for the findings of those assessments. Common security misconfigurations must be addressed first before your organization is ready to pentest.

Exposed services are internet services and ports in your organization's cloud network that an attacker can use to cyber-attack it through the internet. It's vital to make sure that proper access control measures are on all of these points in your public cloud so that no services are exposed. Permissions are an access control component—what are users and machines permitted to do in each application and service your organization has? Cloud integrations are when different cloud platforms in your network (AWS, Azure, GCP) connect with each other, or when any of those parts also connect with an on-premises network. It's essential to secure cloud integrations because they can be especially vulnerable to cyber attacks.

Publicly known security vulnerabilities are recorded in MITRE's CVE database. NIST records the same CVEs in its NVD database and assigns CVSS scores to them that determine how critical they are. FIRST assigns EPSS ratings to those same CVEs that indicate how likely it is that an attacker may exploit them.

As a pentester or red teamer, it's essential for you to communicate and cooperate well with the defensive security team or blue team. Purple teaming is operations the red team and blue team perform together to find security vulnerabilities. Pentest reports should always be written for each and every pentest. They should effectively explain your vulnerability discoveries, their impact, and remediation advice for your organization's executives and defensive security team.

In the next chapter, I'll introduce you to AWS, Amazon's cloud platform. You'll learn about various AWS applications and services and why they're used. We'll also explore Amazon's own built-in AWS security tools, and some third-party tools as well.

AWS is one of the most popular cloud platforms around. You may be surprised by how many different use cases AWS can support. AWS also has many very useful security controls that are important for cloud pentesters to understand.

Further reading

To learn more on the topics covered in this chapter, you can visit the following links:

- *Official AWS penetration testing policies*: `https://aws.amazon.com/security/penetration-testing/`

- *Official Microsoft pentesting rules of engagement*: `https://www.microsoft.com/en-us/msrc/pentest-rules-of-engagement`

- *Official Google pentesting policies*: `https://cloud.google.com/terms/aup`

- *MITRE's CVE database*:

  - `https://cve.mitre.org/cve/`

  - `https://www.cve.org/`

- *A full list of bug bounty programs through HackerOne*: `https://hackerone.com/bug-bounty-programs`

- *NIST's CVSS system*: `https://nvd.nist.gov/vuln-metrics/cvss`

- *FIRST's EPSS system*: `https://www.first.org/epss/`

Part 2: Pentesting AWS

Amazon's AWS is one of the most popular cloud platforms. In this part, we will learn about AWS's various software-as-a-service, platform-as-a-service, and infrastructure-as-a-service applications. We will deploy our own AWS instance in which to test our pentesting skills. We will use AWS Security Hub to check the security posture of our AWS deployment. We will also try out some pentesting tools in AWS, step by step. Then, we'll deploy Docker and Kubernetes containers and test those as well.

This section has the following chapters:

- *Chapter 4, Security Features in AWS*

- *Chapter 5, Pentesting AWS Features through Serverless Applications and Tools*

- *Chapter 6, Pentesting Containerized Applications in AWS*

4

Security Features in AWS

As a cloud pentester, the likelihood of being asked to pentest AWS applications and services is very high. AWS has played a central role in the cloud computing boom of the past 20 years. So, in this chapter, I'll introduce you to AWS. You'll learn about the most popular AWS services, applications, and features and why they're used. We'll also talk about AWS's SaaS, IaaS, and PaaS features, and explore Amazon's own AWS security tools and third-party security tools.

In this chapter, we'll cover the following topics:

- Introduction to AWS

- Frequently used AWS SaaS features

- AWS IaaS features

- AWS PaaS features

- AWS security controls and tools

Let's get started!

Introduction to AWS

AWS stands for **Amazon Web Services**. It's one of the most popular cloud platforms. Amazon started as an online book retailer in 1994, but even in those early days, Amazon founder *Jeff Bezos* said that Amazon.com was a tech company with an objective to simplify online transactions for consumers. The parts of the business akin to traditional retailers, such as maintaining warehouses of inventory and customer service, were just some of the necessary components. The infrastructure that Bezos truly values has always been Amazon's data centers.

As the 1990s went on, Amazon expanded its inventory well beyond books. It started selling music, movies, apparel, home accessories, and so on. In the 21st century, Amazon sells almost everything that can be properly stored at room temperature and legally sold to consumers. They also provide a lot of different internet services for consumers, such as streaming entertainment from **Amazon Prime** and **Kindle eBooks**.

As the 2000s began, Amazon found itself with more computer networking infrastructure than most big corporations. No other company on Earth had so much success selling products through the web. So, by 2002, Amazon started to let other retail businesses use some of its infrastructure and software to deploy their own e-commerce more successfully. That's the origin of AWS, but AWS didn't take its current form until 2006 when it launched **Elastic Compute Cloud (EC2)** and **Simple Storage Service (S3)**. EC2 rents computer processing power and S3 rents data storage to business and enterprise customers.

As of 2023, there's a wide range of AWS applications to serve a variety of business needs. EC2 and S3 have improved over the years and are very commonly used services. There's a whole collection of AWS applications and services for many SaaS, PaaS, and IaaS use cases. Ever since AWS launched about 20 years ago, it has frequently added new services and applications.

Whether your organization uses AWS as its sole cloud provider or has a multi-cloud network, it likely has more than one AWS service or application implemented into its network. Some organizations even use dozens of AWS applications simultaneously.

Describing every AWS service and application in detail is beyond the scope of this book. But when you pentest your organization's AWS network, it's important to understand why many of the most popular AWS services and applications exist. Let's have a look.

Frequently used AWS SaaS features

AWS features, applications, and services fall into a lot of different categories. Some services are offered free of charge or with limited free trials. Most services, especially the ones that businesses are most likely to use, are provided for fees that vary depending on the service and how much a business needs to use it. For example, a cloud application that needs a small amount of bandwidth and serves a few hundred users per month will generally be a lot less expensive than a cloud application that needs a large amount of bandwidth and serves tens of thousands of users per month.

Of course, managing AWS service fees is your organization's responsibility, not yours. So, I'll explain what a pentester needs to understand: the AWS services that businesses frequently use and why they use them.

I'll start with some SaaS features and applications. These applications use AWS's infrastructure, platform, and its own software. SaaS services are the ones Amazon has the most responsibility for and control of. As a pentester, you're not allowed to pentest them in any way whatsoever. Refer to AWS's penetration testing policies (`https://aws.amazon.com/security/penetration-testing/`). However, you should still understand what these applications are, even if you're not allowed to pentest them. It'll help you understand how your organization uses AWS as a whole, which will help you devise more effective red team scenarios and put security testing findings into context.

Amazon Chime is Amazon's equivalent to Zoom or Skype, hosted through the AWS ecosystem. Chime supports pretty much all types of client computers and mobile devices, with native Windows, Mac, iOS, Android, and web applications. Your organization may use Chime to conduct video conferencing between employees and contractors. It can control who has access to its video conferencing meetings and what kind of access they have.

Amazon WorkMail provides email services and integrated calendars. It works kind of like Gmail and Google Calendar. WorkMail can be used with the Microsoft Outlook client or pretty much any email client software that's compatible with the IMAP protocol.

AWS Budgets is designed for small businesses to track their spending. They can set a budget such as $5,000 per month. They can track how much employees or other stakeholders spend from the corporate bank account, and how they spend it. There are a ton of other features, such as the ability to generate highly detailed reports and trigger alerts for spending anomalies.

AWS SaaS services can be very user friendly, and they can help both business customers and consumers get lots of work done. Although you won't be allowed to pentest these applications, there's a strong likelihood that at least some AWS SaaS applications are a part of your company's network. For instance, if a company stores a lot of its data in Amazon S3, it might as well use Amazon WorkMail for the company email servers. AWS service subscriptions make it convenient for companies to use a variety of SaaS, IaaS, and PaaS applications at the same time and pay for them with the same billing.

AWS IaaS features

IaaS or **infrastructure-as-a-service** features are the parts of AWS where enterprises have the most control and the most responsibility. There's more that pentesters are allowed to do with these components than with PaaS and SaaS. But you are still on Amazon's infrastructure, therefore they still have rules of engagement to abide by. Refer to AWS's pentesting policies in *Chapters 2* and *3*, or you can find them on their website (`https://aws.amazon.com/security/penetration-testing/`).

AWS IaaS can be divided into two general categories: *compute* and *storage*.

Compute services

Amazon EC2 is AWS's debut compute service. It stands for Amazon Elastic Compute Cloud. EC2 is largely used by enterprises that develop their own software but need tons and tons of computer processing power to process their databases, conduct scientific research, and so on.

I'll summarize some company testimonials.

Orangetheory Fitness is a popular gym chain in the United States and Canada. It offers its customers "high-tech group workouts that combine high-intensity interval training designed to improve strength and cardio fitness levels." It deploys its in-house software through EC2 to analyze the fitness data it constantly gets from thousands of customers every day.

Toyota Research Institute uses EC2 to train machine learning models. In machine learning, AI processes a large amount of data over time and makes changes to a program according to what it has learned from the data.

Airlines were among the earliest customers of IBM mainframe computers back in the 1960s. Think of all the data an airline has to process constantly – such as ticket sales and flight data. If a flight is late, a computer has to have a record of how late the flight is, where the aircraft is, and why it's late. That's just an example of the kind of information an airline has to compute in its everyday business operations. Cathay Pacific is a very large Asian airline that serves "nearly 200 destinations in 49 countries and territories." And now, using cloud services such as Amazon EC2 is a more effective 21st-century alternative to running massive mainframes on-premises.

Netflix is another example of the sort of large corporation that uses EC2. Its testimonial says that a lot more people were watching Netflix during the beginning of the COVID-19 pandemic. Netflix called it "this unprecedented time." Hypothetically, if 20 million people worldwide were watching Netflix concurrently at a given time and then 50 million people worldwide watched Netflix concurrently at another time, that's a massive increase in the computing and networking resources that would be needed. Therefore, Netflix says it likes EC2 for its scalability.

Amazon **Elastic Container Service (ECS)** is another IaaS computing solution. It is a suitable choice for companies looking for the necessary infrastructure to deploy applications that are containerized, as using containerized applications is a prevalent way to utilize cloud infrastructure.

At the risk of oversimplifying a complex topic, it's a way to deploy an application with a lot of components running in virtual machines, called containers.

What are containers?

Containers are a really precise way to deploy virtualization, a way to simulate computer hardware with software. A container contains only the operating system components that are needed to run a small part of a much larger application. Individual containers can have a lifespan of just a few days or even just a few hours.

Containers can be launched and killed dynamically according to the current needs, a way of providing scalability. Containers often contain a virtualized operating system and a component of a more sophisticated application. But containers need a containerization orchestration solution in order to be managed and to allocate hardware resources. Amazon describes ECS as a "fully managed container orchestration service that helps organizations easily deploy, manage, and scale containerized applications."

Docker is a container orchestration platform. ECS is a service that can be used to deploy such platforms. Think of a company's software as the swimmers, Docker as the water, and ECS as the swimming pool. If your company uses Kubernetes as its container orchestration platform, it can instead choose **Amazon Elastic Kubernetes Service** (**Amazon EKS**) to serve a similar purpose to ECS.

AWS Lambda is another service that AWS permits pentesting on. It's categorized as a compute service. It can be used to help deploy your applications on Amazon's infrastructure as a serverless compute service while dynamically allocating resources according to whatever is needed at any given time. Developers can deploy custom logic in Lambda. For example, if a user leaves an item in their shopping cart without checking it out, send the user an email reminder in three days, and remove the item from their shopping cart in seven days. Lambda can run applications that use any third-party library, and there's also native support for Java, Go, PowerShell, Node.js, C#, Python, and Ruby.

Amazon CloudFront is a **content delivery network** (**CDN**). A CDN is defined as a geographically distributed network of proxy servers and their data centers. CDNs were originally created in the late 1990s to help support the rapidly expanding use of the internet. So, a CDN can dynamically allocate network resources to avoid bottlenecks – points in the transmission path that can slow down performance. So, if one part of a network is managing as much data as it can, the CDN data transmission path will use another part of the network that has room to manage more data. **YouTube** is an example of a very popular streaming media platform that uses a CDN. The data center and servers that are streaming videos to YouTube users can change according to demand and capacity.

Amazon CloudFront supports WebSocket, edge termination, Amazon EC2, Amazon S3, Elastic Load Balancing, and Lambda.

AWS Fargate is a serverless compute solution for containers. Developers can deploy Docker applications through Amazon ECS or Kubernetes applications through Amazon EKS. All the necessary hardware and network resources are dynamically allocated. Just as much memory as is needed at any given time will be used. I'll explain more about containerization in the *AWS PaaS features* section of this chapter and in *Chapters 6*, *9*, and *12*.

AWS Elastic Beanstalk uses Amazon's compute services and infrastructure to deploy web applications. It features native support for Java, .NET, Node.js, PHP, Ruby, Python, Go, and Docker. Developers can use **integrated development environments** (**IDEs**) they're already familiar with, such as Eclipse and Visual Studio, to deploy applications through Elastic Beanstalk.

Let's look at some IaaS solutions for storage.

Storage services

Enterprises can generate petabytes of data. A petabyte is about 1,024 terabytes. You likely have at least a few terabytes worth of storage on your mobile devices, laptop, and external hard drive. Businesses often need petabytes of storage, and sometimes even exabytes! An exabyte is about 1,024 petabytes. Any organization with petabytes or exabytes of data would absolutely need massive data centers in order to store it. Now, it's much more feasible for those data centers to be on the cloud, because even running a data center for several petabytes of storage can be a big hassle.

Amazon S3 is the debut AWS storage service. If a company has huge amounts of data that it needs to store, Amazon S3 is one of the most popular options for that purpose.

Snap, the company that makes **Snapchat**, says that it stores about 2 exabytes of data through Amazon S3. Snap says that's over 1.5 *trillion* photos and videos. So, that's an example of how a company with a huge amount of data may use it. But companies don't have to have anywhere near that much data to use Amazon S3.

Amazon promises that if customers use Amazon S3 as designed, it will keep secure the infrastructure that's used to store their data and make sure that any of their data is easily retrievable as quickly as possible.

One of the more common uses for Amazon S3 is to store data lakes. A data lake is a huge, centralized repository of structured and unstructured data. For instance, all the photos in everyone's accounts in Google Photos could be collected as one data lake in the low exabytes. Big tech companies often use data lakes to train machine learning AI.

Another common reason to use Amazon S3, for large and small businesses alike, is to back up data. There are multiple AWS data centers worldwide, and the data that companies store through Amazon S3 could be physically stored on multiple continents. It's possible for a massive cyberattack, earthquake, or hurricane to destroy a lot of computers in one location. Instead of taking the risk of having all of a company's crucial and critical data stored on its premises, the company can store it through Amazon S3 internationally.

AWS Backup centralizes and automates data backups. It can work with Amazon S3 to store an organization's data, and with Amazon EC2 to create on-demand backup jobs. Imagine a company with thousands of users and PCs in multiple countries. The work they do for the company each day needs to be backed up to the company's AWS network. Most employees work between 9 a.m. and 5 p.m. but may live across a dozen different time zones. So, it may be convenient to execute a backup job at 5 p.m. each day, but 5 p.m. occurs at different moments all across the globe. These are the kinds of complex data backup needs that AWS Backup is designed to handle. AWS Backup is fully compatible with all AWS services.

If your organization has a lot of software developers and IT people, there's a good chance that it can make good use of AWS's IaaS services. AWS IaaS gives organizations a lot of control over their own custom software without the downsides of having to maintain on-premises data centers.

AWS PaaS features

PaaS or **platform-as-a-service** is in the middle between IaaS and SaaS as far as security responsibilities are concerned. AWS provides the infrastructure and a platform, but it doesn't provide all of the software as it would in SaaS. PaaS services are software developer tools most of the time. As a pentester, you generally can only pentest PaaS services under very limited conditions. A lot of what you're permitted to do in IaaS is forbidden in PaaS. When in doubt, assume by default that you're not allowed to do something, and consult the AWS penetration testing policy (`https://aws.amazon.com/`

security/penetration-testing/). In some situations, such as network stress testing, you may submit a form to AWS to request permission to do something. Only proceed with your plans for your red team engagement when you've verified that AWS will permit you to do everything you plan to do. You may have to tweak or adjust your plans according to AWS's response to your inquiry.

As with SaaS, even when you're not allowed to pentest something, it still helps to understand how your company uses AWS PaaS. It'll help you put your red team engagements and their impact into perspective.

The **AWS Command-Line Interface** (**AWS CLI**) is pretty much as it sounds. Just as you can use a command line to administrate your own computer by typing in commands and hitting *Enter*, AWS lets developers manage AWS services in a similar way. Developers often love the CLI because it gives them a lot more control than they'd get from a **graphical user interface** (**GUI**). Or, at least, they can get what they want done much more quickly and efficiently. The AWS CLI has good documentation and support for executing shell scripts (https://docs.aws.amazon.com/cli/latest/reference/). You can use the AWS CLI from an application installed on Windows, Mac, or Linux. Alternatively, you can access the AWS CLI through your web browser with *AWS CloudShell*.

AWS CDK is AWS's **Cloud Development Toolkit**. Software developers are familiar with **software development kits** (**SDKs**). For instance, in order to create Java applications that work well in multiple operating systems, your IDE (a type of application for software development) needs Java SDKs. AWS CDK is conceptually similar, but for the cloud. When an organization develops a cloud application to deploy through AWS in-house, AWS CDK is very useful.

So, AWS CDK helps to support cloud features within in-house-developed cloud applications. Chances are, developers will also need AWS tools and SDKs (https://aws.amazon.com/developer/tools/) to support the other technologies and platforms they may be using. There are AWS SDKs specific to C++, Go, Java, JavaScript, Kotlin, .NET, Node.js, PHP, Ruby, Python, Rust, and Swift.

AWS Cloud9 is Amazon's own IDE for developing cloud applications with AWS CDK and the programming language-specific SDKs and tools that are needed. Cloud9 runs directly in the web browser and developers can use it to work on the applications they're making wherever they happen to be, on any compatible computer they can log in to. That's because Cloud9 stores all of their work through the cloud! How convenient.

What if people are making movies and cartoons instead of cloud-driven software applications? That's what **Amazon Nimble Studio** is for. As with Cloud9, users can work on their projects wherever they go. They can also collaborate on projects with the rest of their team.

All data transmitted on the internet should be encrypted with public key cryptography. **AWS Certificate Manager** is a main component of the **public key infrastructure** (**PKI**) that companies need to deploy in order to encrypt the applications they deploy through AWS with SSL or TLS.

Users often interact with cloud-driven applications with their iPhones and Android phones as endpoints. Software developers know that they can't be sure how well their application will run on a particular device without testing it on that device.

It's a hassle to maintain a collection of iPhones and Android phones of various models. So, developers can use **AWS Device Farm** as an alternative. AWS Device Farm virtualizes a wide variety of phone and tablet models and developers can directly see how their applications will run. They can even interact with their applications exactly how a user would through a touchscreen simulation.

AWS Amplify promises to help developers "build full-stack web and mobile apps in hours." It can be an appropriate solution if the app is relatively simple. For example, luxury retailer Neiman Marcus uses AWS Amplify to create and manage its online retailing.

Databases are often a necessary component for many different kinds of applications. AWS has multiple PaaS database services according to the type of database that's needed. In-depth explanations of different database technologies are beyond the scope of this book, but an experienced development team will usually know what kind of databases they need.

Amazon Aurora supports MySQL and PostgreSQL databases. It also directly integrates with Amazon S3, AWS Backup, AWS EKS, and many other AWS services.

Amazon **Relational Database Service** (**RDS**) is for relational databases. It can use Amazon Aurora as an engine. It can also use MySQL, MariaDB, PostgreSQL, Oracle, and SQL Server directly.

Amazon Redshift is for data warehousing. Whereas data lakes can contain very large amounts of unstructured data, data warehousing is for very large amounts of carefully structured data. It uses SQL to analyze the data in your organization's data warehouses. Deploying large-scale data analytics is a common use case for Amazon Redshift.

Amazon Lightsail promises to help developers deploy web applications "in just a few clicks" using a series of virtual servers. It offers support for managed databases with MySQL or PostgreSQL. It facilitates CDNs on the same infrastructure as Amazon CloudFront. It also supports Docker containers through a Lightsail container service.

AWS CodeDeploy automates code deployment through your organization's on-premises servers, or through Amazon EC2, AWS Lambda, AWS Fargate, or AWS ECS. You can monitor and roll back your applications as needed, configure and orchestrate deployment, and maintain different application releases all at the same time.

AWS PaaS services are popular with software developers. They help developers create custom applications without having to build all the components from scratch. These days, applications are seldom developed from scratch anyway.

AWS security controls and tools

One of the most important things that you need to become familiar with as an AWS pentester is the various security controls AWS uses, and the tools you can use to conduct your pentesting. The details on how to use those tools will be explained in *Chapters 5* and *6*, but I'll introduce the tools here.

Security controls

First, what are security controls, and what security controls does AWS have?

Security controls are components that can help to prevent or mitigate cyberattacks or other possible threats to your organization's data. All security threats are related to the **CIA (confidentiality, integrity, and availability) Triad**. So, a security control is designed to help prevent breaching data confidentiality and the integrity of data, and may also be designed to help maintain the availability of data. A security control can help with one or any combination of these three components.

Examples of security controls include antivirus software, physical door locks to rooms that have computers in them, intrusion detection sensors, security cameras, DDoS mitigation solutions (such as Cloudflare), intrusion prevention systems, firewalls, authentication systems (usernames, passwords, or two-factor authentication), human security guards, and access cards and tokens.

These sorts of tools, systems, and mechanisms can help improve a company's cybersecurity if they're used properly, but no security control guarantees perfect security. Well-used security controls lessen the frequency and negative impact of cyberattacks. As a pentester, you'll often be expected to test the effectiveness of how your organization implements these controls by simulating cyberattacks against them. In your pentesting report, you may have to describe how security controls reacted to your pentests and how your organization can improve their use. Sometimes, you may even work with defensive security professionals to suggest better alternatives or upgrades.

Amazon provides customers with a lot of different security controls that they can use in their AWS networks. As with all security controls, they only work if they use them, and use them properly! Amazon is responsible for the security of its infrastructure, and your organization is responsible for the security of your own code. But Amazon still provides tools your organization can use to help you manage your own security responsibility. I used to do research for a company that provides services for managing machine identities, such as TLS certificates. I discovered that many developers who use cloud platforms don't use the tools those platforms provide to encrypt applications with TLS (`https://venafi.com/blog/want-more-secure-more-effective-cloud-watch-your-machine-identities/`).

Not encrypting the data that's being transmitted from a cloud application is a huge security vulnerability! The cloud platforms are doing everything right. They say, "here's how to encrypt your applications with our tools, and documentation on how to use them." I can't stress enough how important it is that the organization you work for looks at all the security tools that Amazon provides for AWS services, and reads the extensive free documentation they provide on how to use them.

So, with that being said, let's have a look at some of Amazon's most important AWS security tools.

AWS Security Hub is where all of Amazon's native AWS security services come together. Data is aggregated from AWS IAM, Amazon Macie, AWS Health, AWS Systems Manager, Amazon Inspector, AWS Firewall Manager, Amazon GuardDuty, and AWS Config.

Security findings can be correlated between different AWS security services for the full picture. Amazon Detective can be launched from AWS Security Hub to further investigate security alerts and events, and **security orchestration, automation, and response** (**SOAR**) workflows can be initiated once administrators and your organization's security team are familiar with how AWS security services work together, in order to make their work more efficient.

AWS **Identity and Access Management** (**IAM**) offers a console and system to manage all of the user identities and machine identities throughout an organization's AWS account. All of the AWS services that an organization uses through the same account can be managed through the same AWS IAM application. The console is called **IAM Identity Center**.

Some identities can remain relatively unchanged for years, such as user identities for administrators. Other identities may only be needed for a few days or a few weeks, such as machine identities for temporary cloud workloads. IAM can manage all of the different types of identities that your organization's AWS services use. As far as the access management part is concerned, administrators can "fine-grain" customize the permissions and access each identity has.

IAM also supports service control policies to help provide guardrails for the access each identity has. Policies can help limit the access that identities have. Whichever rules or settings are the most restrictive win. This is connected to the principle of least privilege, a common concept in cybersecurity. The principle of least privilege means that users and other entities only have as much access as they absolutely need to do their jobs and no more. This limits not only the harm that a user can cause by their mistakes but also the possible damage that could be done if a cyber threat actor maliciously acquires access to the account.

Using AWS IAM effectively means there are robust logs each time a user or machine logs onto the system, and each time identities are used to access a part of an organization's AWS services. If security professionals suspect that a threat actor may have conducted a privilege escalation attack (when an attacker acquires access to an account and increases their access from that point), AWS IAM is the first place they should check. AWS IAM also generates alerts when anomalies are detected.

AWS Directory Service is another IAM-related tool, but it's specifically for managing Microsoft Active Directory through **Lightweight Directory Access Protocol** (**LDAP**). Active Directory has been the default means for Windows servers to administrate Windows client computers ever since the Windows 2000 Server edition. If your organization manages Windows computers through AWS, AWS Directory Service can be used and also integrated with AWS IAM.

Amazon GuardDuty actively monitors an organization's AWS services for possible cyber threats. GuardDuty receives constant updates about the ever-evolving cyber threat landscape through both AWS and third-party threat intelligence feeds. The system uses a combination of machine learning, behavioral modeling, and anomaly detection to detect possible threats.

For example, GuardDuty may understand that a certain kind of user will transmit a certain amount of data during a session in your organization's application. If, all of a sudden, a user downloads 30 times as much data as an average user, that would probably trigger the anomaly detection mechanisms. Then,

GuardDuty would combine the anomaly data with what the system has learned through machine learning to decide whether or not it's an **indicator of compromise** (**IOC**). Human security professionals may receive an alert. Sometimes, security professionals need to investigate alerts to determine whether a cyberattack is actually happening or whether it's a false positive alert. Is the anti-theft alarm on that parked car triggered because of a real auto theft attempt, or because a cat jumped onto the car? Innocuous mistakes also happen in cloud security.

GuardDuty can continuously monitor and analyze instance and container workloads, user accounts, serverless applications, Amazon S3 resources, and databases. GuardDuty can also scan for malware and generate context for security alerts and the events associated with them.

When security professionals need to investigate activity related to a GuardDuty alert, they can use **Amazon Detective** for help. GuardDuty security findings, and logs from Amazon EKS audits, VPC Flow, and AWS CloudTrail, are all integrated into the system. Not only can GuardDuty alerts be investigated with Detective, but also alerts from AWS Security Hub and integrated security partner products.

Detective can be launched from the AWS Management Console, and then administrators can see visualizations and context for their alerts.

Amazon Inspector is designed for vulnerability management. Remember when I mentioned the importance of frequent vulnerability scanning in *Chapter 3*? Your organization becomes ready for pentesting and red team engagements once a history of vulnerability assessments and security hardening from assessment findings has been established. Then, there should be frequent vulnerability scanning and remediation between pentests and red team engagements as well.

Although there are third-party tools for vulnerability scanning in AWS, Amazon Inspector is the native tool. Inspector detects new cloud workloads automatically, maintains a frequently updated vulnerability database, and scans your organization's entire AWS services continuously. While GuardDuty is for detecting possible threats, Inspector is for detecting vulnerabilities that threat actors could exploit. GuardDuty catches a burglar in action, while Inspector detects the unlocked door that a burglar could use. But like Detective, Inspector will also provide context for the vulnerabilities it detects.

In *Chapter 3*, I discussed the CVE database, which includes records of the majority of known security vulnerabilities found in software, hardware, and networking devices. The Inspector tool utilizes the CVE database and the CVSS to identify vulnerabilities and provide recommendations on their prioritization for mitigation and remediation. For example, a vulnerability with a critical CVSS score of 9.1 should be addressed much earlier than one with a low score of 3.8. Since it is not feasible for the defensive security team to tackle all vulnerabilities at once, prioritizing them is crucial.

Beyond the known vulnerabilities in CVE, Inspector also uses 50 vulnerability intelligence sources to help detect zero-day vulnerabilities. None of these technologies are infallible, but Inspector's ability to detect some zero-day vulnerabilities is a big help. Perhaps your pentesting may help your organization find other zero-day vulnerabilities one day!

AWS CloudTrail monitors user activity and how the **APIs** (**application programming interfaces**, a way for applications to exchange data with each other) throughout an organization's AWS services are used. Unauthorized API usage can be analyzed through "who, what, and when" information in CloudTrail events. Machine learning models are used to detect anomalies in API usage, and logs and audit reports are stored in Amazon S3 to make regulatory compliance easier.

There is a dedicated AWS CloudTrail console, and log files can also be analyzed through Amazon Athena.

Imagine how large and complex your organization's AWS network can be. There can be so many different data assets that it can be difficult to acquire full visibility into them all without the right tools.

Amazon Macie uses machine learning and pattern matching to find sensitive data wherever it happens to be in your organization's AWS network. Amazon Macie continuously scans all of your organization's Amazon S3 storage. Then, administrators don't just get a "new sensitive data discovered" alert. Rather, Macie generates interactive data maps so administrators can find exactly where sensitive data is and how it connects with everything else in your organization's network.

Beyond continuous scans, targeted full discovery scans can also be launched at any time. Macie findings are integrated into AWS Security Hub so they're easy to discover.

AWS Network Firewall can be configured to control how data travels through your organization's AWS services, and in and out of them. **AWS Firewall Manager** is used to create policies based on network firewall rules. The same policies can be applied to any **virtual private clouds** (**VPCs**) your organization may have connected.

Filtering inbound traffic can prevent external cyber threats from making their way into your organization's network. Filtering outbound traffic can prevent sensitive data leaks and malware communications (for instance, spyware reporting keylogger data to a threat actor's command and control servers), and help with regulatory compliance. Firewall rules and policies can also be applied to client devices that connect with your organization's AWS services.

AWS Certificate Manager plays a specialized role in your organization's IAM and PKI. It works with both public and private TLS and SSL certificates. From AWS Certificate Manager, certificates can be deployed and managed.

AWS Certificate Manager can work with any of the **certificate authorities** (**CAs**) in your AWS network, whether certificates are through Amazon Trust Services, AWS Private CA, or public and private certificates that can be imported.

Certificates can be monitored through Amazon CloudWatch and Amazon EventBridge.

AWS Secrets Manager monitors the secrets all throughout your organization's AWS services. Secrets are used for identification and authentication. Secrets include cryptographic keys of various kinds, API keys, access tokens, and other types of credentials.

Secrets can be rotated without disruption to limit the risk of credential breaches without impacting the uptime of your applications and services. Secrets can be integrated with your organization's logging, monitoring, and notification services. AWS Secrets Manager fully integrates with AWS IAM to apply permissions and policies.

All of your organization's secrets are stored in a centralized and highly secured manner.

AWS Audit Manager is designed to facilitate regulatory compliance. It also helps defensive security specialists to perform risk assessments. "How likely is a bad thing to happen, and what would it do?"

Auditing frameworks can be chosen from a collection of prebuilt frameworks or they can be custom-made. Specific scopes can be defined and evidence is constantly collected during an assessment. From there, root causes of security problems can be identified.

So, as you can see, Amazon provides a lot of different security services for your organization to use. Your organization should definitely use as many of them as are applicable to what your organization does. Also, Amazon's security services integrate with each other to manage how the various aspects of network security affect each other.

I strongly recommend that you and the security professionals in your organization explore the official AWS Security documentation (`https://docs.aws.amazon.com/security/`). It covers all of the services I've mentioned here, and all of the other AWS security services and features as well.

Security tools

There are a number of different third-party tools that can be used in your pentesting. Most of the tools I mention here are for AWS specifically. They're also mainly open source, which means the hacker community can constantly improve these tools without having to ask for special permission.

Some of the tedium of your pentesting work can be automated with the right tools, but it's important to understand that pentesting isn't simply a matter of running some tools and then looking at the logs they generate. Some pentests are performed without any automated tools at all, and all pentests require a clever human being to approach their computer networking target the way a human cyber attacker would. That's whether or not any automated tools are used.

Quite often, pentests and red team engagements include matters such as physical security testing (such as breaking physical locks) and **open source intelligence** (**OSINT**). Within the framework of penetration testing, OSINT involves the collection and analysis of publicly accessible information about your target, as well as any vulnerabilities they might possess. OSINT focuses on gathering information legally, sometimes from physical sources such as books and printed records, but predominately from online sources available on the internet.

Most of the concepts that pertain to pentesting computer networks in general apply to pentesting AWS, except perhaps for the shared responsibility model and how Amazon's policies can limit what you may pentest and how. But a lot of the information about pentesting AWS specifically applies to the tools that were developed just for pentesting AWS and other cloud platforms.

How to use these tools will be covered in detail in *Chapters 5* and *6*, but in this section, I'll introduce you to them and explain what they are.

Prowler (`https://github.com/prowler-cloud/prowler`) is an open source command-line utility that has a wide variety of features for pentesting AWS, Azure, and GCP (`https://docs.prowler.cloud/en/latest/`). I will walk you through using Prowler for AWS in *Chapter 5*, Azure in *Chapter 8*, and GCP in *Chapter 11*.

Prowler has prebuilt tests specifically designed for assessing CIS, PCI-DSS, ISO27001, GDPR, HIPAA, FFIEC, SOC2, AWS FTR, and ENS compliance. You can also configure Prowler to work according to custom security frameworks.

Prowler can be executed in many different ways. It can run directly from multiple types of workstation PCs through Linux or macOS. It can also run from Windows, but Cygwin is required. Prowler can also be used from AWS CloudShell, Cloud9, Fargate, and Docker and Kubernetes containers.

Prowler has a multitude of libraries, which include ways to check for exposed secrets, exposed services, and whether any part of your AWS network can be discovered on Shodan.

awspx (`https://github.com/WithSecureLabs/awspx`) is designed specifically for AWS. With this tool, you can generate a detailed visualization of your data resources all throughout your AWS network, and of all of the access relationships.

You can draw possible attack paths from one resource to another. You can explore in-depth which actions impact which resources.

awspx must be run from a Docker container with Linux or macOS, and you'll also need access to the rest of your AWS network from there.

Intruder (`https://www.intruder.io/`) is a commercial vulnerability scanner with monthly or annual subscription fees. It's designed to be used with the OpenVAS and Tenable vulnerability scanning platforms. It has tools for scanning a variety of different types of networks, and it integrates with GitHub, Slack, Jira, and a number of different applications. It also includes integrations for AWS, Azure, and GCP, which is what's relevant to us.

As far as AWS is concerned, Intruder can run automated scans to check for insecure AWS configuration, whether or not your AWS has exposed secrets and where, exposed services, and a frequently updated library to check for authentication and code injection vulnerabilities.

Intruder can perform both external and network scans, and also has tools for scanning web applications.

Acunetix (`https://www.acunetix.com/vulnerability-scanner/`) is also a full-featured vulnerability scanner, but for web applications in particular. AWS is just one of many different technologies it can work with.

According to its developer, Invicti, Acunetix is the first web security scanner, having been in development since 2005. Invicti claims that its proprietary Smart Scan algorithm can detect 80% of the vulnerabilities in a system in the first 20% of a scan.

It has a feature to scan AWS's web application firewall. It also has project management system integration, which may be useful to your organization.

Unlike Intruder, Acunetix can be run as its own self-contained vulnerability scanner. It can be run natively from Linux, macOS, or Windows, but it can also be integrated into OpenVAS. Scans can be executed both internally and externally. Pricing information is available if you request a quote.

Rhino Security Labs Buckethead (`https://github.com/RhinoSecurityLabs/Security-Research/blob/master/tools/aws-pentest-tools/s3/buckethead.py`) is a simple, open source tool that runs as a Python script. It's designed to scan your organization's Amazon S3 buckets to look for exposures and whether or not files can be uploaded to them externally and without authorization.

I looked at the Python script (`https://github.com/RhinoSecurityLabs/Security-Research/blob/master/tools/aws-pentest-tools/s3/buckethead.py`). It's only 258 lines of code. So, all you need is a command-line utility, the ability to run Python, and a connection to your organization's AWS network.

What's really nice about Rhino Security Labs Buckethead is that it can find really serious vulnerabilities without leaving a trace in your network. It probably won't trigger your organization's security controls.

User toniblyx on GitHub worked on the development of Prowler. They also have a collection of other useful AWS pentesting tools on their GitHub. They didn't develop all of these tools themselves, but they're all part of their "arsenal." Here are some of my favorites (found at `https://github.com/toniblyx/my-arsenal-of-aws-security-tools#offensive`):

- **WeirdAAL** (`https://github.com/carnal0wnage/weirdAAL`) is an AWS attack library. Yes, the README file includes a reference to "Weird Al" Yankovic. It has modules for the following AWS components:

  - AWS Lambda

  - CloudFront

  - CloudTrail

  - CloudWatch

  - Config

  - Data Pipeline

  - Database (local)

- DynamoDB

- EC2

- ECR

- Elastic Beanstalk

- EMR

- Firehose

- IAM

- Lightsail

- OpsWorks

- RDS

- Recon

- S3

- SES

- SQS

- **Pacu** (`https://github.com/RhinoSecurityLabs/pacu`) is an entire open source AWS pentesting framework from Rhino Security Labs. It can be run from a Docker container or directly from a Linux or macOS client with Python3.7+ and pip3 support from the command line. It features a collection of 36 plugin modules to perform a variety of simulated attacks in AWS, including privilege escalation, data exfiltration, log manipulation, service exploitation, and enumeration. Each module will require your organization's AWS access keys in order to run its tests.

  Pacu is designed with extensibility in mind, and it encourages other developers to contribute to the project with new modules and improvements.

- **Cred Scanner** (`https://github.com/disruptops/cred_scanner`) is a Python program that can be run from the command line with Python 3.6 support. It has a simple purpose: to find AWS credentials in files.

- **CloudFrunt** (`https://github.com/MindPointGroup/cloudfrunt`) is another useful Python command-line tool. It's designed to find misconfigurations in AWS CloudFront.

- **Redboto** (`https://github.com/ihamburglar/Redboto`) is a collection of scripts to aid in AWS red team engagements. It's a series of Python files that can be installed through pip.

  This particular script may be the most useful:

  ```
  "getEC2Files.py
  ```

It's certainly the most complicated script of the bunch. This script works well in conjunction with `describeInstances.py`, which gives you metadata about instances in EC2. With an API key, you can exfiltrate files from an EC2 instance. The script takes a snapshot of a target volume, spins up an instance to attach to the volume, then spins up and creates an S3 bucket. When the instance finishes launching, it encrypts and copies the chosen files to the S3 bucket, and the script pulls down from the S3 bucket and decrypts the files. The script then tears down the infrastructure that it has created, leaving only logs behind, if enabled.

So, there you have it! The most helpful AWS pentesting tools range from complex commercial vulnerability scanners with monthly subscription fees to simple, open source Python scripts. I look forward to explaining how to use some of these tools in much greater detail in the following chapters.

Summary

AWS is one of the most popular cloud platforms around. You will almost certainly be expected to work with AWS applications and services as a cloud pentester.

AWS includes a lot of its own security controls and tools that your organization may or may not be using. It really ought to be using them, as implementing Amazon's own security controls is a crucial cybersecurity baseline that can prevent a lot of cyberattacks.

Some of the many first-party AWS security applications include Amazon Inspector, AWS Security Hub, and Amazon GuardDuty.

There are also third-party scripts and tools that you can use to conduct vulnerability scans and pentests while abiding by Amazon's policies. They include Prowler, Pacu, CloudFront, and many others.

It's important to understand Amazon's pentesting policies and rules and abide by them. Amazon owns all AWS infrastructure. So, even when you're working with your organization's AWS network, you're metaphorically in Amazon's home. You need to be a considerate guest.

In the next chapter, I'll walk you through AWS's security controls in greater detail. I'll also walk you through actually using Prowler and Pacu, complete with videos. You can set up your own AWS instance to try these tools for yourself.

Further reading

To learn more on the topics covered in this chapter, you can visit the following links:

- *CLI (command line interface) in AWS*: `https://aws.amazon.com/cli/`
- *AWS security products and services*: `https://aws.amazon.com/products/security/`
- *Prowler documentation*: `https://docs.prowler.cloud`

5

Pentesting AWS Features through Serverless Applications and Tools

You've been a very patient reader so far. Understanding concepts and theory is important before you start learning how to conduct the practical aspect of pentesting. You've now reached the first chapter of the book where we'll not just be theorizing but also putting our knowledge into action.

This chapter features step-by-step guides to using the **Amazon Web Services** (**AWS**) first-party security tools to check security configurations and conduct vulnerability assessments to configure the most popular third-party AWS pentesting tools. We will also discuss the pentesting steps to find credentials, enumerate AWS services, conduct vulnerability scans, and discover exposed services with Prowler and Pacu.

This chapter comprises the following main topics:

- How to get an AWS network
- Using AWS PowerShell and the AWS CLI
- Exploring AWS native security tools
- Installing and preparing AWS pentesting tools
- Exploiting AWS applications

Let's get started!

Technical requirements

We will be working with Microsoft's infrastructure. Massive Azure data centers will be doing the bulk of the computer processing work for the exercises in this chapter, so, fortunately, you don't need to have a top-of-the-line workstation. You will need the following:

- A web browser
- A desktop or laptop PC
- An Android or iPhone smartphone
- A good reliable internet connection

Check out the following video to view the Code in Action: `https://bit.ly/3Qo5Ewg`

How to get an AWS network

Before we prepare to pentest AWS services, we need AWS services to pentest! There are two things you could do:

- You can acquire AWS credentials from the organization you work for
- Or if you're just learning and you're not working for an organization yet, you can set up your own AWS instance free of charge

Amazon allows people to do a lot of things on its infrastructure through free services and free trials.

Keep in mind that whether you're using your organization's paid AWS instance or your own free AWS instance, the same AWS pentesting policies apply. Refer to *Chapters 2* and *3* for more details. You may also review AWS's pentesting policies here: `https://github.com/prowler-cloud/prowler`.

If you need to set up a free AWS instance, I'll walk you through the setup process. Follow these steps:

1. Visit `https://aws.amazon.com/` in your web browser.
2. Click on the orange button on the upper-right side of the web page that says **Create an AWS Account**.
3. Under **Root user email address**, enter an email address that you have reliable access to. I would recommend that you use your main personal email account so that you can keep your AWS account even if you switch employers.
4. Under **AWS account name**, enter a unique name that's memorable to you. Make sure it's not something you'd be embarrassed to show a company you're working for. Also, make sure your account name doesn't reveal any of your passwords or other sensitive data. Don't put your social security number in there!

5. You'll be sent a verification code to the email address you used. Check your email to retrieve the verification code, input it into the form field, and click **Verify**. Be quick—it expires in 10 minutes!

6. Create a new password and enter it in both form fields for verification. Your password should be long and complex. I would recommend using a password manager to generate a secure password and remember it for you.

7. Under **How do you plan to use AWS?**, select **Personal**. Enter your full name, phone number, and mailing address in the rest of the form. Make sure that the phone number is connected to a smartphone that belongs to you, in case you need to use it for **multi-factor authentication (MFA)**. Check the **I have read and agree to the terms of the AWS Customer Agreement** box and click on **Continue**.

8. You will be asked to enter your credit card number. AWS will warn you if you try to do something that will result in a credit card charge, and you can always verify whether or not you've been charged for something in the billing section of your account.

> **Note**
>
> None of the tutorials in this chapter will result in a credit card charge, but some of the services I will demonstrate in this chapter (such as Amazon Inspector) have a limited free trial. Be sure to cancel your AWS account before your free trials expire if you don't want to be billed. See the *AWS Free Tier* guide for more details (`https://aws.amazon.com/free/`).

Once you've set up your AWS account or have acquired access to your organization's AWS account, you're ready to move on with the rest of this chapter.

Using AWS PowerShell and the AWS CLI

A lot of the exercises in this chapter can be executed directly from AWS CloudShell. As long as you have a Windows, Linux, or Mac computer with internet access and a web browser, AWS CloudShell is easy to access. Your computer doesn't need to have a workstation or gaming PC hardware specifications, because all the virtualization and computation are conducted on Amazon's infrastructure. But I would definitely recommend that you use some sort of desktop or laptop computer, and not a phone or tablet. AWS CloudShell's UI works best with a physical keyboard.

When you're logged in to your AWS account in your web browser, you can access AWS CloudShell at any time by clicking on an icon at the top of your screen. The AWS CloudShell icon looks like a small square with a command prompt:

Figure 5.1 – AWS CloudShell icon

If you would prefer to access the AWS CLI without AWS CloudShell, you can install the `aws-shell` application from GitHub (`https://github.com/awslabs/aws-shell`). It requires the **Bourne Again Shell** (**Bash**) command line, so a Linux OS or macOS works best.

> **Note**
>
> All demonstrations in this book use CloudShell. But if you'd prefer to install the AWS CLI desktop application, you can find it here: `https://aws.amazon.com/cli/`.

Here's a handy guide to commands you can use at the AWS CloudShell command prompt. These commands will also work directly in the AWS CLI application.

Whether you're in AWS CloudShell or the AWS CLI application, you should always check which command line you have installed first with this command:

```
aws --version
```

The command line will display information about your OS (in AWS, not on your own computer), the version of Python that's installed, and so on. The output will look something like this, but it may say something different depending on what you have installed:

```
aws-cli/2.10.0 Python/3.11.2 Linux/4.14.133-113.105.amzn2.x86_64
botocore/1.13
```

If you have a version of Linux or Mac installed, you can use Bash commands. The particular Bash commands I mention here also work in **Z Shell** (**Zsh**), which is the default for Mac. If you have Windows installed in AWS, you can use Windows PowerShell Command Prompt commands. Bash, Zsh, and Windows PowerShell support is all built into AWS CloudShell and the separate AWS CLI application. You don't need to install anything extra in order to use any of these commands.

Bash commands

Here are some handy Bash (and Zsh) commands:

- This will list all of the files and folders in your current directory:

  - `ls`

- This will change which directory you have open. Don't use the brackets! Enter the path of the directory in that space:

  - `cd <insert directory name here>`

- This will show which directory you're in, in case you get lost:

  - `pwd`

- If you're unsure of what a command does, this will tell you. Don't use the brackets!

  - `man <command name>`

- This handy command will get you out of a shell script you've executed, an SSH session, or will exit you out of AWS PowerShell or the AWS CLI:

  - `exit`

- Get information about whichever processes are running, complete with their **process IDs** (**PIDs**):

  - `ps`

- If there's a process you'd like to stop and you know its PID, use this command:

  - `kill <process ID>`

- If you forget which commands you've used during your session, this command will show you:

  - `history`

- Move or rename a directory:

  - `mv <current directory name> <new directory name>`

- Make a new directory:

  - `mkdir <new directory name>`

- Create a new file with a new filename:

  - `touch <new filename>`

- Read the contents of a file. This will only work for text files and scripts, not for things without text such as media files:

  - `less <filename>`

- Type sudo before your command if you need to do something that requires root permissions. You may need to enter your password afterward:

  - `sudo <command>`

- Use these commands to install programs that are in one of your repositories, or a Python program with the pip package installer:

  - `sudo install <program name in repository>`
  - `sudo pip3 install <program name>`

- `sudo <name of package manager here, such as apt or yum> install <program name>`

Let's look at a few PowerShell commands next.

PowerShell commands

If your AWS server is running Windows, here are some handy Windows PowerShell commands you can use. As long as your AWS instance is running Windows, these commands will work both in AWS PowerShell and the AWS CLI application:

- This is probably the most important Windows command to remember. It'll show you a list of other commands you can use and what they do:

  - `help`

- Just as in Bash (and Zsh), this will change the directory you have open:

  - `cd <directory name>`

- The command for making a new directory in PowerShell is the same as in Bash and Zsh:

  - `mkdir <new directory name>`

- This command moves a file to a new destination:

  - `move <file or directory> <destination directory>`

- This command changes which directory you have open:

  - `chdir <directory>`

- See which processes are running and their PIDs:

  - `ps`

- Get information about your currently open directory:

  - `pwd`

- Remove a file or directory:

  - `rm <filename>`
  - `rmdir <directory name>`

- Displays some of the contents of a file. This works best with text files or files that are scripts:

  - `cat <filename>`

- Create a new file or directory:

  - `ni <new filename or new directory name>`

  If you create a new file, the file may have no contents. However, you can then open the file in a text editor or **integrated development environment** (**IDE**) and create contents in the file.

Now that we have looked into AWS and the AWS CLI, it is time to learn about the tools AWS provides us to help us with cybersecurity.

Exploring AWS-native security tools

AWS provides you with two native tools that will be especially useful to you as a pentester: AWS Security Hub and Amazon Inspector.

First, let's take a look at AWS Security Hub.

AWS Security Hub

AWS Security Hub is an easy way to view all of your AWS security configurations, AWS-native security scan reports, and security alerts. It can combine data from Amazon GuardDuty, Amazon Inspector, Amazon Macie, and AWS Network Firewall.

If there are any major security problems in your AWS instance, AWS Security Hub will notify you! You can mention data you find in AWS Security Hub in your pentest report. But by conducting vulnerability scans and pentests with third-party applications, you may be able to find additional vulnerabilities. I recommend using both the tools AWS provides and third-party tools to get the most thorough data about the security posture of your AWS instance.

Let's take a look at AWS Security Hub for the first time. Follow these steps:

1. Once you've logged in to your AWS account from your web browser, you can find AWS Security Hub by searching for `AWS Security Hub` in the search bar at the top. It's to the left of the icon that you use to launch AWS CloudShell. If you have a Free Tier AWS account, you can sign up for a 30-day free trial. Alternatively, you can find AWS Security Hub under the **Services** tab.

Warning!

Be careful to go to your billing to cancel AWS Security Hub before your free trial expires if this is your own free AWS account for educational purposes.

---

2. On the right, click on **Go to Security Hub**. If you're setting it up for the first time, you will need to select **Enable AWS Config**. Next, where it says **You can enable resource recording manually from the AWS Config console**, click on the **AWS Config console** link.

3. Then, you'll be taken to a page for AWS Config. On the right-hand side, click on **1-click setup**:

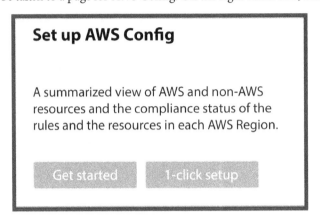

Figure 5.2 – The 1-click setup option

Review the default settings, and then click on the orange **Confirm** button on the lower-right side. An **Amazon Simple Storage Service (S3)** bucket will be created for you. This may take a few moments.

4. When the bucket has been created, you will be taken to the main **AWS Security Hub** dashboard. For now, we can leave all the defaults as they are. Go to your web browser tab that says **Enable AWS Security Hub**.

5. Under the **Security standards** heading, leave the defaults selected:

   • **Enable AWS Foundational Security Best Practices v1.0.0**

- **Enable CIS AWS Foundations Benchmark v1.2.0**

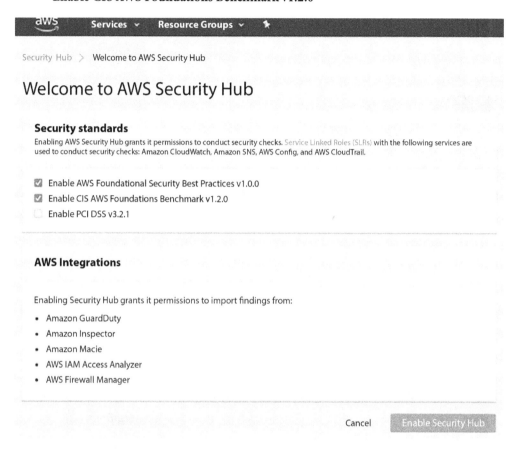

Figure 5.3 – AWS Security Hub setup screen

6. If this was the AWS network for the company you're working for, they may have their own security benchmarks they need to be compliant with. But if you're just using a free AWS account to learn for yourself, you can just leave the default benchmarks as they are. For that reason, also leave **AWS Integrations** and **Delegated Administrator** (the default is no integrations and no additional delegated administrator) as they are. Click on the orange button that says **Enable Security Hub**.

7. Now, you should see the **AWS Security Hub** dashboard.

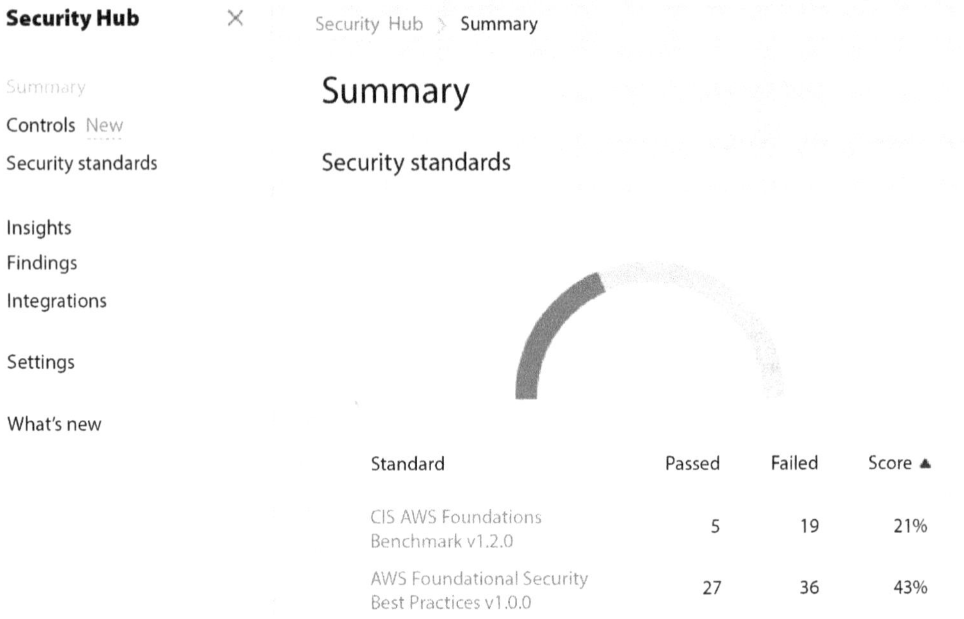

Figure 5.4 – AWS Security Hub dashboard

You should be on the **Summary** page now. No scans have been run so far, so all the possible information sources such as **Findings** and **Insights** will have no data to display.

8. But I did see something interesting. Go to the left menu and click on **Findings**.

It appears that when I enabled AWS Config, the system already performed a number of security checks! There were about a dozen failed checks, with severity ratings ranked LOW, MEDIUM, and CRITICAL. Here's an example of a failed security check. Your results will probably be different:

```
MEDIUM    NEW    ACTIVE    us-east-2    489********(my account
ID)    AWS Security Hub    Network ACLs should not allow ingress
from 0.0.0.0/0 to port 22 or port 3389
```

9. Now, click on **Security standards** in the left menu.

10. I found a box for **AWS Foundational Security Best Practices v1.0.0**. I clicked on **View results**. There were lots of failed checks there. Here's an example of one:

```
CRITICAL    CodeBuild.1    CodeBuild GitHub or Bitbucket source
repository URLs should use OAuth
```

So, AWS Security Hub will give you a lot of very useful vulnerability information from the get-go. You can definitely mention these details in your pentest report, but I would recommend also running some third-party tools, as I'll describe later in this chapter. Multiple tools can find more vulnerabilities, and if more than one tool finds the same vulnerability, that's useful information too. Remember—your pentest report shouldn't just be an output from logs. You will describe in your own words how these vulnerabilities impact your organization and your advice for remediating them.

Now, let's move on to Amazon Inspector.

Amazon Inspector

Amazon Inspector is the built-in vulnerability scanner in AWS. It does a pretty good job of scanning your AWS applications for known vulnerabilities. It can also find the parts of your AWS network that are insecurely exposed to the public internet. I recommend running scans with Amazon Inspector before you conduct scans with third-party applications.

I'll show you how to use Amazon Inspector, step by step:

1. I found Amazon Inspector by searching for Inspector in the top search bar. If you don't have Amazon Inspector set up yet, a white box on the top right will say **Get started with Inspector** and offer you a 15-day trial. Click on the orange **Get Started** button. But if you're just playing around in your free AWS account, then please remember to cancel Amazon Inspector before the 15-day period is over.

2. If you're just trying things out in your free account, then you can leave **Delegated administrator** and **Service permissions** as they are. Click on the **Activate Inspector** button on the bottom right. The activation may take a few moments.

3. Upon activation, you will see a screen that says **Summary** at the top. If you click on the **Manage all accounts** button in the top-right corner, you can get Amazon Inspector working in your **Amazon Elastic Compute Cloud (Amazon EC2)**, **Amazon Elastic Container Registry (Amazon ECR)**, and AWS Lambda instances too.

4. A green notification at the top says **Welcome to Inspector. Your first scan is underway.** So, we'll wait for the automatic scan to complete, then look at the results. My first scan took about half an hour.

   If you get impatient while waiting, there's something fun you can do. Look at the menu on the left side. Click on **Video tutorials**. There's a page with a bunch of embedded YouTube videos, such as **Introduction to the New Amazon Inspector** and **Amazon Inspector for AWS Lambda workloads**. I would recommend watching all of them! The information you'll learn will help you use Amazon Inspector more effectively as a pentester.

5. When your scan is done, click on **Findings** in the left menu. You can sort your findings by vulnerability, by account, by instance, and so on by clicking the tabs at the top. Each finding will show its **Common Vulnerability Scoring System** (**CVSS**) severity rating such as **CRITICAL**, **HIGH**, or **MEDIUM**. **Common Vulnerabilities and Exposures** (**CVE**) numbers for each finding are also shown, and you can click on each CVE database link to read more about it.

As you can see, Amazon Inspector is a really useful tool for pentesting AWS. I really appreciate the CVE data that Inspector shows. It's very useful details to put in a pentest report.

Now, let's move on to some third-party tools. I recommend that you use a variety of tools in your pentests and red team engagements for the sake of being thorough. In these situations, using more tools is generally better because you can get even more information.

Installing and preparing AWS pentesting tools

Let's install and prepare the third-party software we'll be using in the next section.

> **Important note**
> If you encounter problems with disk space while installing any of these tools, you may have to delete old files to make space. Files can be deleted with the Bash commands earlier in this chapter. You also may have to deploy a new AWS EC2 instance. See the official AWS documentation for more information: `https://docs.aws.amazon.com/AWSEC2/latest/UserGuide/EC2_GetStarted.html`.

As much as possible, I will be using AWS CloudShell to install applications.

First, let's start with Prowler.

Prowler

Prowler is a vulnerability scanner for cloud platforms. Prowler can scan AWS for vulnerabilities and security misconfigurations based on the **Center for Internet Security** (**CIS**), **National Institute of Standards and Technology** (**NIST**) 800, NIST **Cybersecurity Framework (CSF)**, the **Cybersecurity and Infrastructure Security Agency** (**CISA**), the **Federal Risk and Authorization Management** (**FedRAMP**), the **Payment Card Industry Data Security Standard** (**PCI-DSS**), the **General Data Protection Regulation** (**GDPR**), the **Health Insurance Portability and Accountability Act** (**HIPAA**), and other security standards.

Open AWS CloudShell by logging in to your AWS account in a web browser (a small square icon with a command prompt).

Before we install Prowler, you may have to update the version of Python in AWS CloudShell to Python 3.9. You can update Python with the commands shown next.

First, check which version of Python you already have:

```
python --version
```

If it says Python 3.9, you're good to go. Otherwise, do this:

```
sudo apt update
sudo apt-get install python3.9
```

Once the installation process is done, you can verify that it works with this command:

```
python --version
```

Here are the commands to enter:

- This uses the yum installer to install some Prowler dependencies. You may be asked to enter your AWS account password:

    ```
    sudo yum -y install gcc openssl-devel bzip2-devel libffi-devel
    ```

- This downloads the package for Python 3.9, a dependency for installing Prowler from pip:

    ```
    wget https://www.python.org/ftp/python/3.9.16/Python-3.9.16.tgz
    ```

- This installs the Python package, configures it, and sets "enable optimizations." Sometimes, a command may take a few minutes to execute:

> **Note**
>
> Be careful to make sure that -- is entered as two hyphens with no space in between. Some web browsers might change -- into one long –. That will cause an error.

```
tar zxf Python-3.9.16.tgz
```

```
cd Python-3.9.16/
```

```
./configure --enable-optimizations

sudo make altinstall

python3.9 --version

cd
```

Now, you're back in your home directory.

- This installs Prowler from `pip`:

```
pip3.9 install prowler

prowler -v
```

Congratulations! Later on, when we actually use Prowler, you can find the output of your pentests and vulnerability assessments by clicking on **Actions** in the top-right corner of the AWS PowerShell screen. Then, go to **Download File** and open the CSV file. It will have a location and filename like this:

```
/home/cloudshell-user/output/prowler-output-<a bunch of numbers>.csv
```

If **Actions | Download File** doesn't work, you may need to open AWS CloudShell in Google Chrome. If you don't have Chrome, install it by visiting `https://www.google.com/chrome/`. Hopefully, you have your AWS root account email address and password recorded somewhere safe so that you can switch web browsers when needed!

Now, let's install Pacu.

Pacu

Pacu is an AWS pentesting application. If you've already followed my instructions for installing Prowler, then you'll already have Python installed. That's great, as we can use `pip` to install Pacu, like so:

```
pip3 install  pip
```

This prepares the `pip` installer:

```
pip3 install  pacu
```

This installs Pacu. Now, let's execute it!

```
Pacu
```

Cred Scanner

Now, let's install Cred Scanner. It's a very simple script to scan the files in your AWS instance for sensitive credentials. You absolutely do not want passwords and the like to be exposed to cyber attackers! Follow the next steps:

1. First, open the Python script in your web browser from GitHub here: `https://github.com/disruptops/cred_scanner/blob/master/cred_scanner.py`.

2. Copy the entire Python script. Paste it into a text editor and make sure the file is saved as `cred_scanner.py`.

3. Next, we need to upload the script from your local computer to your AWS server. Click on **Actions** in the top-right corner of your AWS CloudShell screen. Then, go to **Upload file**, click on **Select file**, navigate to where you saved `cred_scanner.py` on your local computer, and open it.

4. Go to `https://github.com/disruptops/cred_scanner/blob/master/requirements.txt` and do just about the same. It's just one line of code that says `click`. But you still need to save it as a file named `requirements.txt`. Then, upload the file in AWS CloudShell the same way you uploaded `cred_scanner.py`.

5. Now, back to the command line! Make sure Cred Scanner has its requirements by entering the following:

   ```
   pip install -r ./requirements.txt
   ```

6. Then, we can execute the Python script:

   ```
   python cred_scanner.py
   ```

Let's continue with Cred Scanner. Here's what a scan can look like:

```
./venv/lib/python3.9/site-packages/pycparser-2.21.dist-info/top_level.txt
./venv/lib/python3.9/site-packages/pycparser-2.21.dist-info/LICENSE
./venv/lib/python3.9/site-packages/pycparser-2.21.dist-info/RECORD
./venv/lib/python3.9/site-packages/pycparser-2.21.dist-info/WHEEL
./venv/lib/python3.9/site-packages/pycparser-2.21.dist-info/INSTALLER
./venv/lib/python3.9/site-packages/pycparser-2.21.dist-info/METADATA
./venv/lib/python3.9/site-packages/pip-22.0.4.dist-info/LICENSE.txt
./venv/lib/python3.9/site-packages/pip-22.0.4.dist-info/top_level.txt
./venv/lib/python3.9/site-packages/pip-22.0.4.dist-info/RECORD
Found AWS Access Key in ./venv/lib/python3.9/site-packages/pip-22.0.4.dist-info/RECORD
./venv/lib/python3.9/site-packages/pip-22.0.4.dist-info/WHEEL
./venv/lib/python3.9/site-packages/pip-22.0.4.dist-info/entry_points.txt
./venv/lib/python3.9/site-packages/pip-22.0.4.dist-info/INSTALLER
./venv/lib/python3.9/site-packages/pip-22.0.4.dist-info/METADATA
./venv/lib/python3.9/site-packages/dateutil/tz
./venv/lib/python3.9/site-packages/dateutil/__pycache__
./venv/lib/python3.9/site-packages/dateutil/zoneinfo
./venv/lib/python3.9/site-packages/dateutil/parser
./venv/lib/python3.9/site-packages/dateutil/tzwin.py
./venv/lib/python3.9/site-packages/dateutil/utils.py
./venv/lib/python3.9/site-packages/dateutil/_version.py
```

Figure 5.5 – Cred Scanner scan output

Alternatively, you can install Cred Scanner by cloning its GitHub repository. In order to clone a repository, follow the instructions in the GitHub documentation: `https://docs.github.com/en/repositories/creating-and-managing-repositories/cloning-a-repository`.

The code you need to clone can be found here:

`https://github.com/disruptops/cred_scanner`

Then, run this command:

```
pip install -r ./requirements.txt
```

Using Cred Scanner is so simple that I'll show you how to do a scan right now instead of explaining it in the next section:

- This will display Cred Scanner's options:

    ```
    python cred_scanner.py --help
    ```

- This will show you secret keys in the directory you have open at the command line:

    ```
    python cred_scanner.py --secret
    ```

- This will run Cred Scanner in another directory:

```
python cred_scanner.py --path <directory path>
```

Alternatively, you can use the cd command to change to the directory you want to run Cred Scanner in.

CloudFrunt

CloudFrunt is a script developed by MindPoint Group for identifying misconfigurations in AWS CloudFront.

I'm going to show both installing and executing CloudFrunt here as well, due to its simplicity. Remember—you must have AWS CloudFront configured on your AWS server in order for CloudFrunt to work properly.

At the AWS CloudShell command line, download the CloudFrunt script:

```
git clone --recursive https://github.com/MindPointGroup/cloudfrunt
```

Here's the result:

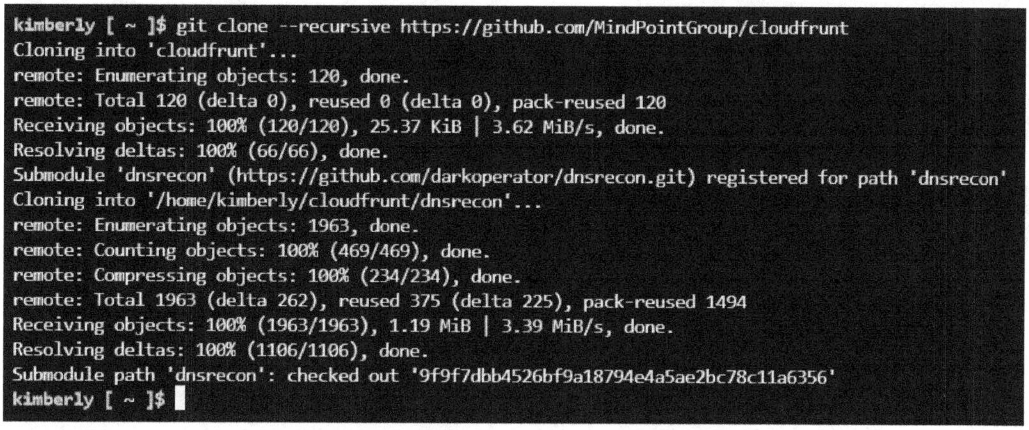

```
kimberly [ ~ ]$ git clone --recursive https://github.com/MindPointGroup/cloudfrunt
Cloning into 'cloudfrunt'...
remote: Enumerating objects: 120, done.
remote: Total 120 (delta 0), reused 0 (delta 0), pack-reused 120
Receiving objects: 100% (120/120), 25.37 KiB | 3.62 MiB/s, done.
Resolving deltas: 100% (66/66), done.
Submodule 'dnsrecon' (https://github.com/darkoperator/dnsrecon.git) registered for path 'dnsrecon'
Cloning into '/home/kimberly/cloudfrunt/dnsrecon'...
remote: Enumerating objects: 1963, done.
remote: Counting objects: 100% (469/469), done.
remote: Compressing objects: 100% (234/234), done.
remote: Total 1963 (delta 262), reused 375 (delta 225), pack-reused 1494
Receiving objects: 100% (1963/1963), 1.19 MiB | 3.39 MiB/s, done.
Resolving deltas: 100% (1106/1106), done.
Submodule path 'dnsrecon': checked out '9f9f7dbb4526bf9a18794e4a5ae2bc78c11a6356'
kimberly [ ~ ]$
```

Figure 5.6 – CloudFrunt installation

Then, install it and its dependencies:

```
pip install -r requirements.txt
```

Now, assuming we have CloudFrunt installed, let's give it a go!

Here's the command structure for using cloudfrunt.py:

```
python cloudfrunt.py -o cloudfrunt.com.s3-website-us-east-1.amazonaws.
com -i S3-cloudfrunt -l list.txt
```

Don't enter that exact command. You'll need to modify it according to your situation. Anything in -<letter> is called an argument.

Replace cloudfrunt.com.s3-website-us-east-1.amazonaws.com with the domain that you're scanning. Replace S3-cloudfrunt with the origin of the vulnerable domain that you're adding. Replace list.txt with a text file of domains to scan.

This is how you display the guide to using CloudFrunt:

```
python cloudfrunt.py --help
```

This is what it will display:

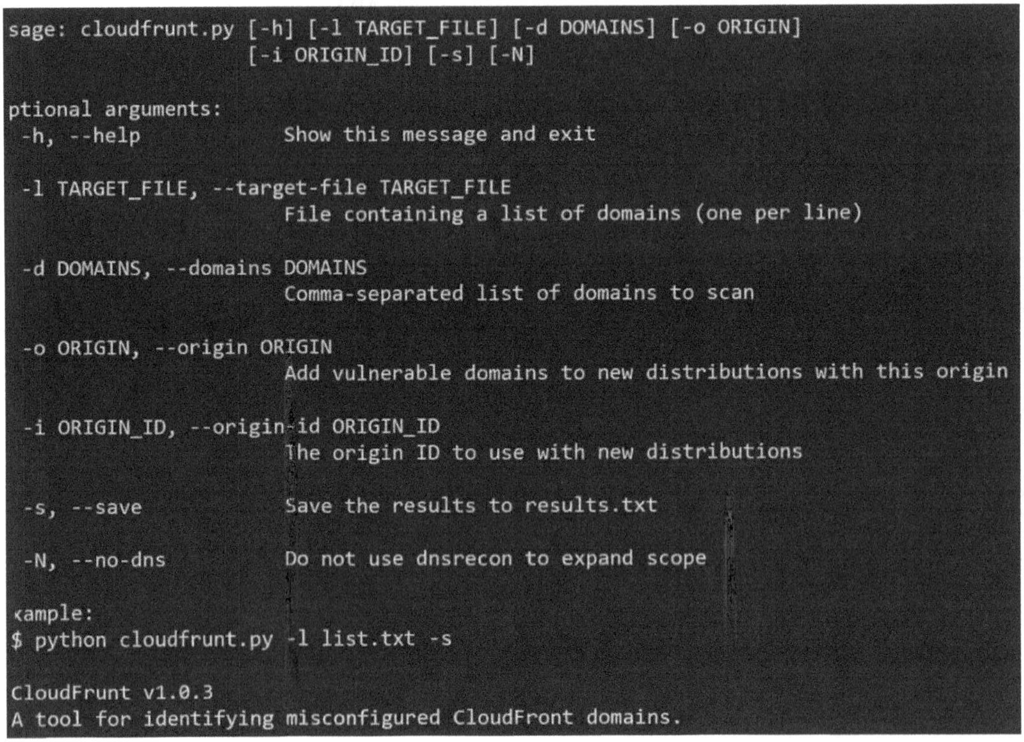

```
sage: cloudfrunt.py [-h] [-l TARGET_FILE] [-d DOMAINS] [-o ORIGIN]
                    [-i ORIGIN_ID] [-s] [-N]

ptional arguments:
 -h, --help            Show this message and exit

 -l TARGET_FILE, --target-file TARGET_FILE
                       File containing a list of domains (one per line)

 -d DOMAINS, --domains DOMAINS
                       Comma-separated list of domains to scan

 -o ORIGIN, --origin ORIGIN
                       Add vulnerable domains to new distributions with this origin

 -i ORIGIN_ID, --origin-id ORIGIN_ID
                       The origin ID to use with new distributions

 -s, --save            Save the results to results.txt

 -N, --no-dns          Do not use dnsrecon to expand scope

xample:
$ python cloudfrunt.py -l list.txt -s

CloudFrunt v1.0.3
A tool for identifying misconfigured CloudFront domains.
```

Figure 5.7 – CloudFrunt help screen

Use this as your guide to executing CloudFrunt. If you use -s or --save when you execute CloudFrunt, you'll be able to find your CloudFrunt scan results by clicking on **Actions** in the top-right corner of the AWS PowerShell screen. Then, go to **Download File** and open the text file. It will have a location and filename like this:

```
/home/cloudshell-user/output/results.txt
```

On to Redboto next!

Redboto

The last third-party tool I'll walk you through installing is the Redboto Python script collection. The scripts perform red team operations against the AWS API. First, let's install its prerequisites:

```
pip install cryptography boto3 texttable
```

Next, open its GitHub collection in another web browser tab:

```
https://github.com/ihamburglar/Redboto
```

Redboto is a collection of scripts. Open each web page for each script you'd like to try. Remember how I walked you through copying scripts from GitHub, pasting the script into a text editor, saving it with its specific filename, and then uploading files with **Actions** | **Upload file** | **Select file** in the AWS CloudShell web UI? Do this with each of the Redboto scripts you'd like to use. The Redboto GitHub repository provides an explanation of what each script does. Then, in the directory you uploaded files to, you can execute each script like this:

```
python checkAWSKey.py

python describeUserData.py

python runSSMShellScript.py

python <insert a different Reboto Python script name here>
```

Afterward, you should be able to go to **Actions** | **Download File** from the AWS CloudShell UI and find output files in this directory:

```
/home/cloudshell-user/output/
```

Remember that directory well because if the tutorials I give you in this chapter are your labor, the contents of that directory are the fruits of your labor. But you won't simply be giving your pentesting client the output in that directory. You will be using the output files as information you'll deploy when you write your pentest report for your client. Being a good pentester isn't simply a matter of executing scripts and sharing outputs and other logs. Your job is to interpret the logs and help your client and the defensive security team understand them and use the vulnerability information to security harden your client's AWS networks and applications.

Alright! Now, it's time to conduct some general pentesting and vulnerability scanning activities in Prowler and Pacu.

Exploiting AWS applications

Now that we've installed a number of pentesting applications and run some simple scripts, let's get deeper into AWS exploitation with Prowler and Pacu.

Prowler

First, let's conduct some pentesting and vulnerability scanning activities in Prowler.

Have your AWS credentials ready. You can verify them by logging in to your AWS account from your web browser. On the top menu bar, look at the far right drop-down menu with your username. Click on **Security credentials** to navigate to the correct AWS **Identity and Access Management** (**IAM**) page. At the top, it should say **My security credentials (root user)**. Make a note of your AWS account ID, access key ID, and secret access key. Then, follow these steps:

1. Now, let's open AWS CloudShell again. Enter this command to configure your key:

    ```
    aws configure
    ```

2. In the AWS_ACCESS_KEY_ID= field, paste the key ID you generated and hit *Enter*. Hit *Enter* for all the other fields too; we'll be leaving them blank.

Note

If you want to save a 0.0003 USD charge to your account per AWS configure occurrence, you can configure AWS with the following:

```
export AWS_ACCESS_KEY_ID=your_access_key_id
export AWS_SECRET_ACCESS_KEY=your_secret_access_key)
```

---

3. Execute Prowler:

    ```
    prowler
    ```

    If that doesn't work, follow the instructions earlier in this chapter to install Prowler again.

    By default, the output of your Prowler scans should be somewhere around here, with a filename like this:

    ```
    /home/cloudshell-user/output/prowler-output-<a bunch of
    numbers>.csv
    ```

The Prowler command on its own will execute a default scan that shows the AWS services that you have (such as EC2, IAM, and so on), whether the scan passed or failed, and the number of critical, high, medium, and low vulnerabilities each service has according to the CVSS score. It'll run through dozens of checks, such as `check121`, `check122`, `check23`, and `check24`. It may print to the screen (and to your CSV logs) all kinds of information that'll be useful in your pentest report, such as the following:

```
[check25] Ensure AWS Config is enabled in all regions - configservice
[Medium]


FAIL! au-north-1: AWS Config recorder disabled
```

In this example, `check25` scanned all of your AWS services to see if they have AWS Config enabled. AWS Config on its own doesn't guarantee security. But it needs to be enabled in order to securely configure it, kind of like how your car must have seatbelts installed. The seatbelts being there doesn't guarantee that the driver and passengers will wear them, but they cannot wear their seatbelts if they aren't there in the first place.

> **Note**
>
> You may encounter AWS secret access key issues. If so, visit `https://console.aws.amazon.com/kms` for **AWS Key Management Service** (**AWS KMS**) and make a new key while making a note of your secret access key. You can also get troubleshooting help in the AWS documentation at `https://docs.aws.amazon.com/kms/latest/developerguide/find-cmk-id-arn.html` and `https://docs.aws.amazon.com/kms/latest/developerguide/programming-keys.html`.

If you want to get more refined, you can start by seeing which specific checks or services you can execute from Prowler with one of these commands:

```
prowler --list-checks
prowler --list-services
```

When you find checks you'd like to execute, you can use this syntax:

```
prowler -c check11,check12
```

Of course, replace `check11` and `check12` with the checks that you'd like to execute.

You can also run all of the checks *except* for some of them, like this:

```
./prowler -E check32,check33
```

That will run all of the checks *except* for `check32` and `check33`.

By default, Prowler will scan your AWS services in all of the regions that have opted in. But you can limit scanning to only some regions, like this:

```
./prowler -f 'eu-west-1 us-east-s'
```

So, in that case, only your servers in eu-west-1 and us-east-s will be scanned.

And those are the basics of executing vulnerability scans and pentests in AWS with Prowler. For more information, refer to Prowler's README file (https://github.com/prowler-cloud/prowler#readme) and documentation.

Pacu

Now, it's time for Pacu. I will walk you through executing a vulnerability scanning module. I will also show you how to find the output reports from your Pacu scans. Follow the next steps:

1. There are one of two methods you can use. You could enter this sequence of commands to prepare your access key to use Pacu free of charge:

```
export AWS_ACCESS_KEY_ID=your_access_key_id
export AWS_SECRET_ACCESS_KEY=your_secret_access_key
```

2. As an alternative to *step 1*, you can enter this command to configure your key:

> **Warning**
> This command may incur a charge of 0.0003 USD to your AWS account.

```
aws configure
```

3. Then, input the key ID that we used for Prowler. Navigate to the directory that we installed Pacu in:

```
cd /Pacu
```

4. At the AWS CloudShell command line, we'll first look at the help options:

```
pacu --help
```

5. If that doesn't work, try the alternative installation instructions here: https://rhinosecuritylabs.com/aws/pacu-open-source-aws-exploitation-framework/. If you installed Pacu that alternative way, you can execute Pacu with this command. Just make sure you're in the correct directory:

```
python3 pacu.py
```

6. When Pacu asks you to name a new session, come up with whatever name for the session you'd like to use, and hit *Enter*. For instance, you can try `TestPacuSession`.

7. See a list of the modules you can try:

    `ls`

    Here's what to expect:

```
Pacu - https://github.com/RhinoSecurityLabs/pacu
Written and researched by Spencer Gietzen of Rhino Security Labs - https://rhinosecuritylabs.com/

This was built as a modular, open source tool to assist in penetration testing an AWS environment.
For usage and developer documentation, please visit the GitHub page.

Modules that have pre-requisites will have those listed in that modules help info, but if it is
executed before its pre-reqs have been filled, it will prompt you to run that module then continue
once that is finished, so you have the necessary data for the module you want to run.

Pacu command info:
    list/ls                            List all modules
    search [cat[egory]] <search term>  Search the list of available modules by name or category
    help                               Display this page of information
    help <module name>                 Display information about a module
    whoami                             Display information regarding to the active access keys
    data                               Display all data that is stored in this session. Only fields
                                         with values will be displayed
    data <service>|proxy               Display all data for a specified service or for PacuProxy
                                         in this session
    services                           Display a list of services that have collected data in the
                                         current session to use with the "data" command
    regions                            Display a list of all valid AWS regions
    update_regions                     Run a script to update the regions database to the newest
                                         version
    set_regions <region> [<region>...] Set the default regions for this session. These space-separated
                                         regions will be used for modules where regions are required,
                                         but not supplied by the user. The default set of regions is
                                         every supported region for the service. Supply "all" to this
                                         command to reset the region set to the default of all
                                         supported regions
    run/exec <module name>             Execute a module
    set_keys                           Add a set of AWS keys to the session and set them as the
                                         default
    swap_keys                          Change the currently active AWS key to another key that has
                                         previously been set for this session
    exit/quit                          Exit Pacu

[ADVANCED] PacuProxy command info:
    proxy [help]                       Control PacuProxy/display help
        start <ip> [port]              Start the PacuProxy listener - port 80 by default.
                                         The listener will attempt to start on the IP
                                         supplied. but some hosts don't allow this. In
```

Figure 5.8 – Pacu help screen

Try whichever modules you'd like. For example, one of the modules is named `backdoor_users_password`. Are there any backdoors into your AWS services that could reveal a user password? You can also look at a full list of modules here: `https://github.com/RhinoSecurityLabs/pacu/wiki/Module-Details`.

Try this command:

```
run <module name>
```

For example, you could try the following:

```
run backdoor_users_password
```

Afterward, you should be able to go to **Actions | Download file** from the AWS CloudShell UI and find output files in this directory:

```
/home/cloudshell-user/output/
```

I recommend checking out the Pacu wiki for more information about getting the most out of using Pacu to pentest AWS:

```
https://github.com/RhinoSecurityLabs/pacu/wiki
```

Summary

Anyone can set up an AWS account under their Free Tier to try out some general AWS pentesting tools.

AWS has its own applications that will be useful to you as a pentester. They include AWS CloudShell, AWS Security Hub, and Amazon Inspector.

AWS CloudShell gives you a CLI you can use from your web browser once you've logged in to your AWS account. Alternatively, you can use the AWS CLI application, which you can install directly on your Windows, Mac, or Linux PC.

AWS Security Hub is a handy unified application for checking all of your AWS security settings, configurations, and reports.

Amazon Inspector is AWS's native vulnerability scanning application. I would recommend using it in addition to the other vulnerability scanners and pentesting applications I demonstrate in this book.

A wide range of vulnerability scans and pentests can be executed with Prowler, Cred Scanner, CloudFrunt, and Pacu. These tools help you find security problems such as exposed services and poor security configurations. Remember—you will need to interpret the outputs of these tools yourself and explain them in your pentesting report. If you just share the CSV output files of scans, you're not doing your job as a pentester!

In *Chapter 6*, we will return to our AWS account to try containerization with Docker and Kubernetes. Then, we'll test the Docker and Kubernetes instances we will make.

Further reading

To learn more about the topics covered in this chapter, you can visit the following links:

- AWS CloudShell documentation: `https://docs.aws.amazon.com/cloudshell/`
- Install Prowler: `https://github.com/prowler-cloud/prowler`
- Prowler documentation: `https://docs.prowler.cloud/en/latest/`
- Pacu: `https://github.com/RhinoSecurityLabs/pacu`

6
Pentesting Containerized Applications in AWS

One of the most common use cases for cloud networks is the deployment of containerized applications. Over the course of your career as a cloud pentester, the likelihood that you'll need to test in containerized environments is very high.

The popular containerization platforms, Docker and Kubernetes, operate the same way within their containerization systems regardless of whether they're deployed in AWS, GCP, Azure, or any other cloud platform. However, the way AWS, GCP, and Azure interface with Docker and Kubernetes is a little bit different in each instance.

Think of it this way. A slice of buttered toast is the same slice of buttered toast whether it's served on a ceramic dish, an aluminum dish, or a paper dish. The toast will taste the same, and you will eat it the same way regardless of what kind of dish it's served on. But after you eat the toast, the way you clean or dispose of the dish will be different.

Hopefully, that makes sense! Well, it will make more sense once you've read this chapter.

In this chapter, I will explain the following:

- How containerization works
- How Docker works in AWS
- How Kubernetes works in AWS
- Docker and Kubernetes pentesting techniques in AWS

Let's get started!

Technical requirements

The wonderful thing about using AWS, whether for containerization or anything else, is that we get to use the computing power of Amazon's infrastructure. That means you don't need a really high-end workstation to do any of the exercises in this chapter. All you need is the following:

- A modern desktop or laptop PC running Windows, macOS, or a common Linux distribution such as Ubuntu or Debian. A MacBook or a Windows 11 OEM PC with at least 4 GB of RAM works great.

- A well-supported web browser such as Safari 15 or later, Microsoft Edge 83 or later, Mozilla Firefox 105 or later, or Google Chrome 115 or later.

- A reliable internet connection.

Check out the following video to view the Code in Action: `https://bit.ly/46VJSp3`

How containerization works

First, there were **virtual machines** (**VMs**). VMs run inside a host operating system, and the host operating system is what runs directly on computer hardware. As far as the host operating system is concerned, the VM is simply an application it's running that has been allocated a certain amount of memory (RAM) and a certain amount of disk space in the form of a virtual disk. VMware and Oracle VirtualBox both make virtualization clients that you can easily run and install on a Windows, Mac, or Linux PC. With those virtualization clients, you can make a VM that runs most versions of Windows, macOS, Linux, or Unix.

There is a plethora of use cases for VMs. My background is in cybersecurity, so the use case I'm most familiar with is malware testing. I can safely execute malware in a VM without harming the host operating system or its hardware. That's because the VM assures that the virtual operating system is "sandboxed" from the host operating system. In a worst-case scenario where the malware in my virtual operating system makes my virtual operating system impossible to boot properly, I can go into my host operating system to uninstall the VM and delete its virtual disk. Then, I can make a new VM and start all over again.

An analogy I often hear about host computers and VMs is "a computer and its pet computer." But basically, the host operating system just treats the VM as any other sort of application.

Virtualization has been possible in computing for a lot longer than people often think. The earliest cases of computer virtualization were found in the late 1960s and early 1970s on IBM mainframe computers. Timesharing systems were common on mainframes and minicomputers of the era because people didn't own their own computers until PCs were invented.

Until the advent of PCs, all computers were shared with multiple people. IBM invented virtualization techniques so that multiple users in a timesharing system could have a layer of abstraction from the

CPU, memory, and disk storage. Each user could have their own virtualized computer that could allocate the host computer's real hardware resources without affecting what the other users were doing on the same host computer.

As with everything else in computer technology, over the past few decades, virtualization has gotten better and better. *Containerization is a similar concept to VMs, but it's not exactly the same thing.* However, progress in the development of virtualization technology is what made the invention of containerization possible.

In a nutshell, containerization is similar to VMs, *but much more lightweight.* If a VM is a house made of bricks, wood, stone, or concrete, a container is a tent that can quickly be erected and taken down as needed.

VMs can be created and removed as needed. But installing and removing a VM isn't an instantaneous process. To install a macOS VM on my Windows PC with Oracle VirtualBox, I still need to go through macOS's installation process for each new macOS VM. That takes at least multiple minutes each time.

Docker and Kubernetes are both containerization orchestration platforms. Docker and Kubernetes have their own systems for allocating hardware resources, load balancing, and process isolation. Setting up a Docker or Kubernetes containerization orchestration system for the first time does take several minutes for installation and configuration. However, once the Docker or Kubernetes containerization orchestration system is ready, containers can be deployed and removed very quickly. And if your AWS services give you enough disk space and network bandwidth, you could possibly run hundreds of containers under the same orchestration platform at any given time.

Your cloud application will immediately benefit from the scalability and efficiency containerization gives it. In typical cloud containerization deployments, containers are deployed and removed constantly according to an application's needs at any given time. Sometimes, an individual container may only exist for a few days or less.

Docker was the first containerization platform to become widely popular. Docker debuted in 2013, and it made containerization easier than ever for developers, enterprises, and hobbyists alike. The Kubernetes team was inspired by Docker, and the first version of Kubernetes was released in 2014.

VMs can run on PCs, server machines, and in cloud environments alike. But although applications such as Docker Desktop make it possible to test multi-container applications locally, containerization was really made for the cloud.

Cloud platforms such as AWS, Azure, and GCP provide organizations with hardware and networking scalability because Amazon, Microsoft, and Google operate lots of massive data centers on every part of the globe (except for Antarctica) that contain millions of server machines and really high-capacity networking infrastructure. If an organization needs the capacity of a dozen server machines one day and several hundred server machines the next, Amazon, Microsoft, and Google can provide it almost instantly for the right amount of money. No hardware resources are wasted, and the allocation of hardware resources can be responsive and dynamic.

Thus, containerization is designed to work in the context of cloud environments. The cloud platform allocates hardware resources at the macro level, and the containerization platform allocates hardware resources at the micro level.

Developers really like containerization because they can design their software to run inside a particular container configuration without having to worry about hardware compatibility.

A container bundles application code with simply the dependencies, libraries, and configuration files it needs to run, whereas if they developed their code for a VM or a host computer, they'd have to worry about the operating system. And if their code was designed to run directly on a host computer, they'd have to know its CPU and hardware specifications. When done properly, containerization saves developers a lot of frustration. So, their time and energy can be focused on making the application better rather than having to waste time troubleshooting hardware and operating system problems.

It's possible to use AWS without containerization. In the previous chapter, I installed a Linux operating system directly in AWS in order to produce that chapter's *Code In Action* videos. When I used Prowler, it was vulnerability scanning a very simple Linux-in-AWS setup. If an AWS customer just needs one or a few servers that they'll maintain on a constant basis, simply using an operating system directly in AWS can fulfill their needs.

However, many AWS customers need to deploy applications that could have thousands—or sometimes even hundreds of thousands—of users at any given time. In those situations, containerization is by far the most practical choice. Cloud platforms help make containerization possible. So, as a pentester, it's important that you understand how to pentest Docker and Kubernetes deployments effectively.

How Docker works in AWS

The layers in a Docker containerization system look like this, from the bottom to the top:

- AWS, Azure, or GCP is the cloud platform.
- The cloud platform runs a service, such as **Amazon Elastic Container Service** (**Amazon ECS**), that supports the Docker host. The Docker host is a server, and the administrator administrates it through their Docker client on their local computer.
- The Docker host runs the Docker daemon, which manages Docker images. The daemon can also download images from the Docker Registry. The registry can be the remote public Docker Hub or the organization's own private registry. The daemon also handles API requests.
- Docker images are instructions for creating Docker containers. Containers are generated from the images.

Here's an example of what a Docker architecture looks like:

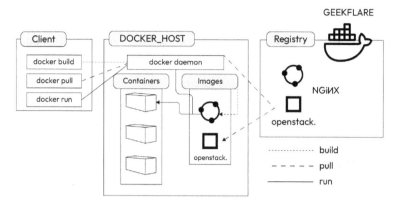

Figure 6.1 – Docker architecture

Docker deployments in AWS use **Amazon Elastic Compute Cloud** (**Amazon EC2**) because that's the main compute platform.

Amazon ECS is the primary service to run Docker in AWS, regardless of the size and scale of your Docker deployment. Amazon ECS is the service you'll be working with directly. It handles the Amazon EC2 work for you.

There are two common ways to install Docker in AWS:

- If you prefer to install Docker with the help of a **graphical user interface** (**GUI**), you can do so with AWS's web application.

- Alternatively, if you prefer to work with a **command-line interface** (**CLI**) as much as possible or if you'd like to use Docker Desktop to test your containerization system locally in addition to deploying it on AWS, you can use the Docker Compose CLI to install Docker in AWS. You may need to install the Docker Compose plugin if it's not already included in your version of Docker Desktop. Read the instructions in *Docker Docs* at `https://docs.docker.com/compose/install/`.

Whichever way you choose to install Docker, you can still use your choice of compatible GUI and CLI applications to use, administrate, and configure your Docker deployment.

Installing a Docker cluster in AWS with Amazon ECS

First, I'll walk you through installing a Docker cluster through AWS's web application GUI:

1. Step one is to launch the Amazon ECS first-run wizard. Log in to your AWS account through your web browser, and the wizard will make launching Amazon ECS and deploying Docker easy.

2. In AWS's web interface, I like to navigate between different AWS services and applications by searching for them by name with the search bar on the top AWS application menu. Search for `Amazon ECS`, click on **Elastic Container Service**, and you'll get to the correct screen quickly.

3. On the right side, there's a white box that says **Deploy your containerized applications**. Click on the orange **Get started** button.

4. You'll be presented with a page that says **Clusters**. Click on the orange button in the top-right corner that says **Create cluster**.

5. Under **Cluster configuration**, give your cluster a name. I chose `AWS-Docker-Test`, but you can choose any name you'd like that's valid.

6. Under **Networking**, leave the default **virtual private cloud** (**VPC**), subnets, and namespace as they are.

7. Under **Infrastructure**, leave the default **AWS Fargate (serverless)** setting as it is. That's the easiest way to have Amazon ECS allocate the hardware resources for your Docker deployment.

8. Likewise, leave the **Monitoring** and **Tags** sections as they are. In the lower-right corner, click on the orange **Create** button.

    A blue bar will appear near the top that says cluster creation is in process. It could take a few minutes. If all goes well, the blue bar will become green and say that the cluster was created successfully. If not, repeat the steps I walked you through and try again. When I tested the cluster creation process myself, my first attempt returned a red bar that said the creation process failed. But on my second attempt, I was successful.

9. Now that your cluster was created successfully, you can see the name of your new cluster in the list. Click on the name of your cluster.

10. You'll be taken to a new page with the name of your cluster (`AWS-Docker-Test`, in my case) at the top. The first section underneath says **Cluster overview**, and the next section has six tabs: **Services**, **Tasks**, **Infrastructure**, **Metrics**, **Scheduled tasks**, and **Tags**. Under the **Services** tab, click on the orange **Create** button in the upper-right corner.

11. On the next page, leave all the default settings in the **Environment** section. In the **Deployment configuration** section, leave **Service** as the application type. Under that, you'll see a **Task definition** area where it says **Select an existing task definition**. To create a new task definition, go to **Task definitions**, and click on **Go to Task definitions**.

12. A new page will load in a new tab in your web browser. On the **Task definitions** page, click on the orange **Create new task definition** button in the upper-right corner. Under **Configure task definition and containers**, give your task definition family a name. I chose `Docker-Test-Task-Definition` because I'm so imaginative. But you can create whatever name you'd like.

13. Under **Container – 1**, name your container (I chose `Docker-Container-Test`). You will also need to enter an image URI (go to `https://docs.aws.amazon.com/emr/latest/EMR-on-EKS-DevelopmentGuide/docker-custom-images-tag.html`

in the AWS documentation to learn how to select a base image URI if you need help). In my case, I'm using Amazon's `us-east-1` data center. So, my image URI is `711395599931.dkr.ecr.us-east-1.amazonaws.com/spark/emr-6.10.0:latest`. Leave all the other default settings as they are. Click on the orange **Create** button in the lower-right corner.

14. Under **Family**, enter your new task definition name (mine is `Docker-Test-Task-Definition`). Leave **Revision** as is. Create a new name under **Service name**. I chose `Docker-Test-Service`. Leave all the other default settings as they are. Click on the orange **Create** button in the lower-right corner.

The deployment of your new service may take a few minutes, as indicated in the blue notification at the top of your screen. All services deployed the way I showed you with Amazon ECS use Docker by default. So, you're making a new Docker instance.

Deploying Docker with Docker Desktop

The other main way to deploy Docker in Amazon ECS is to use Docker Desktop. If that's the way you'd prefer, you'll first need to install Docker Desktop on your local computer. Docker Desktop is an application that's used to run Docker CLI commands. To install it, follow the next steps:

1. Visit `https://docs.docker.com/desktop/install/mac-install/` to install it on Mac, or visit `https://docs.docker.com/desktop/install/windows-install/` to install it on Windows. You may also need to install the Docker Compose plugin in Docker Desktop if it's not already included. There are instructions in *Docker Docs* (`https://docs.docker.com/compose/install/`). If your local computer uses a Linux operating system, you'll need to install the Docker Compose CLI for Linux here: `https://docs.docker.com/cloud/ecs-integration/#install-the-docker-compose-cli-on-linux`.

2. Log in to your AWS account through your web browser. You'll need to make sure that your AWS credentials have access to certain AWS **Identity and Access Management** (**IAM**) permissions. See the AWS documentation on managing permissions (`https://aws.amazon.com/iam/features/manage-permissions/`) if you need more help with this. If you only have your root account, you will need to create a new IAM account that has the permissions listed next. These are the permissions your credentials will need:

   * `application-autoscaling:*`
   * `cloudformation:*`
   * `ec2:AuthorizeSecurityGroupIngress`
   * `ec2:CreateSecurityGroup`
   * `ec2:CreateTags`
   * `ec2:DeleteSecurityGroup`

- `ec2:DescribeRouteTables`
- `ec2:DescribeSecurityGroups`
- `ec2:DescribeSubnets`
- `ec2:DescribeVpcs`
- `ec2:RevokeSecurityGroupIngress`
- `ecs:CreateCluster`
- `ecs:CreateService`
- `ecs:DeleteCluster`
- `ecs:DeleteService`
- `ecs:DeregisterTaskDefinition`
- `ecs:DescribeClusters`
- `ecs:DescribeServices`
- `ecs:DescribeTasks`
- `ecs:ListAccountSettings`
- `ecs:ListTasks`
- `ecs:RegisterTaskDefinition`
- `ecs:UpdateService`
- `elasticloadbalancing:*`
- `iam:AttachRolePolicy`
- `iam:CreateRole`
- `iam:DeleteRole`
- `iam:DetachRolePolicy`
- `iam:PassRole`
- `logs:CreateLogGroup`
- `logs:DeleteLogGroup`
- `logs:DescribeLogGroups`
- `logs:FilterLogEvents`
- `route53:CreateHostedZone`
- `route53:DeleteHostedZone`

- route53:GetHealthCheck

- route53:GetHostedZone

- route53:ListHostedZonesByName

- servicediscovery:*

3. Now, you'll need to run some commands at the Docker Compose CLI. Start with this command:

    ```
    docker context create ecs <name of your ECS context>
    ```

    The following will print on your screen:

    ```
    ? Create a Docker context using:   [Use arrows to move, type to
    filter]
        An existing AWS profile
        AWS secret and token credentials
    > AWS environment variables
    ```

4. Select **AWS environment variables**. Follow the onscreen instructions to configure your ECS context to retrieve AWS credentials. With that, you can now view your Docker context with this command:

    ```
    docker context ls
    ```

5. You can now deploy and manage your Docker containerization in Amazon ECS with the docker compose command.

A guide to Docker Compose CLI commands and configuration help can be found on the *Docker Docs* website (https://docs.docker.com/cloud/ecs-integration/). I strongly recommend referring to the Docker command-line guide as well (https://docs.docker.com/engine/reference/commandline/cli/). But I personally prefer the other Docker deployment method that completely uses AWS's web application GUI.

Refer to the AWS documentation if you ever need to delete your Docker cluster:

https://docs.aws.amazon.com/AmazonECS/latest/userguide/delete_cluster-new-console.html

It's also possible to remove Docker containers when you're not using them anymore. This command (at the Docker CLI) will remove your Docker container and its volumes (**data storage units**, or **DSUs**):

```
docker rm --volumes <name of docker container>
```

So, Docker is one way to deploy containerized applications in AWS. Kubernetes is the other way, and it builds upon Docker's system. But setting it up works differently, as you will see.

How Kubernetes works in AWS

The layers in a Kubernetes containerization system look like this, from the bottom to the top:

- AWS, Azure, or GCP is the cloud platform.

- The cloud platform runs a service, such as **Amazon Elastic Kubernetes Service (Amazon EKS)**, which supports the control plane.

- The next layer is the control plane, which is managed by Kubernetes. This is the root of the cluster.

- The control plane deploys Pods according to changing network application metrics that the cloud administrator can define. Pods are deployed to be able to manage the needs of your Kubernetes application at any given time. For instance, more users and more bandwidth consumption usually result in more Pods.

- Pods deploy containers.

Here's a sample diagram of Kubernetes architecture:

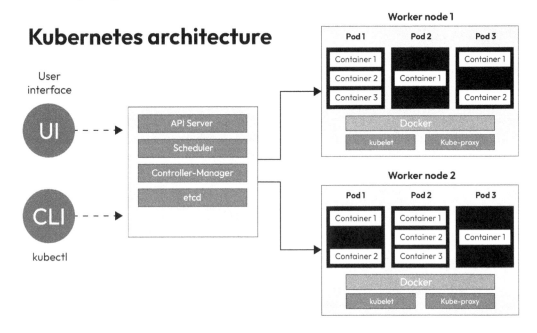

Figure 6.2 – Kubernetes architecture

Kubernetes Deployments in AWS use Amazon EC2 because that's the main compute platform. It's possible to manage Kubernetes directly in Amazon EC2. But more often, organizations choose to use Amazon EKS as an interface with Amazon EC2. It spares administrators the hassle of having to manage etcd and instances.

All the AWS Kubernetes examples I use in this book assume that Amazon EKS is being used.

The simplest way to create a Kubernetes containerization system with an Amazon EKS cluster is to use AWS's web application. It's also possible to launch a cluster at the AWS CLI, but I found it took a lot of extra time to set up IAM and JSON configuration files. If you'd prefer to use the command line, there's a guide in the AWS documentation here: `https://docs.aws.amazon.com/eks/latest/userguide/getting-started.html`. But I presume you're just setting up an environment to practice pentesting. So, launching an EKS cluster through the AWS web interface with all of the default settings should suffice for that purpose. Follow the next steps:

1. Log in to your AWS account through `aws.amazon.com` in your web browser. In the top menu search bar, enter `EKS` or `Elastic Kubernetes Service`. There will be a link to open the Amazon EKS interface. Alternatively, you may see a white box on the right side of your screen that says **Add cluster** for you to click on.

2. You'll immediately be taken to the **Clusters** page. Click on the orange **Create cluster** button in the top-right corner and select **Create** from the drop-down menu. Alternatively, you may need to click on the drop-down menu that says **Create** and click on **Create Clusters**.

3. Now, you're on the **Configure cluster** page. Enter an original name for your cluster. Choose whatever you'd like. I chose `EKS-Pentest`. Leave the default Kubernetes version. Choose a cluster service role from the drop-down menu. If there's no cluster service role to choose from, follow the Amazon EKS user guide instructions (`https://docs.aws.amazon.com/eks/latest/userguide/service_IAM_role.html#create-service-role`) on how to make an AWS IAM role with EKS cluster permissions.

4. Leave the rest of the defaults as they are and click on the orange **Next** button in the lower-right corner.

5. On the next page, there are **Networking** settings to configure. Leave **VPC**, **Subnets**, **Security groups**, and **IP address** at their default settings. Leave **Cluster endpoint access** as public and click on the orange **Next** button in the lower-right corner.

6. On the **Configure logging** page, set the control plane to log **API server**, **Audit**, **Authenticator**, **Controller manager**, and **Scheduler**. For pentesting and red team purposes, more logging is always best! Click on the orange **Next** button in the lower-right corner.

7. Leave the Amazon EKS add-ons as the defaults. They include CoreDNS, Amazon VPC CNI, and `kube-proxy`. Click on the orange **Next** button in the lower-right corner.

8. Leave the default versions for the add-ons. Click on the orange **Next** button in the lower-right corner.

9. Review all of your configurations and click on the orange **Create** button in the lower-right corner.

    You will see a blue notification bar at the top of your screen that says your cluster is being created. It may take a few minutes. When you see a green notification bar, your Kubernetes cluster has been created. Congratulations!

If you ever need to delete your Kubernetes cluster, refer to the AWS documentation here:

`https://docs.aws.amazon.com/eks/latest/userguide/delete-cluster.html`

So, we've now set up Docker and Kubernetes containerization systems in AWS. Now, it's time to pentest them.

Docker and Kubernetes pentesting techniques in AWS

In the previous chapter, I walked you through using Prowler to pentest AWS deployments. I'll show you some scripts and vulnerability checks you can execute to find Docker and Kubernetes vulnerabilities with a few different tools. But first, it's worthwhile mentioning here that Prowler can be executed from a Docker instance! You can use Prowler from Docker containers to help pentest your organization's entire AWS network. *Running Prowler from Docker isn't just for vulnerability assessing Docker.*

The same Prowler CLI commands from the previous chapter can be used when you run Prowler from Docker.

Installation in Docker

Here's how to install Prowler from Docker:

1. Make sure that Docker Desktop is installed on your local computer. Find the Docker Desktop Windows, Mac, and Linux clients here: `https://docs.docker.com/get-docker/`.

2. Have your AWS credentials ready. You can verify them by logging in to your AWS account from your web browser. On the top menu bar, look at the far-right drop-down menu with your username. Click on **Security credentials** to navigate to the correct AWS IAM page. At the top, it should say **My security credentials (root user)**. Make a note of your AWS account ID, access key ID, and secret access key.

3. Navigate to AWS CloudShell by looking at the top menu bar. Launch it by clicking on the Command Prompt-looking icon that's to the left of the bell icon.

4. At the AWS CloudShell CLI, enter `pwd` in order to verify your home directory path. You may need to use the `ls` (list files and folders) command and `cd` (change directory) command to find your home directory.

5. Enter the following commands to install and configure Prowler inside of a Docker container. Make sure that you enter your AWS access keys into the script:

    ```
    docker run -ti --rm -v /your/local/dir/prowler-output:/home/
    prowler/output \
    export AWS_ACCESS_KEY_ID="ASXXXXXXX"
    ```

```
export AWS_SECRET_ACCESS_KEY="XXXXXXXXX"

export AWS_SESSION_TOKEN="XXXXXXXXX"
--name prowler \
--env AWS_ACCESS_KEY_ID \
--env AWS_SECRET_ACCESS_KEY \
```

Replace `/your/local/dir` with the path of your home directory. Enter your access key ID and secret access key after each \ instance.

If you need help generating an `AWS_SESSION_TOKEN` instance, consider using this guide:

`https://www.websitebuilderinsider.com/how-do-i-get-my-aws-session-token/#:~:text=To%20get%20your%20session%20token,best%20to%20contact%20AWS%20support`

Prowler will install in your Docker instance, and you should now be able to execute Prowler from the Docker Compose CLI in Docker Desktop. All of the Prowler commands from the previous chapter will work here. Also, please familiarize yourself with Docker commands with this guide from *Docker Docs*: `https://docs.docker.com/engine/reference/commandline/cli/`.

There is a simple automated pentest script by Vishnu Nair that you can use for both real-world pentesting and for trying out for educational purposes. I recommend giving it a try! It can be found in Docker Hub (`https://hub.docker.com/r/vishnunair/pentest`).

Because I was just trying it out, I decided to run Vishnu Nair's script in the **Play With Docker** (**PWD**) (`https://labs.play-with-docker.com/`) simulation. PWD offers a "*simple, interactive and fun playground*" to experiment with Docker in its own VMs that you can execute from your web browser. But of course, Vishnu Nair's script will work in real Docker instances too.

Vishnu Nair's automated pentest automatically executes dozens of modules including (but not limited to) Nmap, Uniscan, TheHarvester, XSSStrike, Dirb, SSLScan, and DNSmap. Then, it prints results both on screen and in the `/src` folder inside of the container.

It's such a simple script—one of the most user-friendly automated vulnerability scanners for containers I have ever used.

Here are the commands to use:

1. First, create a Docker volume:

    ```
    docker volume create pentest-reports
    ```

2. Then, download the script:

    ```
    docker run -d --name pentest -d -v pentest-reports:/src
    vishnunair/pentest:latest
    ```

3. Execute it like so:

```
docker exec -it pentest bash
```

```
./pentest.sh -d <domain name of your container here>
```

The scan results will print on your screen.

4. Find your Docker volumes in the `/var/lib/docker/volumes` path. You may need to use the `cd` command to navigate to it.

5. Then, find your scan report with this command:

```
docker volume inspect pentest-reports
```

On to Kubernetes!

Installation in Kubernetes

Aqua Security's `kube-bench` is an automated script that runs vulnerability scans based on the **Center for Internet Security (CIS)** Kubernetes Benchmark (`https://www.cisecurity.org/benchmark/kubernetes`). The Benchmark includes a list of checks in these categories:

- Control-plane components

- `etcd`

- Control-plane configuration

- Worker nodes

- Policies

There are multiple ways to run `kube-bench` (`https://github.com/aquasecurity/kube-bench/blob/main/docs/running.md`), including as a Kubernetes Job with a YAML file. In this chapter, I created an **Azure Kubernetes Service (AKS)** cluster for Kubernetes. So, let's try running `kube-bench` there:

1. First, make sure `kubectl-node-shell` is installed in your EKS cluster by following the GitHub instructions here: `https://github.com/kvaps/kubectl-node-shell`.

2. While at the AWS CLI with Docker installed, run the `kube-bench` script:

```
docker run --rm -v `pwd`:/host docker.io/aquasec/kube-
bench:latest install
./kube-bench
```

3. Your benchmark check results will be printed on screen, and you should also find a report in the `/src` folder of your container.

Refer to the `kube-bench` documentation if you need troubleshooting help: `https://github.com/aquasecurity/kube-bench/tree/main/docs`.

> **Tip**
>
> Here's a tip for trying all of the Docker and Kubernetes pentest tools and scripts mentioned in this book. You know how I started this chapter with an analogy about the cloud platform (AWS, Azure, GCP) being like a dish and the containerization orchestration platform (Docker, Kubernetes) being like a piece of buttered toast?
>
> The AWS (*Chapter 5*), Azure (*Chapter 8*), and GCP (*Chapter 11*) pentests are specific to those cloud platforms. But the Docker and Kubernetes pentest tools and scripts mentioned in this chapter, *Chapter 9*, and *Chapter 12* can be run in any Docker or Kubernetes instance regardless of the cloud platform.

So, there are a lot more useful pentest tools and scripts for Docker and Kubernetes further on in this book!

Summary

Cloud platforms such as AWS, Azure, and GCP are popular because they offer organizations lots of scalability in their massive data centers.

Containerization orchestrated by Docker or Kubernetes takes full advantage of cloud infrastructure by helping organizations manage hardware and software resources better for their networked applications. Containers use virtualization but are much more lightweight and portable than VMs. You will almost definitely be working with containerization as a cloud pentester.

In AWS, Docker is usually run through Amazon ECS, and Kubernetes with Amazon EKS. They're both interfaces for Amazon EC2.

Docker and Kubernetes pentesting scripts and benchmarks are interchangeable between cloud platforms.

Now that we've deployed VMs and containerized applications in AWS and pentested them, we will move on to Microsoft Azure in the next chapter.

Further reading

To learn more about the topics covered in this chapter, you can visit the following links:

- Docker on AWS: `https://aws.amazon.com/docker/`
- Kubernetes on AWS: `https://aws.amazon.com/kubernetes/`
- Docker CLI guide: `https://docs.docker.com/engine/reference/commandline/cli/`
- PWD test lab: `https://www.docker.com/play-with-docker/`

Part 3: Pentesting Microsoft Azure

Azure is Microsoft's own cloud platform, and it's been popular with businesses of all kinds for over 15 years. In this part, we will learn about Azure's various software-as-a-service, platform-as-a-service, and infrastructure-as-a-service applications. We will deploy our own Azure instance in which to test our pentesting skills. We will use Microsoft Defender for Cloud to check the security posture of our Azure deployment. We will also try out some pentesting tools in Azure, step by step. Then, we'll deploy Docker and Kubernetes containers and test those as well.

This section has the following chapters:

- *Chapter 7, Security Features in Azure*
- *Chapter 8, Pentesting Azure Features through Serverless Applications and Tools*
- *Chapter 9, Pentesting Containerized Applications in Azure*

7

Security Features in Azure

As a cloud pentester, it's important for you to understand one of the most popular cloud platforms out there—that is, Azure. You'll probably be pentesting Azure networks and applications frequently.

In this chapter, we will first examine some of the most commonly used aspects of the Azure ecosystem along with the most popular Azure services, applications, and features, and why they're used. After that, we'll look into Azure **Software-as-a-Service (SaaS)**, **Infrastructure-as-a-Service (IaaS)**, and **Platform-as-a-Service (PaaS)** features. We will conclude the chapter by discussing Microsoft's own Azure security tools and third-party security tools.

This chapter covers the following main topics:

- Introduction to Azure
- Frequently used Azure SaaS applications
- Azure IaaS applications
- Azure PaaS applications
- Azure security controls and tools

Let's jump right in!

Introduction to Azure

At the beginning of the 2000s, Microsoft's data center infrastructure was smaller than their current cloud platform competitors, Amazon and Google. But Microsoft's pockets were comparatively deep. When it launched Xbox Live in 2002 (now known as the Xbox network), it had built immense backend infrastructure to support what was then the highest-capacity online gaming service ever. From that point on, Microsoft steadily expanded its own data center capacity as it got into the network services business (MSN doesn't count) concurrently with its expansion into the video game console business.

From what I can tell, building Xbox Live/the Xbox network for the consumer market gave Microsoft the experience it needed to start providing network services for the enterprise market. Amazon launched AWS as "*Amazon.com Web Services*" in 2002, its initiative to provide cloud services to the enterprise. Microsoft probably thought, "I'd like a piece of that action."

It took a few more years of research and development and building more infrastructure. But by October 2008, Microsoft was ready to announce "Project Red Dog."

> **Project Red Dog**
>
> Project Red Dog was Microsoft's cloud operating system project that was a precursor to Azure. There is no "Red Dog" operating system; it evolved into the Azure services that are mentioned in this chapter.

By 2010, its new cloud service launched as Windows Azure, and by 2014 it was renamed Microsoft Azure.

As with its main competitors Amazon and Google, over the past several years Microsoft has been steadily adding new features and services to its cloud platform.

One of Microsoft's major advantages is the market dominance of its business operating systems and applications. Companies that run lots of on-premises computers with Windows Server and Active Directory experience great synergy when Azure runs its cloud networks and applications. AWS and GCP can work with Windows Server and Active Directory, but doing that is like eating Italian food made by French people. Windows Server and Microsoft Azure is like eating Italian food made by Italian people! So, it makes sense that many organizations choose to integrate Azure into their networks, whether their cloud is all Azure or multi-cloud.

Before you pentest any Azure network, it's important to make sure that you're abiding by Microsoft's *Penetration Testing Rules of Engagement*. Here's what it says on Microsoft's website (`https://www.microsoft.com/en-us/msrc/pentest-rules-of-engagement`):

"*The goal of this program is to enable customers to test their services hosted in Microsoft Cloud services without causing harm to any other Microsoft customers.*

The following activities are prohibited:

- *Scanning or testing assets belonging to any other Microsoft Cloud customers.*
- *Gaining access to any data that is not wholly your own.*
- *Performing any kind of denial of service testing.*
- *Performing network intensive fuzzing against any asset except your Azure Virtual Machine*
- *Performing automated testing of services that generates significant amounts of traffic.*
- *Deliberately accessing any other customer's data.*

- *Moving beyond "proof of concept" repro steps for infrastructure execution issues (i.e. proving that you have sysadmin access with SQLi is acceptable, running xp_cmdshell is not).*

- *Using our services in a way that violates the Acceptable Use Policy, as set forth in the Microsoft Online Service Terms.*

- *Attempting phishing or other social engineering attacks against our employees.*

The following activities are encouraged:

- *Create a small number of test accounts and/or trial tenants for demonstrating and proving cross-account or cross-tenant data access. However, it is prohibited to use one of these accounts to access the data of another customer or account.*

- *Fuzz, port scan, or run vulnerability assessment tools against your own Azure Virtual Machines.*

- *Load testing your application by generating traffic which is expected to be seen during the normal course of business. This includes testing surge capacity.*

- *Testing security monitoring and detections (e.g. generating anomalous security logs, dropping EICAR, etc).*

- *Attempt to break out of a shared service container such as Azure Websites or Azure Functions. However, should you succeed you must both immediately report it to Microsoft and cease digging deeper. Deliberately accessing another customer's data is a violation of the terms.*

- *Applying conditional access or mobile application management (MAM) policies within Microsoft Intune to test the enforcement of the restriction enforced by those policies.*

Even with these prohibitions, Microsoft reserves the right to respond to any actions on its networks that appear to be malicious. Many automated mitigation mechanisms are employed across the Microsoft Cloud. These will not be disabled to facilitate a penetration test."

In a nutshell, you can pentest in Azure without getting Microsoft's permission. But you're limited in what you're allowed to do. You cannot perform activities that disrupt other Azure customers, such as **distributed denial-of-service (DDoS)** attack simulations or stress tests. You may not even attempt to access Azure data and assets that don't belong to the company you work for. Simulating criminal infrastructure execution exploits is strictly forbidden. You may load-test your company's own services and applications, but you may not generate more data or consume more bandwidth than what would be used for normal operations. Microsoft encourages you to create new user accounts to test for IAM problems, as long as you don't try to access any data that doesn't belong to the company that you work for. Of course, you will also need written permission from the company you work for to perform any sort of pentest, security test, or red team engagement whatsoever.

Microsoft Azure is a unique cloud platform. But in many ways, it's similar to AWS and GCP. As with AWS, GCP, and many other cloud providers, Azure offers a wide range of cloud services that can be categorized according to how much responsibility Microsoft has and how much responsibility the customer (the business you work for) has. As with other cloud platforms, all Azure services can be categorized as either SaaS, PaaS, or IaaS.

No matter whether the service is SaaS, PaaS, or IaaS, organizations are responsible for the security of their own data. If a software vulnerability in a customer's own code is exploited in a cyber attack, it's the customer's problem to deal with. Microsoft offers a lot of very useful security tools that can greatly improve an organization's security posture in Azure, but they have to actually be used in order for them to work.

And no matter what, Microsoft is responsible for the security of its Azure infrastructure. That's why no one is allowed to visit any of its data centers without Microsoft's explicit permission and close supervision. That's also why pentesters are limited in what they're allowed to do when they execute pentesting and red team engagements in Azure. Customers are responsible for their security in the cloud; cloud providers are responsible for the security of the cloud. A customer's own code and applications are their business; Microsoft's servers, networking devices, data center buildings, and Microsoft's own code is its business.

Chapter 3 goes into detail about the shared responsibility model of cloud computing. But for the sake of convenience, you can review Microsoft's *Penetration Testing Rules of Engagement* (`https://www.microsoft.com/en-us/msrc/pentest-rules-of-engagement`) and the *Microsoft Online Subscription Agreement* (`https://azure.microsoft.com/en-us/support/legal/subscription-agreement/`). It's of the utmost importance that you understand and abide by Microsoft's rules before you commence any pentesting in Azure. So, review those resources and re-read *Chapter 3* to make sure you understand what you're permitted to do and what's forbidden. If the organization you're working for asks you to do something that Microsoft forbids, Microsoft's authority trumps theirs. When you pentest Azure, you're a guest in Microsoft's house.

SaaS, PaaS, and IaaS indicate how much of an Azure service is Microsoft's and how much responsibility and autonomy the company you work for has. In SaaS, a lot of the software code belongs to Microsoft. Your company does the least amount of work (relative to PaaS and IaaS). Your company's data is running in Microsoft's online applications. In IaaS, Microsoft is providing its own infrastructure and little else. Your organization has the most flexibility and control, but it also has to build and maintain almost all of the software code and networking configurations that it's using in Microsoft's infrastructure. PaaS is in the middle of those two extremes. PaaS comes with more Microsoft APIs and service features than IaaS. Microsoft is providing an application and services platform, but it's supporting your organization's own software.

Now, let's explore the most frequently used Azure services.

Frequently used Azure SaaS applications

I'll summarize the most popular SaaS applications in Azure. It's unlikely that you will be pentesting them because Microsoft has more responsibility for the security of its SaaS than for its PaaS and IaaS. Your company just inputs its own data into these applications or embeds them in its own applications. But it's important as an Azure pentester to understand the many ways Azure is used so that you can contextualize how SaaS fits in with the rest of Azure and how the company you work for may be using Azure SaaS applications. Plus, the data your organization inputs into Azure's SaaS applications is your organization's security responsibility. For instance, if someone in your organization puts their sensitive bank account information into Microsoft Cost Management outside of the cryptography Microsoft has implemented, that's your organization's problem. If your organization has a PaaS or IaaS application that interfaces with a SaaS application, that data flow can likely be pentested from the PaaS or IaaS end.

Azure Maps

Azure Maps is similar to Google Maps. It offers detailed maps of pretty much every built-up part of the world. There are built-in features that use IP and GPS geolocation so that users can see where they are on the map and where they're going. Azure Maps can be integrated into the mobile and web applications that Azure customers develop. So, for instance, businesses can show a map of the physical location of their premises in an embedded Azure Maps applet on their web pages. Azure Maps has about 250 different code samples hosted on GitHub (`https://samples.azuremaps.com/`) to make integration easy for developers. There are code samples for everything, from animating multiple points on a map to showing different map layers with different kinds of geographic and meteorological data to implementing maps of indoor spaces with Azure Maps Web Control:

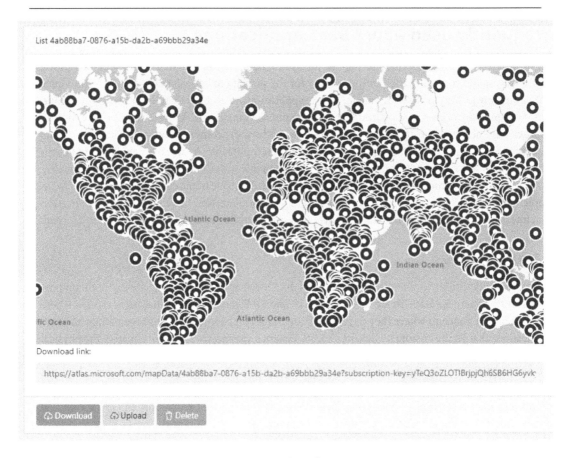

List 4ab88ba7-0876-a15b-da2b-a69bbb29a34e

Download link:

https://atlas.microsoft.com/mapData/4ab88ba7-0876-a15b-da2b-a69bbb29a34e?subscription-key=yTeQ3oZLOTIBrjpjQh6SB6HG6yvk

Figure 7.1 – Screenshot of Azure Maps

Azure Maps has multiple data feeds for traffic, weather, photographic imagery, and data visualization. For instance, where are the tallest mountain peaks and deepest canyons? Which areas get the most precipitation in a given year? Where are all of a retailer's stores located? Azure Maps's data visualization features work with a business customer's own data.

Azure Digital Twins

Azure Digital Twins uses a customer's own IoT devices to create digital models of physical objects, business processes, and places. When the IoT devices detect changes in a physical environment, Azure Digital Twins can adjust the digital models accordingly. It integrates with REST APIs, Azure IoT Hub, Logic Apps, Event Hubs, Azure Data Explorer, and Azure Synapse Analytics. It's kind of weird but also kind of cool.

Azure Monitor

The two previous applications (Azure Maps and Azure Digital Twins) are more specialized. But **Azure Monitor** is a lot more generalized. Azure Monitor can be configured so that organizations can see a wide range of business networking data through dynamic dashboard interfaces. Metrics, logs, changes, and traces are fed into Azure Monitor. Then, administrators can watch a variety of different network events, and not all of them are directly related to security events. You can also display live data for metrics such as "*How many users are using which applications, and when?*"

Azure Monitor integrates into every Azure service and application possible. You can also implement data from other cloud provider services (multi-cloud environments) and on-premises networks through Azure Arc.

Microsoft Cost Management

Microsoft Cost Management gives Azure customers very detailed information about how much they're spending on their various Azure services, applications, and features. There are detailed panels for cost analysis, cost alerts, budgetary data, billing charges and usage, and Azure costs related to company departments and accounts.

Graphs can be shown that show trends and patterns in a customer's spending on Azure services. Accountants and **chief financial officers** (**CFOs**) love this sort of stuff. It's not just "*Our company spent $25,657 on Azure this month.*" Microsoft Cost Management shows every possible Azure spending metric that can be shown on an accountant's ledger. So, of course, customers can see pie graphs that break down overall Azure spending into all the applicable categories.

Azure Advisor

Azure Advisor is similar to Microsoft Cost Management, but instead of budgetary and billing information, it shows a variety of metrics related to security, reliability, performance, operational excellence, and cost:

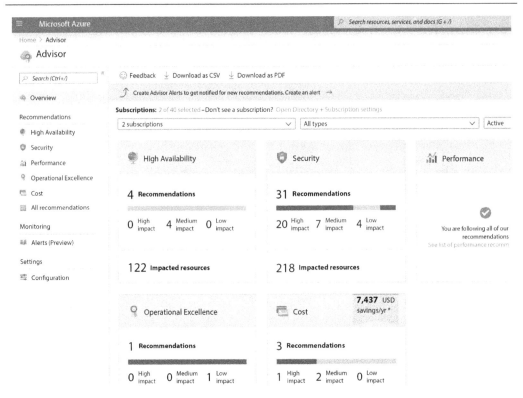

Figure 7.2 – Screenshot of Azure Advisor

Azure Advisor can be launched through the **Azure command-line interface** (**Azure CLI**), the Advisor API, or the Azure portal to show metrics that are relevant in context. If an administrator asks "*How can we manage our Azure resources and applications more effectively?*", Azure Advisor will provide the information they need in order to make those kinds of decisions.

Network Watcher

Network Watcher is an overall network performance monitoring and diagnostics solution. It shows dashboards with dynamic real-time networking metrics from **virtual machines** (**VMs**), **virtual private networks** (**VPNs**), and network traffic patterns.

See how much network bandwidth each part of your organization's Azure cloud uses! View general security metrics, resource security hygiene, security alerts, and compliance data through Security Center. Network Watcher can also be used to diagnose various connectivity issues.

Now that we have looked at SaaS, let's get into IaaS. While SaaS gives Microsoft the maximum control and security responsibility, IaaS gives most of the control and security responsibility to the organization that you work for.

Azure IaaS applications

Azure IaaS gives your organization just the very basics as far as software code is concerned. The vast majority of the code your organization deploys in IaaS belongs to your organization and is your organization's responsibility as far as cybersecurity is concerned.

Here are some of the most commonly used IaaS applications in Azure.

Azure Virtual Machines

Azure Virtual Machines enables your organization to deploy VMs with Windows and Linux. You can deploy lots and lots of virtualized Windows and Linux servers to do anything and everything Linux and Windows servers do, from running huge enterprise applications to deploying web servers and other kinds of internet services.

Azure Kubernetes Service

Azure Kubernetes Service (**AKS**) supports Kubernetes containerization orchestration in Azure (`https://azure.microsoft.com/en-ca/products/kubernetes-service/`).

AKS is specially designed for Kubernetes clusters, so it is the best way to deploy Kubernetes-based applications in Azure. I was able to deploy Kubernetes with AKS in Azure within minutes, whereas deploying Kubernetes in Azure without AKS is at least hours of work and a lot of hassle:

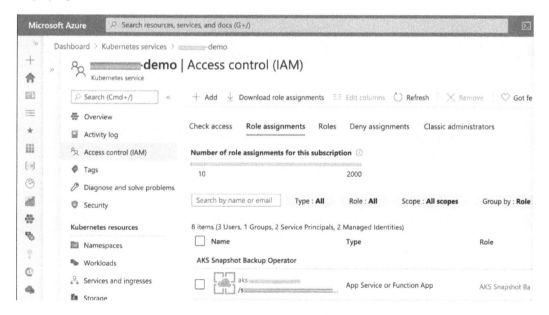

Figure 7.3 – Screenshot of AKS

There will be a lot more information about AKS in *Chapter 9*!

Azure Container Instances

Azure Container Instances (**ACI**) empowers Azure customers to develop and deploy their own software applications without having to manage VMs or learn new tools:

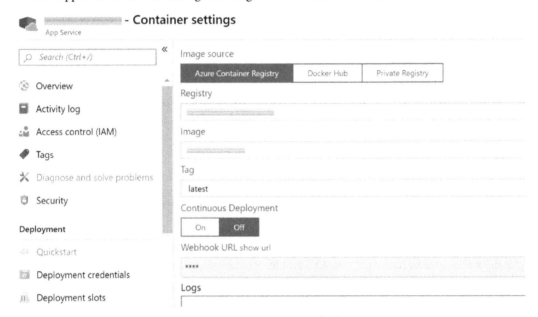

Figure 7.4 – Screenshot of ACI

ACI can work with AKS and Azure Functions (more on that in the immediate next section) to support complex applications with lots of containers.

Azure Dedicated Host

Azure Dedicated Host is a dedicated physical server to host Azure VMs running Windows and Linux. Yes—with Azure Dedicated Host, your organization gets its very own physical server machine on Microsoft's premises. That's a relatively expensive option for enterprises that have the budget for it, but it gives them the maximum control they can possibly have within the Azure ecosystem:

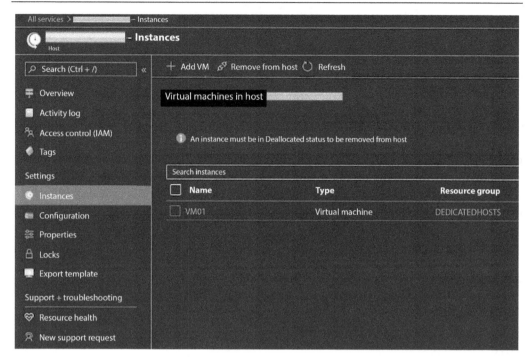

Figure 7.5 – Screenshot of Azure Dedicated Host

Now, let's take a look at PaaS in Azure.

Azure PaaS applications

Azure PaaS is in between SaaS and IaaS as far as the amount of control and autonomy of Azure customers (such as the business organization you work for) is concerned.

In PaaS, Azure provides a platform. Only Azure SaaS provides Azure's own complete applications that customers deploy their data in, whereas Azure IaaS basically provides Azure's server hardware and networking infrastructure with absolutely minimal Azure code. The vast majority of the code in an IaaS deployment belongs to the customer and is their responsibility.

Here are Azure PaaS services where customers run the applications they develop, but within platform systems that Microsoft develops.

Azure SQL Database

Azure SQL Database enables customers to build applications with SQL databases. SQL is one of the top vendor-neutral database development technologies. A wide variety of types of applications that need support from backend services use SQL, not just mobile apps or web apps.

Web Apps

Web Apps is used to host ASP.NET web applications. ASP.NET is a developer platform of tools, programming languages, and libraries for building web apps. It uses HTML, CSS, JavaScript, Node.js, Python, Java, and C#.

Mobile Apps

Mobile Apps is Microsoft Azure's service for deploying the backend for all kinds of apps for iOS and Android. It deploys **single sign-on** (**SSO**) authentication with Azure Active Directory. It integrates with Facebook, Twitter, and Google APIs. It also enables apps to work offline for extended periods of time, although mobile apps should be online periodically for synchronization.

Azure Logic Apps

Azure Logic Apps is a very specialized logic application development tool. A logic app creates and automates workflows without having to write a lot of code. Logic apps can be built with diagrams where events trigger actions.

Azure Functions

Azure Functions is a serverless compute platform, which means that Azure customers can deploy applications without their having to manage a server. Azure Functions is event-driven, which means that if certain defined events occur in the applications your organization develops, Azure Functions will respond to those events in a way that your organization defines (`https://azure.microsoft.com/en-us/products/functions/`).

Now, let's look at the applications Microsoft provides Azure users with for managing cybersecurity.

Azure security controls and tools

It's possible to use Microsoft Azure to deploy cloud networks with excellent security. But cybersecurity is everyday work. As a cloud pentester, you'll be deploying pentests, red team engagements, and vulnerability scans that will give the organization the vulnerability data it needs to continuously security harden its networks and applications. Defensive security specialists need to put your security recommendations into practice. They also need to actually use the variety of security tools that Microsoft provides for Azure.

Excellent cybersecurity is possible with Azure. But you've got to do the work and use the tools Microsoft gives you!

Security controls

Microsoft provides a number of applications to help your organization maintain the cybersecurity of its applications and services in Azure. They are also useful for pentesters to check, to look for security alerts and vulnerabilities that Microsoft's own security controls can find.

Here are the main security controls that Microsoft provides for securing Azure.

Microsoft Defender for Cloud

Microsoft Defender for Cloud is its main unified cloud-native application protection platform. If you're already familiar with Microsoft Defender in Windows, Microsoft Defender for Cloud includes a lot of those features and expands upon them for functionality that's required for securing cloud networks.

Microsoft Defender for Cloud provides visibility into your security posture not only in Azure, but also in AWS, GCP, and your organization's on-premises network. It provides antimalware and security monitoring for a variety of services. Administrators can see critical risks prioritized with context-aware security. It also provides **extended detection and response** (**XDR**) to detect and respond to cyber attacks. You can even see real-time data about your network's regulatory compliance.

If Microsoft Defender for Cloud is running in the services you're pentesting, your organization should see detailed information about the cyber attacks you're simulating!

Microsoft Defender External Attack Surface Management

Microsoft Defender External Attack Surface Management (**Defender EASM**) builds upon Microsoft Defender's basic features. Organizations can have unique external cyber-attack surfaces. Defender EASM discovers unknown resources so that organizations can have full visibility into their security posture.

Defender EASM works dynamically and in real time, so administrators can be alerted to new external-facing resources as they appear.

> Note
>
> Shadow IT is a huge problem in many organizations. Shadow IT refers to when employees, contractors, and other people internal to an organization use their own applications and devices with a company's network. The problem with shadow IT is that the new technologies that insiders introduce to a company's network aren't managed by their cybersecurity or IT team. So, shadow IT can introduce new attack vectors, vulnerabilities, and malware that an organization is often completely unaware of. Shadow IT is one of the many kinds of external risks that Defender EASM can detect and mitigate.

Azure DDoS Protection

Azure DDoS Protection is as it sounds. In a DDoS attack, cyber attackers overwhelm your applications and networked services with an overwhelming volume of malicious data in order to shut them down. It's a major attack on the availability of data in the CIA triad of cybersecurity. The *distributed* part means that the attacker leverages a number of distributed machines in order to execute their attacks. The most common method for DDoS attacks is to use a botnet of zombie malware-infected computing devices, which can include any combination of PCs, servers, phones, tablets, IoT devices, and routers. The attacker controls their botnet through their **command and control** (**C2**) server. So, botnets offer a lot of computing power that can be used to execute DDoS attacks.

Azure DDoS Protection uses adaptive **threat intelligence** (**TI**) with **artificial intelligence** (**AI**) and DDoS mitigation capacity. The latter feature uses Microsoft's data processing and networking infrastructure to absorb an attacker's large volumes of malicious data before it can harm your organization's own Azure services and applications.

Azure Bastion

Azure Bastion makes it possible for organizations to deploy remote access to their VMs in a secure way. That's a common need because these days, businesses support more remote workers than ever before. If an employee connects to their employer's Azure-hosted VMs from their home, it should be routed through Azure Bastion.

A direct connection for RDP and SSH (common remote networking internet protocols) sessions in the Azure portal can be launched at any time. Your organization's VMs don't need any additional software to use Azure Bastion. Azure Bastion integrates into your firewalls and other security controls. And most importantly, Azure Bastion prevents the IP addresses assigned to your VMs from being exposed to the public. That makes it much harder for external cyber attackers to access and harm your organization's VMs.

Azure Firewall

Azure Firewall is designed to securely manage and limit access to your organization's Azure **Virtual Network** (**VNet**). Traffic can be dynamically denied from malicious IP addresses and domains. It uses **Transport Layer Security** (**TLS**) to prevent malware transmission through encrypted sessions. Network and application firewall rules can be managed throughout all of your organization's virtual networks.

Azure Firewall also features built-in **Intrusion Detection and Prevention System** (**IDPS**) capabilities to generate security incident alerts and output logs and block many kinds of attacks in real time. So, it has not only the basic firewall functionality of blocking or filtering traffic according to a series of security rules, but it also uses **Machine Learning** (**ML**) to improve its functionality over time by learning from your organization's network traffic patterns.

Azure Web Application Firewall

Azure Web Application Firewall (**WAF**) is a specialized firewall for web applications. **Open Web Application Security Project** (**OWASP**) is an organization that maintains web security standards including their Top 10 security risks. Azure WAF is specifically designed to mitigate those risks.

There are a variety of technologies that are particular to web applications and web servers, so Azure WAF is designed to work natively in that use case.

Azure Firewall Manager

Azure Firewall Manager is listed as its own application. It simply works as a configuration and management interface for Azure Firewall. It presents administrators with a unified control plane dashboard so that they can see everything that Azure Firewall is doing at any given time, and also see their security alerts. Multiple Azure Firewall instances can be managed through one Azure Firewall Manager control plane. It can also integrate with third-party **Security-as-a-Service** (**SECaaS**) applications.

Microsoft Sentinel

Microsoft Sentinel is a **Security Information and Event Management** (**SIEM**) system that's directly integrated into Azure. Your organization may use it if they have a **Security Operations Center** (**SOC**).

What does a SOC do?

A SOC is a defensive cybersecurity team and department that watches for security events and incidents in real time and responds to them.

A SIEM system analyzes the various network and server logs that are fed into the SIEM system and shows the SOC analysts security alerts when it looks like a security incident could be occurring, which are generally cyber attacks.

The SOC plays an integral role in **incident response** (**IR**). Their job is to mitigate or contain an attack or breach as soon as possible while it's happening to mitigate as much harm as possible.

In layperson's terms, with Microsoft Sentinel, SOC analysts can view a control plane and dashboard that shows through network and application activity that something bad is happening. When something really bad appears to be happening, the SOC analysts get a notification that says something to the effect of "*Danger, danger!*" Then, they can use Microsoft Sentinel to investigate the incident to help stop the bad thing from happening.

Key Vault

Key Vault stores the various cryptographic keys and secrets that your organization uses in Azure. Keys and secrets are used to acquire privileged access to sensitive data and applications. It would be super dangerous for any of those keys to fall into the wrong hands. So, they're kept in a metaphorical vault!

Key Vault ensures that applications have no direct access to keys. Keys can both be created by and imported to Key Vault.

As much of your organization's data in transit and in storage as possible should be encrypted. That's a part of *Cybersecurity 101*. Scrambling plaintext data into ciphertext gibberish protects both the confidentiality and integrity components of the CIA triad.

Azure has all the tools your organization needs to make sure that all data in storage and in transit is strongly encrypted. Key Vault should be used so that unauthorized parties and cyber attackers cannot "unlock" any of it.

Microsoft Azure Attestation

Microsoft Azure Attestation exists because the Azure clouds organizations deploy don't only implement entities within the Azure ecosystem. Many organizations also implement third-party services and applications into their Azure networks. Microsoft Azure Attestation verifies the identities and security postures of third-party platforms before they're interacted with.

Your organization has a lot of different security policies, baselines, and standards. Microsoft Azure Attestation will verify if they can be established in third-party platforms. If so, Microsoft Azure Attestation can make sure that those security policies, baselines, and standards are enforced through them.

Active Directory is what Windows Server uses to manage the security of user accounts, user groups, and administrative accounts. **Azure Active Directory** extends those sorts of IAM features into Azure.

Controlling what user accounts are allowed to do is a major part of security operations, as is making sure those accounts have proper authentication and authorization. A control plane provides full visibility of how accounts are being used. Azure Active Directory also implements SSO and **multi-factor authentication (MFA)** systems. MFA is absolutely crucial! MFA often isn't a default, but it should be. Even the best passwords are vulnerable to data breaches and certain kinds of cryptoanalysis attacks. Augmenting passwords with additional authentication vectors such as biometrics and **one-time password (OTP)**/PIN applications greatly improves account security.

Azure Information Protection

Azure Information Protection (AIP) is another generic name for a service that explains exactly what it does. It conducts a lot of **Data Loss Prevention** (DLP) features by classifying data according to sensitivity labels and then making sure that data is only shared outside of your organization as it's permitted to do so.

AIP can protect documents, many other types of files, and email. As cybersecurity practitioners, we think about email attachments as a malware vector all the time. We're also aware of how often phishing emails with links to dangerous phishing websites are sent and received. But email is also a major vector for breaching confidential or sensitive data! AIP helps protect against sensitive data being breached by email.

Azure Dedicated HSM

Azure Dedicated HSM is a very specialized Azure cybersecurity application. **HSM** stands for **hardware security module**. An HSM is a physical computing device, often the size of a RAM or graphics card, that protects cryptographic keys, performs encryption and decryption for digital signatures, and assures strong authentication in additional ways.

Organizations can use HSM devices with their endpoint and client computers and in their on-premises networks. Azure Dedicated HSM is a backend to support those HSMs that run in Azure's cloud platform. Azure Dedicated HSM can be used to manage access to HSMs within your organization and also to configure them with your Azure services.

VPN Gateway

VPN Gateway enables organizations to integrate their own VPN infrastructure with their Azure services. A VPN is a way to implement **end-to-end** (**E2E**) encryption between two endpoints through a computer network, most often through the internet. Enterprises often have their own VPN servers so that they have full control over how that technology is used.

Many organizations mandate that VPNs be used in situations such as people working remotely from home and connecting to their employer's network, and also to protect use cases such as employee travel and **Bring-Your-Own-Device** (**BYOD**) policies. A good VPN can protect against **man-in-the-middle** (**MITM**) attacks whereby a cyber attacker intercepts a network session to breach confidentiality or tamper with the integrity of network-transmitted data.

App Configuration

App Configuration is for organizations that develop and deploy their own apps in Azure. App Configuration enables organizations to unify security configuration settings across all of their own Azure apps and app users. That's especially useful for both regulatory compliance and for complying with an organization's own security policies.

If there's a critical problem with an app's configuration, the problem can be fixed in real time without having to redeploy the app. Distributed components shared between multiple apps can also be troubleshooted and remediated if they have security vulnerabilities or misconfigurations.

So, that's all of the major security controls that Microsoft provides to Azure customers so that they can improve the security of their Azure networks, applications, and services.

Now, let's examine some top third-party Azure pentesting and vulnerability scanning tools!

Security tools

There are a lot of third-party-developed vulnerability assessment and pentesting tools for Azure. You'll probably be using at least a few of these as a pentester! In *Chapters 8* and *9*, I'll walk you through using some of these tools so that you can discover Azure cybersecurity vulnerabilities in a way that's permitted by Microsoft's Azure policies.

Prowler

If you've read *Chapters 5* and *6* about pentesting AWS, you're already familiar with **Prowler** (`https://github.com/prowler-cloud/prowler`). Prowler can also be used to pentest Azure! Prowler can be run from the CLI to check for common security misconfigurations and also conduct vulnerability scans based on CIS Benchmarks.

As with AWS, when you use Prowler with Azure, you can generate vulnerability scanning logs that give you data that you can use directly in your pentesting reports, complete with **Common Vulnerability Scoring System** (**CVSS**) vulnerability scoring in critical, high, medium, and low categories.

MicroBurst

MicroBurst is a collection of Microsoft Azure security assessment scripts, developed by NetSPI (`https://github.com/NetSPI/MicroBurst`).

It can discover Azure services in your network, audit weak configurations, and simulate cyber-attacker actions such as credential dumping.

MicroBurst works with Az, AzureAD, and MSOnline PowerShell modules. PowerShell is the CLI that Microsoft uses for administrating both Windows Server and Azure.

MicroBurst uses the Az module to acquire sensitive passwords, keys, certificates, and other sensitive authentication and authorization secrets from App Services, Storage accounts, Cosmos DB, Key Vault, Automation accounts, and AKS.

AzureAD

AzureAD is a depreciated PowerShell module, so well-patched Azure deployments that don't support legacy systems won't be using it. But if you're pentesting an Azure instance with legacy systems (which tend to be extra vulnerable in the first place!), the AzureAD module will help MicroBurst exploit vulnerabilities that pertain to how Active Directory is implemented in Azure. Insecure Active Directory configurations can lead to dangerous privilege escalation attacks! And they can also lead to attackers acquiring unauthorized access to privileged user accounts. Active Directory is central to how IAM works in Azure and Windows Server, so discovering Active Directory vulnerabilities and mitigating them is extremely important.

MSOnline

MSOnline is another depreciated PowerShell module, so it's only useful for Azure networks that support legacy systems with the first outdated version of Azure Active Directory. The MSOnline module enables MicroBurst to support similar IAM-related exploits as in the AzureAD module.

PowerZure

PowerZure (`https://github.com/hausec/PowerZure`) is another useful Azure pentesting tool that works with PowerShell, developed by hausec.

As with MicroBurst, PowerZure uses the `az` PowerShell module to scan for Active Directory vulnerabilities in Azure. PowerZure can exploit vulnerabilities for information collection, data extraction, and malicious credential access. Once PowerZure is installed, it can be executed with a few simple commands at the CLI.

ScoutSuite

ScoutSuite (`https://github.com/nccgroup/ScoutSuite`) is a CLI application that's developed by nccgroup. nccgroup used to develop Azucar, a *"security auditing tool for Azure environments."* As it no longer maintains Azucar, it recommends using ScoutSuite instead.

ScoutSuite is a multi-cloud security auditing tool. So, as with Prowler, it can also be used for AWS and GCP. ScoutSuite is also developing support for Alibaba Cloud and **Oracle Cloud Infrastructure (OCI)**, two cloud platforms that aren't covered in this book.

ScoutSuite scans APIs for common vulnerabilities, and using the tool can give pentesters a more accurate scope of the external cyber-attack surfaces of their cloud environments.

Azurite

Azurite (`https://github.com/FSecureLABS/Azurite`) is developed by FSecureLABS, and it features two components—*Azurite Explorer* and *Azurite Visualizer*. Azurite is a novel way to use PowerShell for pentesting Azure. Let's look at its components in a bit more detail:

- *Azurite Explorer* can import PowerShell modules to fingerprint an Azure instance and retrieve sensitive configuration data. That's bad news and something you need to watch out for and simulate as an Azure pentester. A real cyber attacker can do a lot of harm if they know how your organization's Azure services and accounts are configured!

- *Azurite Visualizer* takes the output from Azurite Explorer and generates a visualization of the data. Visualizations can help pentesters and security administrators better understand the relationships between different Azure vulnerabilities.

Azurite scans the following Azure components:

- VNets

- Subnets

- VNet gateways

- Azure SQL servers

- Azure SQL databases
- Azure websites
- Azure key vaults

Cloud Katana

Cloud Katana (`https://github.com/Azure/Cloud-Katana`) is an open source tool with development led by Microsoft. Cloud Katana (`https://cloud-katana.com/intro.html`) is used to assess and evaluate the security tools that customers use in their Azure networks. It's a serverless application that's built on top of Azure Functions.

SkyArk

SkyArk (`https://github.com/cyberark/SkyArk`) is developed by CyberArk and it's used to discover, assess, and secure the most privileged entities in Azure. It also works in AWS.

SkyArk's AzureStealth module is what's used to scan Azure environments.

SkyArk's purpose is simple—discover the most privileged cloud users!

If a cyber attacker can acquire malicious access to a highly privileged Azure account, they can do enormous damage. They can install all sorts of malware in an Azure environment, they can acquire very sensitive data, and they can even make an Azure network completely dysfunctional. Data breaches and ransomware deployment are two of the major cybersecurity problems that attackers can execute with ease if they have access to an administrative account!

Cloud shadow admins are a major security risk, and SkyArk will help pentesters and security administrators discover them and protect against vulnerabilities that give attackers privileged and administrative access.

MFASweep

MFASweep (`https://github.com/dafthack/MFASweep`) is a tool developed by dafthack to see whether MFA is enabled in a variety of Microsoft services, including those used in Azure.

Unlike cloud shadow admins, which are a very, very bad thing, MFA is a very, very good thing! Hopefully while using MFASweep, you'll find MFA enabled on all of your organization's Azure accounts!

Passwords are frequently exposed in data breaches, so the cybersecurity community believes in the consensus that securing accounts with MFA is necessary. A second factor to a password can be a biometric scan (such as with fingerprints and irises) or an OTP sent to a user's device that expires within minutes.

MFASweep scans the following services:

- Microsoft Graph API

- Azure Service Management API

- Microsoft 365 Exchange Web Services

- Microsoft 365 web portal (Windows, Linux, macOS, Android Phone, iPhone, Windows Phone)

- Microsoft 365 ActiveSync

- **Active Directory Federation Service (ADFS)**

Azure AD Connect

The **Azure AD Connect** password extraction (`https://github.com/dirkjanm/adconnectdump`) toolkit is developed by Foxit. It's exactly what it sounds like. It exploits vulnerabilities in how Active Directory is configured in Azure to extract passwords. If a real cyber attacker can do it, your organization's Azure network has some very dangerous Azure vulnerabilities!

The toolkit can extract highly privileged credentials from Azure Active Directory.

CloudBrute

CloudBrute (`https://github.com/0xsha/CloudBrute`) is a multi-cloud enumerator tool that's developed by 0xsha. If your organization has a public URL for your websites and web applications, it's very important that sensitive parts of your cloud networks aren't exposed to cyber attackers that way.

CloudBrute not only works with Azure and other Microsoft services, but also with AWS, GCP, DigitalOcean, Alibaba, Vultr, and Linode.

CloudBrute will help you find if there are sensitive cloud entities that your organization is exposing through the internet. Exposed services are a major cloud network attack vector! Ideally, no services should be exposed in a way that makes them susceptible to cyber attacks.

BlobHunter

BlobHunter (`https://github.com/cyberark/blobhunter`) is another tool from CyberArk. While CloudBrute looks for exposed cloud services in general, BlobHunter looks for Azure Blob Storage containers that are publicly accessible on the internet.

It can find poorly configured containers that can store lots of sensitive data. Find misconfigurations before an attacker gets to them!

As you can see, there's a wide range of applications in Azure, and also third-party tools for pentesting Azure.

Summary

Microsoft Azure offers a wide variety of SaaS, PaaS, and IaaS applications and services. Your organization will choose which Azure components you use according to your specific business needs.

Microsoft also provides a variety of security controls so that Azure instances can have effective cybersecurity. That includes protecting IAM through Active Directory, preventing exposed services, and protecting highly sensitive cryptographic keys and other kinds of authentication data and components.

Several third parties develop open source Azure pentesting and vulnerability scanning tools that you'll use as a pentester. Using those tools is an effective way of finding vulnerabilities in Azure environments while avoiding activities that violate Microsoft's pentesting policies.

In the next chapter, we'll deploy our own Azure network and run some pentests in it.

Further reading

To learn more on the topics covered in this chapter, you can visit the following links:

- *A listing of Microsoft Azure services*: `https://azure.microsoft.com/en-ca/products/`

- *Microsoft Azure's definition of PaaS*: `https://azure.microsoft.com/en-ca/resources/cloud-computing-dictionary/what-is-paas`

- *Microsoft Azure's definition of IaaS*: `https://azure.microsoft.com/en-ca/resources/cloud-computing-dictionary/what-is-azure/azure-iaas/`

- *Kyuu-Ji's collection of Azure pentesting tools on GitHub*: `https://github.com/Kyuu-Ji/Awesome-Azure-Pentest`

Pentesting Azure Features through Serverless Applications and Tools

In the last chapter, we looked at the various SaaS, PaaS, and IaaS services Azure has to offer.

Now, it's time to actually practice some vulnerability scanning and pentesting in your very own Azure deployment! This will be fun and educational. If you have gone through *Chapter 5, Pentesting AWS Features through Serverless Applications and Tools*, we're going to be doing the same kind of work in this chapter, but in Azure.

This chapter features a step-by-step guide to using Azure's own first-party security tools to check security configurations and conduct vulnerability assessments. The featured tools are Microsoft Defender for Cloud and Azure Firewall Manager. After that, we will learn how to configure the most popular third-party Azure pentesting tools. The featured tools are Prowler, MFASweep, and ScoutSuite. Lastly, we'll have a look at the pentesting tutorials to find credentials, enumerate Azure services, conduct vulnerability scans, and discover exposed services with Prowler, MFASweep, and ScoutSuite.

The following topics will be covered in this chapter:

- Setting up an Azure instance
- Setting up an Azure account
- Using Azure Cloud Shell and PowerShell
- Azure native security tools
- Azure pentesting tools
- Exploiting Azure applications

So, let's get into some practical exercises!

Technical requirements

We will be working with Microsoft's infrastructure. Massive Azure data centers will be doing the bulk of the computer processing work for the exercises in this chapter. So, fortunately, you don't need to have a top-of-the-line workstation. You will need the following:

- A web browser

- A desktop or laptop PC

- An Android or iPhone smartphone

- A good, reliable internet connection

Check out the following video to view the Code in Action: `https://bit.ly/3rUulqT`

Setting up an Azure instance

Anyone can set up their own Microsoft Azure account. Many Azure services are free of charge. I strongly recommend deploying your own Azure instance to practice vulnerability scanning and pentesting in Azure before you do paid work for a client so that you can practice your skills. And chances are that your Azure test deployment is simpler than the Azure network the organization you work for operates!

Thanks to the magic of the cloud and the fact that the computer processing, data storage, and bandwidth are on Microsoft's infrastructure, you don't need to have a powerful workstation computer to try the exercises I will demonstrate in this chapter. A typical desktop or laptop PC with Windows, macOS, or Linux, good web functionality, and a modern web browser will do.

First, open your web browser and go to Microsoft's guide to free Azure services (`https://azure.microsoft.com/en-ca/free`). Here are most of the Azure services that are free as of the time of this writing in 2023:

- **Azure Active Directory** is always free, but you're limited to 50,000 stored objects with a **single sign-on** (**SSO**) authentication interface. Again, this shouldn't be a problem with your test deployment.

- **Azure Advisor** services are always free and unlimited. Advisor makes personalized recommendations and identifies best practices for using Azure.

- You get 12 months of **Anomaly Detector** services for free. Anomaly Detector uses **artificial intelligence** (**AI**) and **machine learning** (**ML**) to help you troubleshoot technical problems in Azure.

- **Azure App Configuration** is always free, but there's a limit of 1,000 requests per day with 10 MB of storage. It's very unlikely that your Azure test deployment will make more than 1,000 requests per day. App Configuration manages and stores the configurations of your Azure apps.

- **Azure App Service** is always free. App Service makes it possible to create apps for any platform or device using tools such as PHP and Node.js. You are limited to 10 apps with 1 GB of storage and 1 hour per day, though. This is unlikely to be an issue with your test deployment.

- **Azure DevOps** is always free but with a limit of five users. Azure DevOps facilitates building apps with CI/CD methodologies, using Git repositories. Basically, if your app needs to deploy several updates per day, Azure DevOps helps to make it happen.

- **Azure Files** is free for the first 12 months. It makes it possible to migrate your files across platforms without changing any code. But you're limited to 100 GB of **locally redundant storage** (**LRS**) transactions and 2 million file operations. That may be restrictive to some corporate clients, but it's unlikely to be a problem with your test deployment. (LRS is about synchronously replicating data to three disks.)

- **Azure Kubernetes Service** (**AKS**) is always free. That's very important because Kubernetes containerization is one of the most common use cases for cloud networks! You'll learn about pentesting Kubernetes containerizations in Azure in *Chapter 9*.

- **Azure Lighthouse** is always free. It allows you to manage different service providers interfacing with your Azure network under the Zero Trust network security model. Zero Trust is a more secure alternative to the old perimeter model of security. Instead of having a perimeter with your trusted computers inside, the internet and other untrusted computers outside, and authentication at the perimeter, Zero Trust creates authentication vectors at all possible points and distrusts all unauthenticated data transmissions by default, even if they're coming from inside your own network.

- **Azure Maps** is an equivalent to Google Maps in the Azure ecosystem. It has many APIs and features and integrates natively with all Azure applications. You can do things with custom embedded maps on your own mobile, desktop, and web applications alike. Using Azure Maps in the applications you develop is always free, but you're limited to 1,000 to 5,000 transactions for specific mapping and location insights features.

- **Azure Migrate** is always free. It helps you migrate your **virtual machines** (**VMs**) from your premises or other cloud platforms to Azure.

- **Azure Policy** helps you comply with data privacy and cybersecurity regulations. This is likely more of an issue for your employer than for your Azure test deployment. But you do get free access to configuration and change tracking features.

  You get 15 GB of outbound data transfer bandwidth free for the first 12 months, and 100 GB of inbound data transfer for free always.

- **Blobs** are a kind of unstructured data object. You get 5 GB of LRS storage in Blob Storage, with 20,000 read and 10,000 write operations for free for the first 12 months. But I don't anticipate you using Blob Storage for your test deployment anyway.

- As far as **Cloud Shell** is concerned, you get 5 GB of free storage in Azure Files for free for the first 12 months. It's the Azure equivalent of AWS CloudShell, which I demonstrated in *Chapters 5* and *6*. Having access to a CLI in your web browser is very important, and you almost certainly will be using Azure Cloud Shell in your Azure test deployment too!

- **Container Apps** is always free but with some limits. Container Apps makes it possible to deploy apps and microservices in serverless containers, and you're limited to 180,000 vCPU seconds, 360,000 GiB seconds, and 2 million requests. That's unless you're ready to pay extra.

- **Container Registry** stores and manages your container images throughout Azure's ecosystem. It's free for the first 12 months, but you're limited to one Standard tier registry with 100 GB storage and 10 webhooks.

- **Cost Management** is always free. So, you won't be paying extra to save money and optimize your Azure cloud services expenses with full visibility into your expenditures. And of course, if you always stay within the free services and their limits, then there won't be any expenditures in the first place! But you can always check with Cost Management anyway.

- **Database Migration Service** makes it easier to migrate databases from on-premises servers to the cloud. It's unlikely you'll be doing that with your test deployment, but the Free Standard Compute level is always free.

- **DevTest Labs** enables developers to test their work in dev/test environments. It's always free.

- **Event Grid** assures reliable event delivery at a massive scale, to facilitate service integration. It's always free, but you're limited to 100,000 operations per month. You should be fine!

- **Functions** makes it possible to process events with a serverless code architecture. Just in case you want to use it, 1 million requests are always free.

- **Key Vault** safely stores the encryption keys you use in your Azure services. Its services are free for the first 12 months, but you're limited to 10,000 transactions, RSA 2048-bit keys, or secret operations at the Standard tier.

- You get some amount of **Linux VMs** for free for the first 12 months. The limit is 750 hours of B1s burstable VMs.

- **Load Balancer** assures that the usage of your Azure deployment is balanced across servers according to demands at any given time. For the first 12 months, you get 750 hours, 15 GB of data processing, and up to five rules with Standard Load Balancer.

- **Managed Disks** is a service used for Azure Virtual Machines block storage. For the first 12 months, you get 2 drives of 64 GB SSD storage, plus 1 GB snapshot and 2 million I/O operations for free. Anything more is going to cost you!

- **Media Services** makes it possible for you to deploy streaming media to any kind of device, such as streaming video or audio. It's unlikely that you'll be doing that with your test deployment. But just in case, you get 5 hours each of Standard Passthrough, Live Transcription, and Standard Streaming endpoints free for the first 12 months.

- **Monitor** gives you full visibility and observability into your applications, infrastructure, and network. There are different limits per feature, but otherwise, it's always free.

- **Network Watcher** helps you monitor, diagnose, and otherwise understand your network performance in Azure. It's always free, but you're limited to 5 GB storage with 1,000 checks, 10 tests, and 10 connection metrics.

- **Notification Hubs** allows you to send push notifications to any mobile device (iOS and Android). You're limited to 1 million push notifications, but that much is free. This should only be a concern if you're using your Azure instance to deploy mobile apps, though.

- **Private Link** lets you privately access your Azure services from any of your own endpoints. It's always free.

- **Resource Manager** lets you see how your app resources are being used and enables you to manage it all. It's always free.

- **Security Center** makes it possible to prevent, detect, and respond to threats across all your Azure deployments. Policy assessments and recommendations are always free!

- It's highly likely that your web apps and other database-driven apps will need **SQL Database**. For the first 12 months, you get a 250 GB S0 instance with 10 database transaction units for free.

- **SQL Server 2019 Developer Edition** makes it possible to build, test, and demonstrate applications outside of your production environment. It's always free.

- You also get some amount of **Windows VMs** for free for the first 12 months. Again, the limit is 750 hours of B1s burstable VMs.

- You get 50 instances of **Virtual Network** for free, always. But that's for provisioning private networks and connecting them to a data center that's on your premises. That's not likely something you'll need for your test deployment.

- **VPN Gateway** makes it possible to deploy VPNs across data centers and cloud services. That encrypts your data in transit in a very effective way. You get 750 hours for free for the first 12 months. But that's probably a service that's much more useful for the organization that you're working for than for your Azure test deployment.

Let's deploy an Azure instance for you to use for testing purposes.

Setting up an Azure account

Everything you need to do to launch your first Azure instance to practice your pentesting skills can be done from your web browser. Here's how:

1. While you're on the Azure free services web page (`https://azure.microsoft.com/en-ca/free`), click on the green **Start free** button:

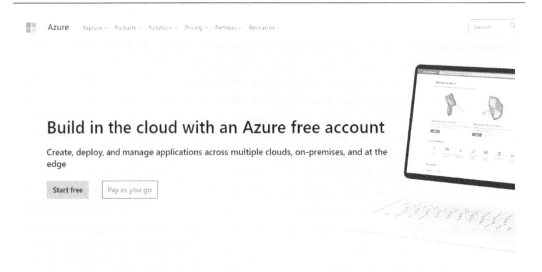

Figure 8.1 – Azure free account creation page

You'll be taken to a screen to sign in to a Microsoft account. If you use Windows 10 or Windows 11 at home, chances are you already have a Microsoft account. You can choose to use your existing Microsoft account, create a new Microsoft account (which you may do even if you already have another Microsoft account), or sign in with your GitHub credentials if you have them.

I decided to use a Microsoft account that I already have. I'm cautious when it comes to cybersecurity, so I already had **multi-factor authentication** (**MFA**) set up on my Android phone with Microsoft Authenticator. I used my password and a code sent to my phone through Microsoft Authenticator, and I was logged in. Microsoft Authenticator is free for both Android and iOS, and I strongly recommend using it for your Azure services. Here's where you can learn more about Microsoft Authenticator: `https://www.microsoft.com/en-ca/security/mobile-authenticator-app`.

Just to make sure there's no confusion, I use my phone for Microsoft Authenticator, but I use my Windows 11 laptop to work with Azure through its web interfaces. It's not very practical to manage your cloud services from your phone. Fortunately, a MacBook or a Linux PC works just as well as a Windows PC for this work.

2. Once I logged in, I was taken to a form where I entered my name, my region (in my case, Canada), and my phone number. I even got $200 USD of credit to use in my first 30 days! Thank you, Microsoft. My phone number was confirmed via an SMS text message. Then, I entered my home mailing address and agreed to the customer agreement. At the bottom of the form, click on **Next**.

3. Then, you'll see a screen where you enter your credit card information. Even if you're using free services, this step is mandatory. Your card will be charged if you incur any number of paid services or consume over your free services limits. I recommend using Azure's Cost Management app to watch that carefully!

At the bottom, click on the blue **Sign up** button.

4. Wait a few moments, and your account will be set up. Then, you'll see a screen that says **You're ready to start with Azure**. Click on the blue button that says **Go to the Azure portal**. It sounds very exciting! We're going on a cloud services journey together.

The QuickStart Center will show you a lot of different options for you to get started. You can take an online course, follow setup guides, or start a project. The project options under the **Projects and guides** tab are:

- **Create a web app**
- **Deploy a virtual machine**
- **Deploy and run a container-based app**
- **Set up a database**
- **Get started with data analytics, machine learning, and intelligence**
- **Store, back up, or archive data**
- **Build, deploy, and operate a serverless app**

You can see an overview of this here:

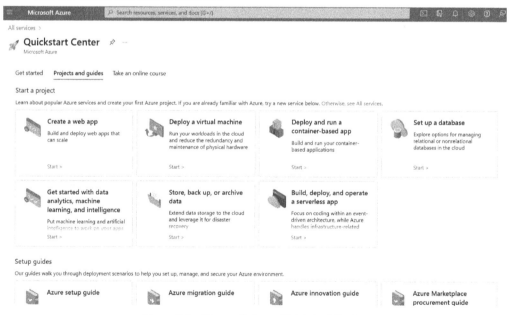

Figure 8.2 – Microsoft Azure Quickstart Center

For now, let's deploy a VM. (We'll deploy and run a container-based app in *Chapter 9*.)

5. Next, you'll be given the option to create a Windows VM or a Linux VM:

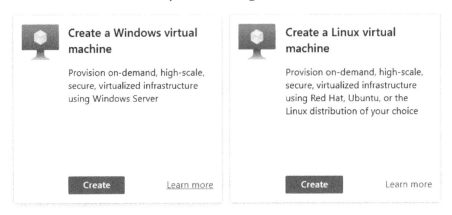

Figure 8.3 – Screen to deploy a VM from Quickstart Center

Because I used a Linux VM in the AWS chapter, we'll shake things up and choose a Windows VM here. But if you create a Linux VM, you can use the Linux Bash commands at the CLI that I used in *Chapter 5* for AWS.

6. The next screen says **Create a virtual machine** at the top. You'll have a form to fill out:

   •   Under **Project details**, leave the subscription as default or **Azure subscription 1**. Under resource group, leave it at **(New) Resource group**.

   •   Under **Instance details**, give VM an original name that you'll remember. I entered `PentestingWindowsVM`. Spaces and special characters aren't allowed!

   •   I chose **(US) East US** as my region. But you can choose any region that you'd like. It doesn't even need to be near your physical location. You can be in India and choose **(Europe) Norway East** if you want!

   •   Under **Availability options**, I chose **No infrastructure redundancy required**. That's your safest bet if you want to avoid service charges. However, the organization you work for has much greater needs than your test deployment and would probably choose a different option.

- Under **Security type**, I chose **Standard**. That's the safest bet for your own test deployment to avoid service charges, but a business, institution, or enterprise should probably choose a greater security level.

- I left the default Windows Server 2016 Datacenter as my image. x64 is the only VM architecture option for that image. Besides, ARM64 isn't a free service option.

- I chose the smallest possible size (1 vCPU, 3.5 GiB memory for $91.98 per month). I'm only going to be using my instance for a month, and this will fit into my $200 USD of free credit. Fingers crossed! You don't need a large size for your own test deployment.

7. On the next screen, create a username and password for your administrator account. Make sure your password is strong! I used a password manager to generate a complex password with lots of characters. I recommend using a password manager too, perhaps one built into your web browser. Then, you won't have to remember your complex passwords.

8. On the next screen, I disabled public inbound ports. Then, at the bottom left, I clicked on the blue **Review + create** button because I decided to leave the rest of the defaults for **Disks**, **Networking**, **Management**, and **Monitoring**. Your view may look similar or a little different. Look at the words on your screen carefully. I plan to cancel my Azure account in about a month. But if you need to keep your Azure test deployment longer, then I recommend clicking on **Next** instead of **Review + create** and consider your options carefully.

9. If the options on your screen look good, click on the blue **Create** button in the lower-left corner. Otherwise, click on the **Previous** button to change your configuration accordingly.

    It takes a few moments for your deployment to be ready. Be patient!

Your mileage may vary. But for me, my deployment took about a minute to take effect. Then, the screen said **Your deployment is complete**. So, I clicked on the blue **Go to resource** button.

In *Chapter 9*, we will pentest the VM we just deployed.

If you're really technical, you'll love the screen that appears after clicking **Go to resource**. You can browse all of the technicalities of your VM and other Azure services. But for now, let's get into Azure Cloud Shell.

Using Azure Cloud Shell and PowerShell

Wherever you are in the web interface for managing your Azure services (the URL in your address bar should say `portal.azure.com`), as long as you're logged in, there will be a blue menu bar at the top. To the right of the search bar, there's an icon that looks like a command prompt (something like this: >_):

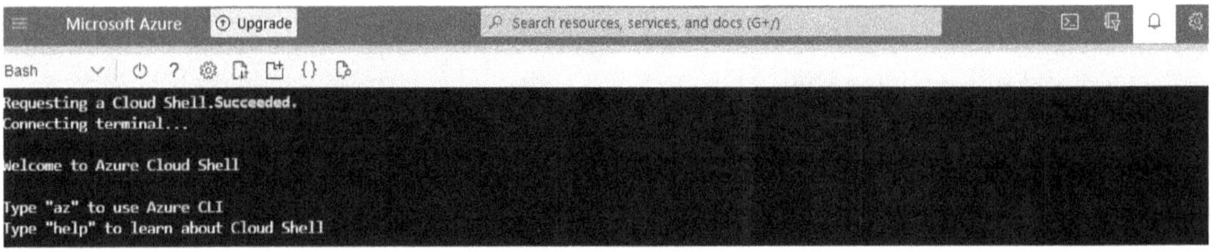

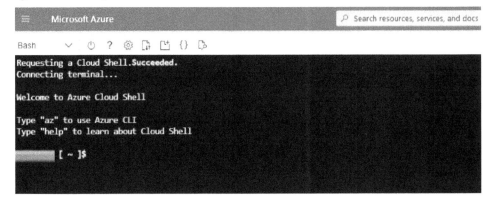

Figure 8.4 – Azure menu bar and Cloud Shell

Click on it to launch Azure Cloud Shell. In Azure Cloud Shell, you can switch back and forth between PowerShell and Bash at the drop-down menu in the top-left corner. You may have to choose **Create storage** the first time you launch Cloud Shell:

Figure 8.5 – Azure Cloud Shell screen

You'll find some Bash commands in *Chapter 5, Pentesting AWS Features through Serverless Applications and Tools*. We will be using Bash when installing and executing the tools in this chapter. But let's review some useful PowerShell commands that you can use at the Azure Cloud Shell CLI. They're handy to know, and you may need to use PowerShell commands when conducting some other activities in Azure Cloud Shell:

- Similar to Bash, you can use the following commands to change which directory you have open:

  - `cd`

  - `chdir`

- Copy an item with one of the following commands before the filename of the item you're copying:

  - `copy`

  - `cp`

- You can move an item with any of the following commands. You'll also need to enter the file path and filename that you're moving and the destination file path in the command:

  - `mi`

  - `move`

  - `mv`

- Remove an item with one of the following commands and the name of the file or files you'd like to remove. Remember, this will delete your files:

  - `del`

  - `erase`

  - `rd`

  - `ri`

  - `rm`

- This command will remove an entire directory. Be careful when you use it:

  - `rmdir`

- If you want to create a new item, use the following command. I'll usually only use it for text-based documents that can be modified in Notepad, though. Using this command will create an empty file with the filename you choose in your command:

  - `ni`

- Set a new value on an item with this command:

  - `si`

  For instance, you can enter `si path <string>` to a string or `si value <object>` to an object, such as `https://ss64.com/ps/set-item.html`.

- Start a background job (executable task) with this command:

  - `sajb`

- Suspend the job with this command:

  - `sujb`

- Resume the job with this command:

  - `rujb`

- Start a stopped service:

  - `sasv`

In Azure Cloud Shell, whether you run PowerShell or Bash, the following guide will be displayed the moment you launch Cloud Shell. The commands I've shown here so far work in the Azure CLI, and checking out the built-in help guide is always a good use of your time:

```
Type "az" to use Azure CLI
Type "help"" to learn about Cloud Shell
```

Up next, let us take a look at some of the native Azure security tools.

Azure native security tools

Here's what's built into Azure that can help you with security.

Microsoft Defender

Microsoft Defender for Cloud is an important application for checking your security posture in Azure. It will give you security recommendations based on your current configuration and let you know about some of the security vulnerabilities you have. This is information that you can use in your pentest report.

Let's open Microsoft Defender and see what we can learn about how secure our Azure deployment is:

1. To execute the application, first, make sure that you're logged in to your Azure account in your web browser. Visit `portal.azure.com`. You should then see this screen.

2. Next, at the blue menu bar at the top, enter `Defender` in the search bar. A link to Microsoft Defender for Cloud should populate. Click on it.

   You may need to add Microsoft Defender for Cloud as a paid service. If you haven't signed up for it already, there will be a handy **Upgrade** button on the main page of the application. Be careful to check the subscription fees before you commit!

3. Once you're in Microsoft Defender for Cloud, there will be a menu on the left-hand side with a number of different sections (*Figure 8.6*). They represent different tools for understanding your security posture in Azure:

   - **Recommendations** will show you some security improvement recommendations, classified as **High**, **Medium**, and **Low** in severity.

- **Attach path analysis** will show if Defender has identified an attack path to your Azure instance that a threat actor could use. Hopefully, this page will say **No attack paths were found**. Whether or not an attack path was found, you can include this information in your pentest report.

- **Security alerts** is similar to **Recommendations**. Alerts are classified as **High**, **Medium**, and **Low** in severity.

- **Cloud Security Explorer** will show you a bunch of query templates you can execute:

  - Internet-exposed VMs

  - Internet-exposed VMs with high-severity vulnerabilities

  - VMs vulnerable to a specific vulnerability

  - Internet-exposed SQL servers with managed identity

  - User accounts without MFA and with permissions to storage accounts

  - Azure Kubernetes pods running images with high-severity vulnerabilities

  - Key Vault keys and secrets without any expiration period

  - User accounts with permission to vulnerable VMs

  - Internet-exposed SQL servers tagged as production

  - External users with permission to SQL VMs that allow code execution on the host

  - VMs with Log4Shell vulnerability that has permissions to storage accounts

  - Kubernetes namespaces that contain vulnerable pods

  - Internet-exposed **Simple Storage Service** (**S3**) buckets with sensitive data that allow public access

  - Internet-exposed storage account containers with sensitive data that allow public access

- **Diagnose and solve problems** offers a number of automated troubleshooters to resolve issues in these areas:

  - Defender **cloud security posture management** (**CSPM**) plan

  - Defender for servers

  - Onboarding and settings

  - Pricing, billing, and usage

  - Secure score and recommendations

- Security alerts

- **Vulnerability assessment (VA)**

The latter two troubleshooters should be especially useful for you to make sure your security alerts and vulnerability assessments work properly!

- Under **Cloud Security**, **Security posture** will present an overview with a secure score and environment indicators (Management groups, Subscriptions, Unhealthy resources, and Recommendations). You can also generate a governance report from the top of the screen. This data may be useful to include in your pentest report.

- From the left menu in Microsoft Defender for Cloud, you can also view **Azure Firewall Manager**, which will show you monitoring reports and overviews.

- You can also manage **Azure Firewall Policies**, **distributed denial-of-service (DDoS) Protection Plans**, and **Web Application Firewall Policies**.

In the next section, I'll walk you through the installation processes we'll use when we exploit our own Azure test deployments.

Azure pentesting tools

In the previous chapter, I listed several different third-party applications that you can use when you pentest Azure.

Everything that I'll demonstrate here is permitted under Microsoft's policies, as long as you're either conducting these activities in your own Azure instance or you have permission from the owner of the Azure instance you're working with to conduct vulnerability scanning and pentesting there.

But I believe there's no such thing as being too cautious. So, I'm linking to Microsoft's policies again (`https://www.microsoft.com/en-us/msrc/pentest-rules-of-engagement`). Please read and understand those policies so that you can abide by them, whether or not the Azure instance you're working in is yours, because ultimately, you're still working in Microsoft's infrastructure either way!

Prowler

In the AWS section (*Chapter 5*), we found Prowler to be a very useful vulnerability scanning tool. Prowler is also good for vulnerability scanning in Azure, so I'll walk you through Prowler's installation process in Azure:

1. Launch Azure Cloud Shell by looking to the right of the search bar at the top. There's an icon that looks like a command prompt (something like this: >_).

    Click on it!

2. Instead of launching the PowerShell CLI in Azure Cloud Shell, we'll need to run Bash instead. At the top left of the Azure Cloud Shell display, there's a drop-down menu to switch back and forth between PowerShell and Bash. Make sure Bash is selected.

3. We're going to use `pip` to install Prowler, so it might be useful to make sure the version of `pip` that you have installed in Azure is up to date. Try this command first:

```
pip install --upgrade pip
```

4. Now, we're going to install Prowler with one simple command. First, make sure you're in your home directory or the directory you'd like to run and install Prowler in. Use the `cd` command if you need to do so. Then, use `pip` to install Prowler, like this:

```
pip install prowler
```

You'll see the various Prowler components downloaded at the command line, and then all of the necessary packages should be installed. Hopefully, you will be good to go! If you need more help, check out the official Prowler documentation (`https://docs.prowler.cloud/en/latest/`) and the official pip documentation (`https://pip.pypa.io/en/stable/`).

Next, let's install MFASweep (`https://github.com/dafthack/MFASweep`).

MFASweep

MFASweep is a PowerShell script that attempts to log in to various Microsoft services using a provided set of credentials and will attempt to identify if MFA is enabled. It's very important for all user accounts in Azure to have MFA enabled to protect those accounts from cyber attackers.

Let's install it!

1. In another web browser tab, make sure you're logged in to your GitHub account at `github.com`. If necessary, create a new GitHub account.

2. Next, run this command to link your GitHub account to your Azure account. You may need to add a **one-time password** (**OTP**) in order to do so. If that's the case, an OTP for you to enter into GitHub (in the other web browser tab) will be generated:

```
gh auth login
```

3. Now, enter this command to use Git to install MFASweep:

```
gh repo clone dafthack/MFASweep
```

```
PS /home/█████> gh repo clone dafthack/MFASweep
To get started with GitHub CLI, please run:    gh auth login
Alternatively, populate the GH_TOKEN environment variable with a GiHub API authentication token.
PS /home/█████> gh auth login
? What account do you want to log into? GitHub.com
? What is your preferred protocol for Git operations? HTTPS
? Authenticate Git with your GitHub credentials? Yes
? How would you like to authenticate GitHub CLI? Login with a web browser

! First copy your one-time code: █████
Press Enter to open github.com in your browser...
! Failed opening a web browser at https://github.com/login/device
  exec: "xdg-open, x-www-browser, www-browser, wslview": executable file not found in $PATH
  Please try entering the URL in your browser manually
√Authentication complete.
- gh config set -h github.com git_protocol https
√Configured git protocol
√Logged in as █████
PS /home/█████> gh repo clone dafthack/MFASweep
Cloning into 'MFASweep'...
remote: Enumerating objects:  45, done.
remote: Counting objects:  100%  (45/45), done.
remote: Compressing objects:  100%  (45/45), done.
remote: Total 45 (delta 22), reused 2 (delta 0), pack-reused 0
Receiving objects: 100% (45/45), 623.27 KiB | 27.10 MiB/s, done.
Resolving deltas: 100% (22/22), done.
PS /home/█████>
```

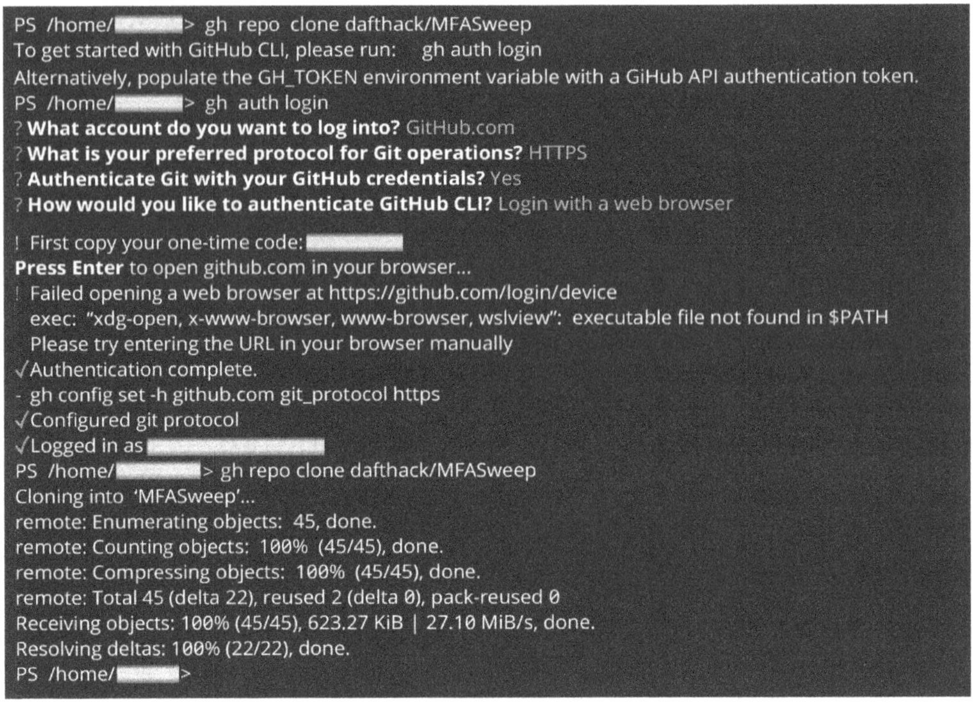

Figure 8.6 – MFASweep installation process in Azure

In the preceding screenshot, you can see the GitHub repository cloning process and installation of MFASweep at the command line.

ScoutSuite

Now, let's install ScoutSuite. ScoutSuite is useful for auditing the security posture of our Azure instance. In Bash, enter this command:

```
pip install scoutsuite
```

Various ScoutSuite components will be downloaded and installed. But if that doesn't work properly, I recommend checking out the ScoutSuite page on GitHub (https://github.com/nccgroup/ScoutSuite) for additional help:

```
kimberly [ ~ ]$ source venv/bin/activate
(venv) kimberly [ ~ ]$ pip install scoutsuite
Collecting scoutsuite
  Downloading ScoutSuite-5.13.0-py3-none-any.wh1 (3.5 MB)
                            ──────────── 3.5/3.5 MB 31.9 MB/s eta 0:00:00
Collecting google-cloud-container>=2.1.0
  Downloading google_cloud_container-2.26.0-py2.py3-none-any.wh1 (233 kB)
                            ──────────── 233.6/233.6 KB 18.9 MB/s eta 0:00:00
Collecting azure-mgmt-web==1.0.0
  Downloading azure_mgmt_web-1.0.0-py2.py3-none-any.wh1 (1.4 MB)
                            ──────────── 1.4/1.4 MB 27.8 MB/s eta 0:00:00
Collecting azure-mgmt-web==1.3.0
  Downloading google_cloud_kms-1.3.0-py2.py3-none-any.wh1 (65 kB)
                            ──────────── 65.3/65.3 KB 3.1 MB/s eta 0:00:00
Collecting google-cloud-monitoring==1.1.0
  Downloading google_cloud_monitoring-1.1.0-py2.py3-none-any.wh1 (235 kB)
                            ──────────── 235.3/235.3 KB 12.6 MB/s eta 0:00:00
Collecting msgraph-core==0.2.2
  Using cached msgraph_core-0.2.2-py3-none-any.wh1 (15 kB)
Collecting policyuniverse>=1.3.2.0
  Downloading policyuniverse-1.5.1.20230703-py2.py3-none-any.wh1 (470 kB)
                            ──────────── 470.2/470.2 KB 14.6 MB/s eta 0:00:00
Collecting botocore>=1.20.21
  Downloading botocore-1.31.3-py3-none-any.wh1 (11.0 MB)
                            ──────────── 11.0/11.0 MB 40.6 MB/s eta 0:00:00
Collecting azure-mgmt-resource==15.0.0
  Downloading azure_mgmt_resource-15.0.0-py2.py3-none-any.wh1 (1.6 MB)
                            ──────────── 1.6/1.6 MB 28.2 MB/s eta 0:00:00
Collecting azure-mgmt-redis==12.0.0
  Downloading azure_mgmt_redis-12.0.0-py2.py3-none-any.wh1 (58 kB)
                            ──────────── 58.8/58.8 KB 2.0 MB/s eta 0:00:00
```

Figure 8.7 – ScoutSuite installation process

Now, let's use the tools we installed!

Exploiting Azure applications

Now, let's run some security tests with the tools we've installed.

Prowler

First, let's run a default Prowler scan in Azure. The default scan is an effective general vulnerability assessment. Follow these steps:

1. Launch Azure Cloud Shell and make sure you're using Bash. At the top left of the Azure Cloud Shell display, there's a drop-down menu to switch back and forth between PowerShell and Bash. There you go!

2. I like to just make sure that Prowler is installed properly before I commence a scan. Check the version of Prowler you have with this command:

    ```
    prowler -v
    ```

3. Next, let's see which security checks you can run with Prowler in Azure with this command:

    ```
    prowler azure --list-checks
    ```

4. Now, let's run some of the checks that were listed as a response to the previous command. Make sure `--az-cli-auth` is at the end of your `prowler azure` command so that you can execute it with the necessary permissions.

    If you experience technical problems with IAM at the command line, you can check your IAM settings by visiting this page in another web browser tab (Make sure you're logged in to your Azure administrative account properly!):

    ```
    https://portal.azure.com/#view/Microsoft_AAD_IAM/
    RolesManagementMenuBlade/~/AllRoles/adminUnitObjectId//
    resourceScope/%2F
    ```

5. Run a few checks from the `--list-checks` output, like this:

    ```
    prowler azure --checks defender_ensure_defender_for_app_
    services_is_on defender_ensure_defender_for_storage_is_on
    storage_infrastructure_encryption_is_enabled --az-cli-auth
    ```

    In between `--checks` and `--az-cli-auth`, you can input the names of any checks that are displayed as a result of the `prowler azure --list-checks` command. Give them a try! Try as many checks as you want.

    The result of the checks scan will print on screen according to whether they passed or failed. You can also acquire logs from your scan in HTML, CSV, and JSON formats by going to the `/home/<your_name_here>/output/` directory.

6. Next, you can see which services you can scan with Prowler in Azure with this command:

    ```
    prowler azure --list-services
    ```

    The Azure services you can scan will output in a list at the command line.

7. Next, let's scan those services! Use a command like this:

    ```
    prowler azure --services defender iam storage --az-cli-auth
    ```

    Between `--services` and `--az-cli-auth`, you can enter the names of any services you'd like printed on screen from the `prowler azure -list-services` command:

As with the checks scan, you can also acquire logs from your scan in HTML, CSV, and JSON formats by going to the `/home/<your_name_here>/output/` directory.

Let's run an MFA check with MFASweep.

MFASweep

Making sure that MFA is enabled on all of the accounts linked to your (or your client's) Azure instance is very important! Passwords are a relatively weak method of authentication. Passwords are frequently cracked or breached. Implementing MFA is crucial to ensuring that your accounts are still secure, even when cyber threat actors threaten your passwords. I use Microsoft Authenticator on my phone as my second factor of authentication. In cybersecurity speak, my password is "something I know," while Microsoft Authenticator (via my phone) is "something I have." If I were to implement some sort of biometrics, such as a fingerprint scanner, that'd be "something I am."

Let's execute MFASweep to check to see if the user accounts in Azure have MFA enabled. This command will make MFASweep check both my main Azure account and **Active Directory Federation Services (ADFS)**:

```
Invoke-MFASweep -Username <insert_username_of_account_email_address_
here>@<insert_domain_name_here> -Password <insert_password_here>
-Recon -IncludeADFS
```

Notice how careful I am not to share my Azure credentials in that example! That's the kind of thinking you need to use to be effective at cybersecurity. We call that **OPSEC**, otherwise known as **operational security**.

A new command line will be populated that starts with >>. I found that it took several minutes to see the results of my scan, so you may need to be patient:

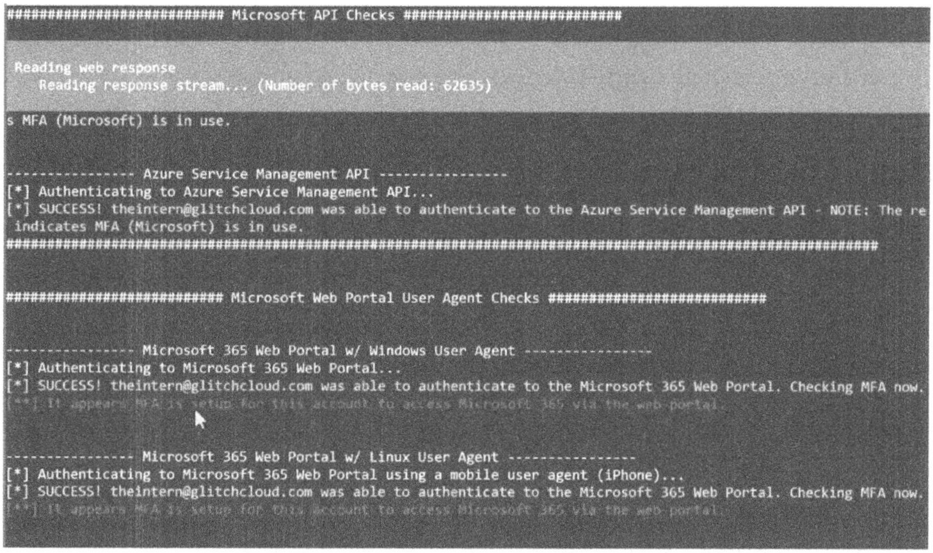

Figure 8.8 – MFASweep scan results

ScoutSuite

Now, it's time to conduct a basic ScoutSuite scan in Azure. Your authentication credentials should already be set from using the previous tools.

Run the scan with the following command:

```
scout azure --cli
```

A number of actions will output at the command line, like this:

```
(venv) ▓▓▓▓▓▓ [ ~ ]$ scout azure --cli
2023-07-17 18:31:05 cc-1990f3e2-59f6dbbd67-r6bxc scout[1793] INFO Launching Scout
2023-07-17 18:31:05 cc-1990f3e2-59f6dbbd67-r6bxc scout[1793] INFO Authenticating to cloud provider
2023-07-17 18:31:07 cc-1990f3e2-59f6dbbd67-r6bxc scout[1793] INFO No subscription set, inferring
2023-07-17 18:31:07 cc-1990f3e2-59f6dbbd67-r6bxc scout[1793] INFO Running against subscription 23a702ce-b083-499e-8d22-0b29f5e93f43
2023-07-17 18:31:08 cc-1990f3e2-59f6dbbd67-r6bxc scout[1793] INFO Gathering data from APIs
2023-07-17 18:31:08 cc-1990f3e2-59f6dbbd67-r6bxc scout[1793] INFO Fetching resources for the Azure Active Directory service
2023-07-17 18:31:08 cc-1990f3e2-59f6dbbd67-r6bxc scout[1793] INFO Fetching resources for the RBAC service
2023-07-17 18:31:08 cc-1990f3e2-59f6dbbd67-r6bxc scout[1793] INFO Fetching resources for the Security Center service
2023-07-17 18:31:08 cc-1990f3e2-59f6dbbd67-r6bxc scout[1793] INFO Fetching resources for the SQL Database service
2023-07-17 18:31:08 cc-1990f3e2-59f6dbbd67-r6bxc scout[1793] INFO Fetching resources for the Storage Accounts service
2023-07-17 18:31:08 cc-1990f3e2-59f6dbbd67-r6bxc scout[1793] INFO Fetching resources for the Key Vault service
2023-07-17 18:31:08 cc-1990f3e2-59f6dbbd67-r6bxc scout[1793] INFO Fetching resources for the Network service
2023-07-17 18:31:08 cc-1990f3e2-59f6dbbd67-r6bxc scout[1793] INFO Fetching resources for the Virtual Machines service
2023-07-17 18:31:08 cc-1990f3e2-59f6dbbd67-r6bxc scout[1793] INFO Fetching resources for the App Services service
2023-07-17 18:31:08 cc-1990f3e2-59f6dbbd67-r6bxc scout[1793] INFO Fetching resources for the MySQL Database service
2023-07-17 18:31:08 cc-1990f3e2-59f6dbbd67-r6bxc scout[1793] INFO Fetching resources for the PostgresSQL Database service
2023-07-17 18:31:08 cc-1990f3e2-59f6dbbd67-r6bxc scout[1793] INFO Fetching resources for the Logging Monitoring service
```

Figure 8.9 – ScoutSuite scanning at the command line

When that's all done, logs in JS, JSON, and HTML formats will be written here:

```
scoutsuite-report/scoutsuite-results/scoutsuite_results_azure-tenant-
<unique_identifier_here>.<file_extension_here>
```

Prowler, MFASweep, and ScoutSuite should produce command-line output and logs that you will find very useful when pentesting Azure. Make sure to include these results in your pentest report and interpret them in your own words.

Summary

There are a number of handy tools you can use to check your security posture in Azure, run vulnerability scans, and conduct simple pentests. All of the information you can acquire from these tools can be useful to include in your pentest report.

Microsoft Defender for Cloud is your main security posture hub. It provides security recommendations, security alerts, attack path analysis, troubleshooters, and security configuration information. Azure Firewall Manager is also built in. Azure Firewall helps to allow and deny activity in your Azure instance. You definitely want to deny activity that could help a cyber threat actor!

The Azure Cloud Shell CLI can be executed in your web browser while you're logged in to Azure's web application. We can install and run third-party pentesting tools from Azure Cloud Shell.

Prowler is just as useful for pentesting Azure as it is for pentesting AWS.

MFASweep is specifically for Azure. It's the most effective way to make sure MFA is set up to protect all accounts that have access to your Azure instance.

ScoutSuite is another tool with a lot of very useful scans and checks for Azure built right in.

In the next chapter, we'll deploy containerized applications in Azure, and pentest them too.

Further reading

To learn more about the topics covered in this chapter, you can visit the following links:

- *A list of free services in Azure*: https://azure.microsoft.com/en-ca/free
- *A cheat sheet with PowerShell commands*: https://www.comparitech.com/net-admin/powershell-cheat-sheet/
- *Prowler documentation*: https://docs.prowler.cloud
- *MFASweep*: https://github.com/dafthack/MFASweep
- *ScoutSuite*: https://github.com/nccgroup/ScoutSuite

9

Pentesting Containerized Applications in Azure

In the previous chapter, we went through the process of setting up a Microsoft Azure environment for us to practice pentesting and vulnerability scanning in. We then deployed a **virtual machine** (VM), learned some PowerShell commands, and conducted some scans with some applications using Bash, while in the Azure Cloud Shell CLI.

Sometimes, organizations simply run their applications in Azure from ordinary Windows and Linux VMs. However, very often, organizations need a highly scalable cloud configuration where application components can be launched and shut down quickly and responsively. That's especially true in DevOps applications, and that's where *containerization* comes in.

Because a lot of companies use containerization in their Azure networks, it's important for you to learn how to pentest them. That's what this chapter is all about.

In this chapter, I will explain what containerization is, why containerization is used, and how containerization works in general. We will also discuss how Docker and Kubernetes work in Azure, along with the pentesting techniques to test them.

The following topics will be covered in this chapter:

- How containerization works
- Docker and Kubernetes pentesting techniques in Azure

So, let's get into it!

Technical requirements

We will work with Microsoft's infrastructure. Massive Azure data centers will do the bulk of the computer processing work for the exercises in this chapter. So, fortunately, you don't need to have a top-of-the-line workstation. You will need the following:

- A web browser
- A desktop or laptop PC
- An Android or iPhone mobile
- A good, reliable internet connection

Check out the following video to view the Code in Action: `https://bit.ly/3QmGlKX`

How containerization works

VMs are simulated computers. Instead of directly running on PC or server machine hardware, a VM imitates all of the hardware components that are needed to run an operating system. So, one physical computer can run several simulated computers, and each simulated computer runs as if it were an application in a hypervisor in a host operating system, or in a hypervisor that runs directly on the hardware.

You can use an application on your own PC, such as Oracle VirtualBox or VMware Workstation Player, to work as a hypervisor for your VMs. All you need is a disk image file of an operating system you'd like to run in your VM and configure it in your hypervisor. The operating systems don't have to match your host operating system, and very often, they don't. I could run a Kali Linux VM on my Windows 11 PC. You could run a Windows 11 VM on your MacBook. And I could run a macOS VM on my Ubuntu Linux desktop.

However, it does take a few minutes to set up a VM, as we did in *Chapter 8*, and when you set up a VM, a disk image of the entire operating system needs to be used.

It's also possible to run a VM on a cloud platform, as we did in the previous chapter. Even though I used Microsoft's computers and not my own to run the VM, it still took a few minutes to set one up on Azure. Also, a conventional VM on a cloud platform is functionally similar to a VM on your own computer; the entire operating system is used.

Running a VM like that on a cloud platform works great when a company wants to keep the same VM running for months at a time or longer. Running a simple web server on a cloud platform is a great use case for that.

However, nowadays, DevOps and CI/CD application development methodologies make it possible for companies to deploy dynamic applications that need to scale rapidly. These applications can have backends that are radically different from one day to another, reponding to whatever the current production network needs are at any given moment.

Containers are a really precise way to deploy virtualization. A **container** contains only the operating system components that are needed to run a small part of a much larger application. Individual containers can have a lifespan of just a few days, or even just a few hours.

Docker and *Kubernetes* are the two commonly used containerization orchestration platforms companies use today. A containerization orchestration platform will automatically launch and kill containers without needing direct human interaction. These platforms manage how containers are deployed and also handle the load balancing within the virtualized hardware, allocating hardware resources such as CPU and memory only when they are needed.

Cloud platforms have made containerized applications possible for companies and other sorts of enterprises. Microsoft has massive hardware and networking capacity in its various Azure data centers around the world. So, if a containerized application needs a capacity of 1,000 machines one day, 200 the next, and 2,000 the following day, Azure makes it possible so the company doesn't have to deploy and decommission all of those machines on their own premises.

You will very likely be expected to pentest Docker- and Kubernetes-based applications in Azure.

As AWS has its own ways of managing Docker and Kubernetes, so does Azure. Therefore, let's learn about that.

How Docker works in Azure

You can launch a Docker instance in Azure from your local computer using Docker Desktop, or directly from the Azure CLI. Docker Desktop requires you to install the Docker Desktop application on your computer (`https://docs.docker.com/cloud/aci-integration/`), but it's also possible to launch a Docker instance directly from Azure Cloud Shell (a way to access the Azure CLI) in your web browser. Personally, I prefer the latter option. That's probably the most convenient way if you just want to launch Docker in the simplest way possible for testing purposes. If you were to launch Docker for a specialized business purpose and have more control over it, Docker Desktop may be the better option.

Let's work from Azure Cloud Shell and use one of the Docker images Azure makes available by default (it's also possible to acquire or create your own Docker images, but that's not necessary for the exercises in this book; a Docker image is like a disk image used in conventional VMs but specialized for a container):

1. Log in to the Azure account we set up in the previous chapter, from your web browser.

    The native way to deploy Docker in Azure is to use Azure Container Instances, which is a serverless service. There is technically a server, but Azure manages it, not you! That's what will be running in the background while you follow these instructions.

2. From the blue menu bar at the top of the web page, go to the first icon to the right of the search bar. It should look something like >_.

3. Click on it to launch Azure Cloud Shell. From there, we'll work in Bash instead of PowerShell because that's what the pentesting tools in this chapter use. Choose **Bash** from the top bar of the Azure Cloud Shell screen.

4. Then, make sure you have the necessary version of the Azure CLI. Input the following command:

```
az version
```

As long as you've got version 2.0.55 or later, you're good to go. I have version 2.50.0, so I don't need to upgrade. If you do need to upgrade, input the following:

```
az upgrade
```

5. Containers in Azure use a resource group in order to manage Azure's resources for your purposes. Let's set one up. Input this command:

```
az group create --name <resourceGroupNameOfYourChoiceHere>
--location eastus
```

`eastus` can be replaced by whichever Azure data center region name you'd like. For instance, you could choose `canadacentral`, `brazilsouth`, or `westus` if you want.

6. Then, we need to create a container! For the purposes of the exercises in this chapter, using one of Microsoft's default Docker container images is fine. Do so with this command:

```
az container create --resource-group
<resourceGroupNameOfYourChoiceHere> --name mycontainer --image
mcr.microsoft.com/azuredocs/aci-helloworld --dns-name-label
<dns-name-label-of-your-choice-here> --ports 80
```

Make sure that the name of your resource group is the same name you created in the previous command.

7. Now, you can verify your container's status to see whether all that worked! Enter this command:

```
az container show --resource-group
<resourceGroupNameOfYourChoiceHere> --name mycontainer --query
"{FQDN:ipAddress.fqdn,ProvisioningState:provisioningState}"
--out table
```

If all of that worked, something like this will be printed on the command line:

```
FQDN                                        ProvisioningState
--------------------------------            ------------------
aci-demo.eastus.azurecontainer.io           Succeeded
```

If not, start all over again from the `create resource group` command. Now, we have a Docker instance running that we can test our pentesting skills in! Congratulations!

There's just one last command that's very useful to pentest your new Docker instance. A lot of the vulnerability data we can mention in a pentest report comes from logging. You can use the following command to pull container instance logs:

```
az container logs --resource-group <resourceGroupNameOfYourChoiceHere>
--name mycontainer
```

You will get a message on the command line that says `listening on port 80` (the TCP/IP port for HTTP), and eventually, you will see HTTP `GET` requests displayed on the command line as they are made for your Docker instance from your computer or other computers on the internet.

You can remove your Docker container with this command:

```
docker rm <name of folder with container here>
```

Now, let's move on to Kubernetes.

How Kubernetes works in Azure

Azure has services that are specifically designed to deploy Kubernetes! Azure Kubernetes Service (`https://learn.microsoft.com/en-us/azure/aks/intro-kubernetes`) makes deploying Kubernetes containerization on Azure's platform easy.

Kubernetes is the most popular containerization orchestration platform today. However, here's a fact that may confuse some newcomers – Kubernetes expands on some of the technologies that were pioneered by Docker. It's also possible to run Docker containers in Kubernetes! So, Docker and Kubernetes are often intertwined in enterprise DevOps and CI/CD applications that run in the cloud.

In the previous section, we deployed a purely Docker-based containerization system, with Azure's serverless Azure Container Instances service running in the background to support it all. Now, we will deploy containerization in Azure Kubernetes Service.

Kubernetes has a very particular architecture (as discussed in *Chapter 6*).

> **Note**
> Kubernetes architecture is the same regardless of the cloud platform.

At the base of a Kubernetes deployment is the control plane. That's the parent of everything else that runs on top of it. It features an API server to manage connections to external applications, and a controller manager. We will give it commands through *kubectl*, the Kubernetes CLI.

The control plane's children are *Nodes*. They share compute, network, and storage resources. The children of Nodes are *Pods*, and the children of Pods are the *individual containers*. So, think of it this way – containers are the great-grandparents of containers.

Containers are the most dynamic component; they change most frequently. They're generated responsively from container images, according to whatever an application needs at the time. They contain only the configuration files, libraries, and dependencies that are required for the code they execute to run. That's because the Nodes handle the load balancing of hardware resources, and the control plane has ultimate control over everything and is also the gateway to systems outside of your Kubernetes containerization system.

If you want to sound like you're a real Kubernetes expert, call it *K8s*. That's the nickname Kubernetes developers and administrators have given it. However, I prefer to call it by its formal name.

Okay, let's deploy Kubernetes in our Azure network! We can use it for pentesting later in this chapter:

1. First, we need to launch Azure Cloud Shell again. From the blue menu bar at the top of the web page, go to the first icon to the right of the search bar. It should look something like >_.

2. Click on it to launch Azure Cloud Shell. From there, we'll work in Bash instead of PowerShell. Choose **Bash** from the top bar of the Azure Cloud Shell screen.

3. Then, make sure you have the right version of the Azure CLI. Use this command:

   ```
   az -version
   ```

   As long as you have version 2.0.55 or later, you're good to go. Otherwise, enter this command:

   ```
   az upgrade
   ```

   While working with Kubernetes at the Azure CLI, I learned that I needed to create a service principal with access to my container registry first so that everything else would work properly.

4. Copy this script, and paste it into a text editor, such as Notepad. Replace where it says $containerRegistry with a name of your choice (e.g., acrKim). Replace $servicePrincipal with a name of your choice (e.g., KIM_KUBERNETES):

   ```
   #!/bin/bash

   # This script requires Azure CLI version 2.25.0 or later. Check
   version with `az --version`.

   # Modify for your environment.
   # ACR_NAME: The name of your Azure Container Registry
   ACR_NAME=$containerRegistry

   # SERVICE_PRINCIPAL_NAME: Must be unique within your AD tenant
   SERVICE_PRINCIPAL_NAME=$servicePrincipal

   # Obtain the full registry ID
   ACR_REGISTRY_ID=$(az acr show --name $ACR_NAME --query "id"
   --output tsv)
   # echo $registryId
   ```

```
# Create the service principal with rights scoped to the
registry.
# Default permissions are for docker pull access. Modify the
'--role'
# argument value as desired:
# acrpull:   pull only
# acrpush:   push and pull
# owner:     push, pull, and assign roles
PASSWORD=$(az ad sp create-for-rbac --name $SERVICE_PRINCIPAL_
NAME --scopes $ACR_REGISTRY_ID --role acrpull --query "password"
--output tsv)
USER_NAME=$(az ad sp list --display-name $SERVICE_PRINCIPAL_
NAME --query "[].appId" --output tsv)

# Output the service principal's credentials; use these in your
services and
# applications to authenticate to the container registry.
echo "Service principal ID: $USER_NAME"
echo "Service principal password: $PASSWORD"
```

5. If yours won't be thrown away soon, change your password to something complex with a lot of random characters.

   Now, we can finally deploy our Kubernetes cluster! Replace kimAKSCluster with a cluster name of your choice. Replace acrKim with the ACR name you used in the ACR_REGISTRY_ ID=$(az acr show --name $acrKim --query "id" --output tsv) line of the previous script:

   ```
   az aks create \
       --resource-group myResourceGroup \
       --name kimAKSCluster \
       --node-count 2 \
       --generate-ssh-keys \
       --attach-acr acrKim
   ```

6. After a few minutes, a JSON output will display confirmation of the metrics of your Azure Kubernetes Service deployment.

   The Kubernetes CLI, otherwise known as *kubectl*, is already installed in Azure Cloud Shell.

7. Then, we need to connect to our Kubernetes cluster with kubectl. Enter the following command, but replace myResourceGroup with the resource group name you used previously, and replace kimAKSCluster with the cluster name you used previously:

   ```
   az aks get-credentials --resource-group myResourceGroup --name
   kimAKSCluster
   ```

8. Now, we can verify that everything worked and our Nodes are running. Input this command:

```
kubectl get nodes
```

Now, we have a vanilla Docker instance in Azure using Azure Container Instances, and a basic Kubernetes instance using Azure Kubernetes Service.

In the following section, we'll run some vulnerability scans and pentest scripts in those instances. This is the fun stuff!

Docker and Kubernetes pentesting techniques in Azure

Let's explore some tools to pentest containers in Azure.

kube-hunter

The first pentesting application we'll try is `kube-hunter` by Aqua Security on GitHub. The introduction in the kube-hunter `README` file at `https://github.com/aquasecurity/kube-hunter/blob/main/README.md` states the following:

"kube-hunter hunts for security weaknesses in Kubernetes clusters. The tool was developed to increase awareness and visibility for security issues in Kubernetes environments. You should NOT run kube-hunter on a Kubernetes cluster that you don't own!"

Absolutely! That's why we set up our own Kubernetes cluster in our own Azure services in this chapter. When you're actually doing paid work as a pentester, you will need signed legal permission from the company that owns the Azure network and Kubernetes instance.

There are lots of different kinds of scans you can do with kube-hunter. First, let's install it. Then, we'll run a quick scan.

Let's clone the `git` repository for kube-hunter with this command in Bash within Azure Cloud Shell:

```
git clone https://github.com/aquasecurity/kube-hunter.git
```

Now, we'll install its dependencies:

```
cd ./kube-hunter
pip install -r requirements.txt
```

kube-hunter is a Python application, so we can launch it with this command:

```
python3 kube_hunter
```

There's another installation method that I like to use. It uses the `pip` repositories. Try this:

```
pip install kube-hunter
```

And if you installed kube-hunter that way, you could launch it with this command:

```
kube-hunter
```

You can also run kube-hunter while specifying a certain log level. Try this command:

```
kube-hunter --active --log WARNING
```

That will output the WARNING level logs. Those are the events you should really pay attention to, which can be very useful to mention in your pentest report. Alternatively, you can output DEBUG logs with this command:

```
kube-hunter --active --log DEBUG
```

The default when you launch kube-hunter is to log INFO-level events. If you changed the logging to WARNING or DEBUG and you'd like to switch back to INFO, use this command:

```
kube-hunter --active --log INFO
```

As we're working in our own Kubernetes instance for educational purposes, feel free to play around with the different logging options.

When you run a quick scan with the kube-hunter command, this is what will output at the command line:

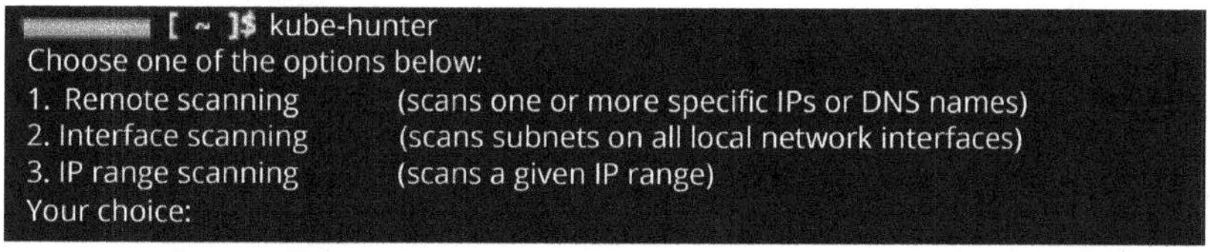

Figure 9.1 – Running kube-hunter in Azure

So, then, you enter 1, 2, or 3 for the type of scanning you'd like to execute. If you use options 1 or 3, you will need to enter IP addresses at the following prompt.

I often forget about the IP addresses that I use with my Azure instance when I'm playing around. We're in Bash, so the simplest way to check your IP addresses in Azure is with this command:

```
ifconfig
```

Something like this should output at the command line:

```
[ ~ ]$ ifconfig
eth0: flags=4163<UP, BROADCAST, RUNNING, MULTICAST>  mtu 1450
       inet             netmask 255.255.252.0  broadcast
       inet6                          prefixlen 64  scopeid 0x20<link>
       ether              txqueuelen 1000  (Ethernet)
       RX packets 105014  bytes 591232764 (563.8 MiB)
       RX errors 0  dropped 0  overruns 0  frame 0
       TX packets 93124  bytes 32685563 (31.1 MiB)
       TX errors 0  dropped 0  overruns 0  carrier 0  collisions 0

lo  : flags=73<UP, LOOPBACK, RUNNING>  mtu 65536
       inet 127.0.0.1  netmask 255.0.0.0
       inet6 ::1  prefixlen 128  scopeid 0x10<host>
       loop  txqueuelen 1000 (Local Loopback)
       RX packets 1179  bytes 116298 (1135.5 KiB)
       RX errors 0  dropped 0  overruns 0  frame 0
       TX packets 1179  bytes 116298 (113.5 KiB)
       TX errors 0  dropped 0  overruns 0  carrier 0  collisions 0

kimberlery [ ~ ]$
```

Figure 9.2 – The ifconfig command in Azure

Yes, I know the character X isn't used in IPv4 or IPv6 IP addresses. I replaced some of the characters in my IP addresses for the sake of operational security. You can never be too careful!

You can also install and run kube-hunter inside Docker containers! Install kube-hunter in Docker with this command:

```
docker run -it --rm --network host aquasec/kube-hunter
```

By default, kube-hunter outputs the logs from all of your scans through an entity called stdout. Therefore, you can find your logs through the Azure Monitor interface:

1. Go back to your Azure account interface at portal.azure.com.

2. At the blue menu bar at the top, enter Monitor in the search bar.

3. On the left-hand side, there's a list of sections under **Monitor**, such as **Overview** and **Activity log**. Click on **Activity log**.

The following screen will show your logs like this:

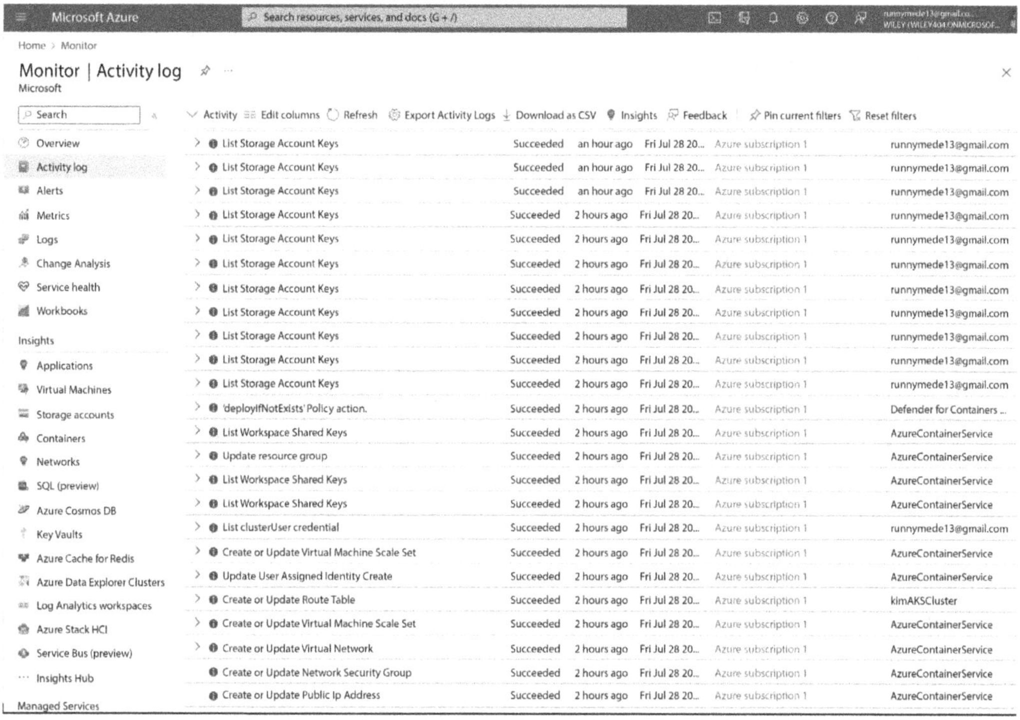

Figure 9.3 – Activity log in Azure

Your actions in kube-hunter will be recorded there. My actions produced a lot of entries named **List Storage Account Keys**. That's the sort of sensitive information kube-hunter was looking for!

Explore the kube-hunter documentation (`https://aquasecurity.github.io/kube-hunter/`) to find out other things you can do.

Now, let's try *kdigger*.

kdigger

kdigger is a multipurpose Kubernetes pentesting tool. It's capable of *digging* around in your Kubernetes instance to see which entities it can find. Of course, being able to fingerprint and enumerate a containerization deployment is a very dangerous ability for a cyber threat actor to have, as they'll then know how to proceed with their attacks.

The data you acquire from using kdigger can also be used to conduct better-informed pentests in Kubernetes.

kdigger can also be used for fuzzing. That means inputting invalid, unexpected, or random data into an application to see whether it's breakable. If the application is designed to validate inputs and handle exceptions in code, it won't be susceptible to fuzzing attacks. To learn how to use kdigger for fuzzing and other possibilities, check out their documentation: `https://github.com/quarkslab/kdigger`.

Let's install kdigger and do some digging.

Depending on your configuration, you may find one of these two installation methods works best:

- The first method is the default Git source technique:

```
git clone https://github.com/quarkslab/kdigger
cd kdigger
```

  Then, you need to move your binary into a working directory in your path:

```
sudo install kdigger </usr/local/bin or enter your path name
here>
```

  That method will require you to remember your `sudo` password.

- This simpler installation method uses `go`:

```
go install github.com/quarkslab/kdigger@main
```

Now, let's give kdigger a try!

Navigate to the directory where your Pods are and where kdigger is installed. When I get lost in Bash, I enter this command to list the contents of my current directory:

```
ls
```

And then I enter this command to change to the directory that I'm looking for:

```
cd go/bin
```

When you're in the directory that kdigger is installed in, you can do a general scan with a very simple command:

```
./kdigger dig all
```

For me, this is what was outputted at the command line. I have replaced some characters in the DNS names and IP addresses with X for operational security reasons:

```
; <<>> DiG 9.16.33 <<>>
;; global options: +cmd
;; Got answer:
;; ->>HEADER<<- opcode: QUERY, status: NOERROR, id: 33463
;; flags: qr rd ra; QUERY: 1, ANSWER: 13, AUTHORITY: 0, ADDITIONAL: 27
```

```
;; OPT PSEUDOSECTION:
; EDNS: version: 0, flags:; udp: 1224
;; QUESTION SECTION:
;.                              IN      NS

;; ANSWER SECTION:
.                     7048      IN      NS      XXX.net.
.                     7048      IN      NS      XXX.net.
.                     7048      IN      NS      XXX.net.
.                     7048      IN      NS      XXX.net.
.                     7048      IN      NS      XXX.net.
.                     7048      IN      NS      XXX.net.
.                     7048      IN      NS      XXX.net.
.                     7048      IN      NS      XXX.net.
.                     7048      IN      NS      XXX.net.
.                     7048      IN      NS      XXX.net.
.                     7048      IN      NS      XXX.net.
.                     7048      IN      NS      XXX.net.
.                     7048      IN      NS      XXX.net.

;; ADDITIONAL SECTION:
XXX.net.    1461    IN      A       198.XX.X.X
XXX.net.    1461    IN      AAAA    2001:503:XXXXX
XXX.net.    1461    IN      A       192.58.XX.XX
XXX.net.    1461    IN      AAAA    2001:503:XXXXX
XXX.net.    1461    IN      A       192.XXX.XX.XX
XXX.net.    1461    IN      AAAA    2001:XXXXX
XXX.net.    1461    IN      A       199.X.XX.XX
XXX.net.    1461    IN      AAAA    2001:XXX

;; Query time: 0 msec
;; SERVER: 168.63.129.16#53(168.XX.XXX.XX)
;; WHEN: Fri Jul 28 21:56:48 UTC 2023
;; MSG SIZE  rcvd: 824
```

If you want to scan all the buckets, try this:

```
dig all
```

You can mention any exposed Kubernetes entities that kdigger found in your pentest report.

Summary

Organizations often deploy containerization on their cloud platforms because it is a very responsive and dynamic way to use virtualization to implement rapidly scalable and ever-evolving applications, using DevOps or CI/CD methodologies.

A container contains just the parts of an operating system that are required to execute the code it processes. The load balancing and managing of hardware resources are done by the parent, grandparent, or great-grandparent of the containers within the containerization platform.

Now, we know how to deploy Docker and Kubernetes containerization instances in Azure and test them for security vulnerabilities. Docker and Kubernetes are two of the most used containerization platforms. Kubernetes basically extends Docker's features further and can even work with Docker images and containers.

In the following chapter, I'll introduce you to Google Cloud Platform and its various services.

Further reading

To learn more about the topics covered in this chapter, you can visit the following links:

- *Deploy a container instance in Azure using the Azure CLI*: `https://learn.microsoft.com/en-us/azure/container-instances/container-instances-quickstart`

- *What is Azure Kubernetes Service?*: `https://learn.microsoft.com/en-us/azure/aks/intro-kubernetes`

- *kube-hunter documentation*: `https://aquasecurity.github.io/kube-hunter/`

- *kdigger documentation*: `https://github.com/quarkslab/kdigger`

Part 4:
Pentesting GCP

GCP is **Google's Cloud Platform**! However, those in the know use the acronym. In this part, we will learn about GCP's various software-as-a-service, platform-as-a-service, and infrastructure-as-a-service applications. We will deploy our own GCP instance in which to test our pentesting skills. We will use Security Command Center to check the security posture of our GCP deployment. We will also try out some pentesting tools in GCP, step by step. Then, we'll deploy Docker and Kubernetes containers and test those as well.

This section has the following chapters:

- *Chapter 10, Security Features in GCP*
- *Chapter 11, Pentesting GCP Features through Serverless Applications and Tools*
- *Chapter 12, Pentesting Containerized Applications in GCP*

10
Security Features in GCP

Welcome to **Google Cloud Platform**, or **GCP** for short. GCP is the last of the top three most popular cloud platforms mentioned in this book. A lot of how GCP works is similar to AWS and Azure, but there are definitely some aspects to GCP that are unique and important for pentesters to understand before they pentest in the platform.

First, let's examine some of the most commonly used aspects of the GCP ecosystem. In this chapter, you'll learn about the most popular GCP services, applications, and features, and why they're used. Next, we'll look into GCP **Software-as-a-Service** (**SaaS**), **Infrastructure-as-a-Service** (**IaaS**), and **Platform-as-a-Service** (**PaaS**) features. We will conclude the chapter by discussing Google's own GCP security tools and third-party security tools.

Before we pentest GCP, it helps to understand how the company we're working for may use GCP, and what security features Google provides that can help pentesters understand the security posture of the GCP deployment they're working with.

This chapter covers the following main topics:

- Introduction to GCP
- Frequently used GCP SaaS applications
- GCP IaaS services
- GCP PaaS services
- GCP security controls and tools

Let's get into it!

Introduction to GCP

The first service that Google launched was its eponymous search engine. That was back in 1998, during a time in which ordinary people were starting to use the internet in large numbers. The very first server (`http://infolab.stanford.edu/pub/voy/museum/pictures/display/0-4-Google.htm`) that founders Larry Page and Sergey Brin used for Google featured 10 4 GB HDDs, and their hardware was held in a frame made out of LEGO bricks! Their first server ran on Stanford University's networking infrastructure and premises.

Google's first service that was specifically targeted to business customers was its AdWords advertising platform, now known as Google Ads (`https://ads.google.com/home/`). In the years since, it has launched a handful of services that are still very popular, such as Gmail, and it has killed a much greater number of services (`https://killedbygoogle.com/`).

One collection of services that should hopefully endure and evolve for many years to come is GCP.

GCP started as simply App Engine back in 2008 (`https://cloudplatform.googleblog.com/2008/04/introducing-google-app-engine-our-new.html`). That was about two years after Amazon launched AWS as we now know it. App Engine is a way for businesses and other entities to launch their own web applications within Google's platform. At the beginning of App Engine's history, Google limited its use to 10,000 customers. That gave Google the opportunity to fix bugs and gradually expand its infrastructure so that it could be more competitive against Amazon's AWS and Microsoft Azure.

By November 2011, Google made App Engine an officially supported product, available to anyone or any entity that's willing to pay for its services and abide by its policies. Google gradually launched more cloud services, and App Engine became one of many products under the GCP banner.

As of 2023, you can get more disk storage (5 GB of cloud storage) in GCP's Free Tier (`https://cloud.google.com/free`) than the entire capacity of a single HDD in Google's first server machine (4 GB). We sure have come a long way in 25 years of Google services!

Before you do any pentesting in GCP, it's important to review Google's *Google Cloud Platform Acceptable Use Policy* to make sure that we abide by it. This is taken from Google Cloud (`https://cloud.google.com/terms/aup?sjid=12831346254261876451-NA`):

Customer agrees not to, and not to allow third parties to use the Services:

- *to violate, or encourage the violation of, the legal rights of others;*

- *to engage in, promote or encourage illegal activity, including child sexual exploitation, child abuse, or terrorism or violence that can cause death, serious harm, or injury to individuals or groups of individuals;*

- *for any unlawful, invasive, infringing, defamatory or fraudulent purpose including Non-consensual Explicit Imagery (NCEI), violating intellectual property rights of others, phishing, or creating a pyramid scheme;*

- *to distribute viruses, worms, Trojan horses, corrupted files, hoaxes, or other items of a destructive or deceptive nature;*

- *to gain unauthorized access to, disrupt, or impair the use of the Services, or the equipment used to provide the Services, by customers, authorized resellers, or other authorized users;*

- *to disable, interfere with or circumvent any aspect of the Services, Software, or the equipment used to provide the Services;*

- *to generate, distribute, publish or facilitate unsolicited mass email, promotions, advertisements, or other solicitations ("spam"); or*

- *to use the Services, or any interfaces provided with the Services, to access any other Google product or service in a manner that violates the terms of service of such other Google product or service.*

In a nutshell, you can pentest in GCP without asking Google for permission. But what you're allowed to do is limited. You absolutely cannot conduct any types of pentests that could disrupt GCP for other GCP customers. That means no DDoS attack simulations, no malware distribution, no attempting access outside of the assets the company you work for owns, and—obviously—no breaking the law. Encouraging illegal activity and distributing malware can also harm people who don't use GCP. Vulnerability scanning and looking for exposures and unprotected sensitive data within the resources your company owns are permitted in GCP. Just make sure that your company gives you written legal permission to do that.

Now, let's explore what GCP has to offer.

Frequently used GCP SaaS applications

There are a large number of applications and services within the GCP ecosystem. Many of those services are classified as SaaS. That means that Google provides the infrastructure, the platform, and the application that runs in it. As a user or organization, you're only responsible for the code or data you enter into its applications.

As Google has more responsibility and control over its SaaS services, your ability to pentest those services while abiding by their policies is very limited to nonexistent. Google Support says the following (`https://support.google.com/cloud/answer/6262505?hl=en#zippy=%2Cdo-i-need-to-notify-google-that-i-plan-to-do-a-penetration-test-on-my-project`):

Do I need to notify Google that I plan to do a penetration test on my project?

If you plan to evaluate the security of your Cloud Platform infrastructure with penetration testing, you are not required to contact us. You will have to abide by the Cloud Platform Acceptable Use Policy and Terms of Service, and ensure that your tests only affect your projects (and not other customers' applications). If a vulnerability is found, please report it via the Vulnerability Reward Program.

That pertains to infrastructure, not applications. You will have more freedom to pentest and vulnerability scan Google's PaaS and IaaS services.

Nonetheless, it's still important for cloud pentesters to understand which SaaS services are available within the GCP ecosystem. Understanding SaaS in GCP will help give you context into how the organization you work for uses GCP as a whole. Organizations will usually use some PaaS or IaaS services in addition to SaaS, and GCP services are able to connect to each other. Plus, sometimes, an organization's IaaS and PaaS applications interface with GCP's SaaS applications. If an organization's data flows from an IaaS or PaaS application to a SaaS application, the security of that data may be able to be pentested from the IaaS or PaaS end.

Here are some of the most commonly used GCP SaaS services.

Google Workspace

Google Workspace (`https://workspace.google.com/`) is more or less Google's equivalent to Microsoft 365 for Business. Google Workspace's defining feature is that it integrates well-known Google productivity applications, such as Gmail, Google Calendar, Google Meet, Google Chat, Google Drive, Google Docs, Google Sheets, Google Slides, and Google Forms.

If that all sounds familiar to you, that's because the collection was previously known as G Suite. Google sure loves to change its branding every so often! It keeps us on our toes! Businesses, whether or not they subscribe to GCP, get a 14-day free trial if they're using Google Workspace for the first time. Google Workspace and its components have a much greater usage capacity and enterprise-specific features that aren't available in the consumer versions of Gmail, Google Docs, and so on.

Google App Engine

Google App Engine was mentioned at the beginning of this chapter, as it was Google's first cloud services offering for the enterprise market and the first ever GCP component.

App Engine (`https://cloud.google.com/appengine`) is a "serverless" way to deploy web applications on Google's infrastructure. There is technically a server, but App Engine users aren't supposed to manage or configure it.

Because App Engine users don't manage its platform or its infrastructure, it's by its very definition a SaaS service. App Engine users can build their applications in Node.js, Java, Ruby, C#, Go, Python, and PHP, which are all very commonly used application development technologies. If developers are already well experienced in one or more of those languages in other platforms, learning how to use App Engine should be pretty easy.

Cost Management

AWS and Azure both have applications that users of their platforms can use to manage their spending on cloud services in those platforms. Google also offers such an application for GCP—**Cost Management**.

Cost Management (`https://cloud.google.com/cost-management`) doesn't just say "You spent $364.24 last month." Rather, it offers a lot of charts and graphs so that you can make sense of your spending trends on every GCP component that you use.

When I walk you through deploying a GCP environment for pentesting educational purposes in *Chapter 11*, I strongly recommend checking Cost Management every so often to make sure you won't be incurring any surprise charges. Free services can become paid services if you're not careful!

Google Cloud app

The **Google Cloud app** (`https://cloud.google.com/app`) can be installed on your iPhone or Android phone to give you an easy on-the-go way of checking your GCP services and network.

A laptop or desktop PC with a physical keyboard is the best interface for doing serious, detailed development and administrative work in your GCP services. But the Google Cloud app can help you understand and discover production issues, manage your resources such as projects, billing, App Engine apps, and Compute Engine VMs, receive and respond to production-related alerts, and make general changes to your GCP deployment.

The Google Cloud app's features include alerts, error reporting, incident management, a customizable dashboard, billing, and a way to check your use of Compute Engine, Cloud Storage, Cloud SQL, and App Engine.

Google Marketing Platform

Google's earliest monetization schemes were based on advertising revenue (Google AdWords, now known as Google Ads), and data-mining services to advertisers. So, Google knows marketing as well as it knows tech. Therefore, **Google Marketing Platform** can be useful for businesses.

Google Marketing Platform (`https://marketingplatform.google.com/about/enterprise/`) includes Analytics 360 for metrics about how users use your applications, Optimize 360 for testing your applications with marketing needs in mind, Search Ads 360 to better understand the effectiveness of your marketing campaigns, Tag Manager 360 to understand the effectiveness of the tags you use in your marketing, and Campaign Manager 360 to understand the effectiveness of your marketing efforts per campaign.

Now, let's get into IaaS. Those are the kinds of cloud services that give companies the most control, while also delegating them the most responsibility in operating their services and keeping them secure.

GCP IaaS services

With GCP IaaS services, you get maximum control, but you also have maximum responsibility. Google provides its networking infrastructure and the hardware and tools for deploying VMs.

The main difference between using IaaS services and deploying an on-premises cloud network is that the organization you work for won't have physical access to the infrastructure. No one in the organization you work for will be allowed to touch the physical power button on any of the computers in the GCP data centers. You aren't even allowed to physically enter those data centers.

But you have a lot more freedom to conduct penetration testing activities in IaaS services. You should still make sure that you abide by the *Google Cloud Platform Acceptable Use Policy*. But don't fret, because all of the pentesting tutorials that I give in *Chapter 11* and *Chapter 12* are policy compliant!

Here are the GCP components that give your organization Google's infrastructure and let your organization do the rest. (These services can sometimes also be combined with other services for PaaS and SaaS offerings.)

Compute Engine

Compute Engine (`https://cloud.google.com/compute`) is the GCP component that lets your organization run its VMs on Google's infrastructure. Compute Engine is what it sounds like. It handles computer processing. Compute Engine also drives many GCP PaaS and SaaS services. But if you're just using Compute Engine and Cloud Storage as is, then what you have is an IaaS solution.

Compute Engine is very useful for a wide range of cloud network application use cases because Google has way more hardware in their GCP data centers than most companies could ever have. Compute Engine is especially used for lots of DevOps and **Continuous Integration/Continuous Deployment (CI/CD)** needs. But you can also just deploy simple VMs in Compute Engine.

Cloud Storage

While Compute Engine basically serves the CPU function, **Cloud Storage** (`https://cloud.google.com/storage`) serves the disk function. A lot of SaaS and PaaS solutions also use Cloud Storage, but Cloud Storage can also be used as is for IaaS setups.

Google says that with Cloud Storage, you can store any amount of data and retrieve it as often as you'd like. That's a bold statement, but Google has the infrastructure to store petabytes worth of your data if you'd like. Just not for free—it'll cost you! When we deploy a GCP network for educational purposes in the next chapter, I'll get 5 GB for free. That's enough for my temporary testing needs.

Shielded VMs

If your organization deals with extra-sensitive data, such as—for instance—if you were in healthcare, law, or the public sector, Shielded VMs may be what's best suited for your cloud security and regulatory compliance needs.

Shielded VMs (`https://cloud.google.com/shielded-vm`) are specially configured to implement security controls that protect against bootkits and rootkits. Rootkits are malware that grants attackers malicious root (administrative) access, whereas bootkits are persistent malware that executes upon the operating system boot process.

Shielded VMs run off of specialized hardware that uses special **Unified Extensible Firmware Interface** (**UEFI**) firmware (the firmware that's used to boot a physical machine before it boots the operating system or hypervisor), a virtual trusted platform module, and integrity monitoring.

It's possible to run VMs in GCP's standard Compute Engine configurations in a way that's very secure and regulatory compliant, but Shielded VMs go a step further with their specialized hardware and other features. Organizations will often spend a bit more on Shielded VMs if their security needs are extra high and they have the budget for it. You will get in trouble for trying to pentest the extra security controls in Shielded VMs, so don't even consider it!

Sole-tenant nodes

Sole-tenant nodes are another possibly very expensive IaaS option to deploy extra sensitive applications on Google's infrastructure.

Cloud platforms such as GCP can be used to deploy public clouds and private clouds. The majority of GCP users implement public cloud services, which simply means that our applications are running on hardware that's also used for other GCP customers. Every time I walk you through deploying a cloud network for educational purposes in this book, we're using public cloud services.

Private clouds can be hosted on a company's own premises, but GCP and other cloud platforms also offer machines that can be dedicated to one customer only. By customer, I mean a person or company that subscribes to cloud services to host their own applications, not to a customer's customers, if that makes any sense. I as a hypothetical GCP customer can pay for GCP services to host my shoe store e-commerce website. My customers who buy shoes from my GCP-hosted site aren't GCP customers in that sense; I'm the GCP customer. Whew!

Anyway, what GCP calls sole-tenant nodes (`https://cloud.google.com/compute/docs/nodes/sole-tenant-nodes`) are another way to deploy private cloud services in GCP's ecosystem. Some industries and companies are required to use private cloud services only, for the sake of regulatory compliance. So, they may pay Google the big bucks to make sure their machines aren't shared with other GCP customers.

So, those are GCP services that can be used for IaaS deployments. Now, it's time for PaaS.

GCP PaaS services

PaaS is the space between SaaS and IaaS. SaaS means you're basically just running your code, commands, documents, or media in Google's applications, on Google's platform, and on Google's infrastructure. IaaS means Google is letting you use its hardware, but you're responsible for providing your own platforms and applications. PaaS means Google is offering you a platform you can run your own applications in.

PaaS is not quite as much responsibility and work as deploying with IaaS, but it's still more work than SaaS. Here are some services in GCP that provide customers with Google's platforms to support a customer's own custom applications.

Cloud SDK

Cloud SDK (`https://cloud.google.com/sdk`) is a standard development kit for developers. It includes client libraries for Java, Python, Node.js, Ruby, Go, .NET, C++, PHP, and **Advanced Business Application Programming** (**ABAP**). It has special tools that can be integrated into the Google Cloud CLI.

In a nutshell, Cloud SDK is a collection of tools so that a developer can make their own custom applications that use various technologies in GCP's ecosystem.

Cloud SQL

Cloud SQL is for hosting **Structured Query Language** (**SQL**) databases on GCP. The vast majority of backend-driven applications, web-based or otherwise, require at least one database of some sort. And the vast majority of databases these days use some type of SQL.

Cloud SQL (`https://cloud.google.com/sql`) is a managed relational database service for MySQL, PostgreSQL, and SQL Server. It takes away a lot of the hassle of deploying SQL servers. Cloud SQL streamlines the SQL server deployment and management processes.

Cloud Run

Cloud Run (`https://cloud.google.com/run`) makes deploying containerized applications easier. Cloud Run can use Docker images if you want. (**Google Kubernetes Engine** (**GKE**) might be an even better option for Kubernetes deployments, though.)

Cloud Run supports Go, Python, Java, Node.js, .NET, Ruby, and many other popular application development programming languages.

GKE

So, that segues nicely into GKE.

Kubernetes is a containerization orchestration platform that builds upon Docker's core features. Kubernetes is open source and uses many open standards, but it was initially developed by a team at Google, including Joe Beda, Brendan Burns, and Craig McLuckie. So, although one can definitely deploy Kubernetes in AWS and Azure with native support, one might argue that GCP is Kubernetes' true home. GKE (`https://cloud.google.com/kubernetes-engine`) is the most convenient way to deploy Kubernetes in GCP.

Anthos

Anthos (`https://cloud.google.com/anthos`) is designed to help organizations deploy multi-cloud and hybrid-cloud networks.

As explained in the first two chapters of this book, hybrid clouds are when a company has services on a cloud platform and servers on its own premises, and the two aspects are integrated with each other. Multi-cloud is when organizations use more than one cloud provider, and their cloud services from multiple providers are integrated with each other.

So, an organization could have GCP services and some servers on their own premises, and that's a hybrid cloud. They could have services on AWS, Azure, and GCP, and that's multi-cloud. They could also have servers on their own premises and services in AWS, Azure, and GCP. That's both a hybrid cloud and multi-cloud. That's a hybrid multi-cloud!

Anthos makes managing all of those different kinds of cloud configurations easier.

Next, let's look into some important GCP security controls and applications.

GCP security controls and tools

Let's get into the applications and features Google makes available to GCP customers for the sake of improving their security. Your organization really ought to be using them! Then, we'll get into some useful third-party security tools.

Security controls

Google provides a lot of useful applications that can help us manage our security posture in GCP. Let's have a look at them.

Identity and Access Management

Identity and Access Management (IAM) (`https://cloud.google.com/iam`) is one of the crucial cloud security components, and GCP is no exception.

Users and groups of users are granted certain permissions and rights regarding what they're allowed to do with your organization's files, applications, and other sorts of cloud resources. Your organization should implement the **Principle of Least Privilege (PoLP)**, so users and groups only have as much access as they need to perform their jobs, and no more.

IAM works with Cloud Identity to sync user accounts between applications and projects. **Two-Factor Authentication (2FA)** can be set up directly from the Google Admin console. That's really useful because cloud security benchmarks and some data regulations require users to have more than just their password for authentication.

Requiring 2FA (or **multi-factor authentication, MFA**) isn't just some silly rule to annoy administrators and users. Passwords are considered to be a weak method of authentication, as they're often breached or cracked. Adding another factor of authentication can be as simple as a user installing Google Authenticator on their phone, and entering an OTP from that application when they're logging in to their company's GCP services.

IAM also features robust and detailed user account logging. Each and every user must be accountable for their actions, and IAM makes it possible for administrators to see who's done what. These logs can also be fed into other security tools, such as an **Intrusion Detection System (IDS)**.

Cloud IDS

Speaking of IDS, there's **Cloud IDS**, GCP's native IDS.

When Cloud IDS (`https://cloud.google.com/intrusion-detection-system`) is used properly, it can detect many kinds of malware attacks and cyber attacks that are executed from **Command and Control (C2)** servers.

Cloud IDS can monitor both east-west traffic and north-south traffic within your GCP deployment. East-west traffic is between different services and machines inside of your cloud network, whereas north-south traffic is between your cloud network and the public internet and other external networks. Cyber attacks can travel between east and west and north and south!

Cloud IDS can generate alerts for administrators so that they can mitigate cyber attacks as they're happening.

Data produced by Cloud IDS can also be used for investigating cyber incidents in the wake of their occurrence.

Cloud Firewall

Cloud Firewall can be configured to filter or restrict certain kinds of traffic or network activities within your cloud network.

Google says that Cloud Firewall (`https://cloud.google.com/firewall`) can provide *"granular control, including micro-segmentation without network re-architecting."* That's a lot of fancy computer networking language that I'll be happy to translate into plain English—Cloud Firewall lets administrators control really small activities and the smaller components of larger activities, including the ability to divide a network into even smaller administrative sections without the organization's network having to be completely changed in how it's set up.

There are so many ways that firewalls can regulate traffic, including Cloud Firewall. Traffic can be managed according to its TCP/IP ports, IP addresses, domain names, and user accounts. Cloud Firewall can use **Threat Intelligence** (**TI**) from third parties to determine IP addresses, domain names, and users to block.

Secret Manager

Secret Manager (`https://cloud.google.com/secret-manager`) offers GCP customers a secure way to manage their secrets. These aren't secrets such as "I used a calculator when I wasn't allowed to in math class when I was a kid." Rather, Secret Manager protects secrets such as passwords, cryptography certificates, API keys (they let applications communicate with other applications), and other sorts of sensitive authentication data.

So when you set up TLS certificates for a web server or a user creates a password for their account through IAM, they are stored in Secret Manager. Think of it as a massive bank vault with a thick bulletproof door, and all of your keys are inside. Protecting those keys is absolutely necessary so that cyber criminals and other malicious entities can't do bad things to your GCP applications and data.

Cloud DLP

Cloud DLP (short for **Data Loss Prevention**) (`https://cloud.google.com/dlp`) helps to make sure that your important data within GCP isn't lost! Yes—its name is descriptive of its function, but obviously, the technology it uses takes a bit more effort to describe.

Cloud DLP can use masking and tokenization to obfuscate your data. So, for instance, if a credit card number going through the **Point-of-Sale** (**POS**) system of your e-commerce application is G2F69 Cloud DLP may disguise it as B7K31 (No real credit card numbers use that format; I'm being extra safe!)

Cloud DLP can also show security administrators that bit of data went through here, then over there, then out through that other component even further over there. Except, of course, it wouldn't be that vague. Cloud DLP can also track data as it leaves your cloud and prevent sensitive data that's not supposed to leave your cloud from doing so.

Security Command Center

Security Command Center (`https://cloud.google.com/security-command-center`) is a unified interface that combines those GCP security controls and other GCP security controls as well.

Theoretically, you could have an IAM panel on one monitor, acting separately from a Cloud Firewall panel displaying on another monitor.

However, it helps security administrators immensely when all of these security applications are integrated with each other. It helps so much to defend against cyber attacks when administrators can see how one security component is working with another, or how a cyber attack is trying to do one type of bad thing, and then another.

Security Command Center makes it possible to identify security misconfigurations and many kinds of security vulnerabilities so that they can be addressed as quickly and effectively as possible.

In addition to helping administrators detect cyber threats, Security Command Center can also be set up to help a company make sure they're being compliant with data security regulations that apply to them.

Now, onto the third-party stuff that you can use when you're vulnerability scanning and pentesting in GCP.

Security tools

Many very talented pentesters have developed third-party pentesting and security testing tools that are designed to be used in GCP. All the tools mentioned here are open source and available through GitHub. In this section, you'll find the GCP pentesting tools that I've found to be the most useful.

GCPBucketBrute

GCPBucketBrute (`https://github.com/RhinoSecurityLabs/GCPBucketBrute`) is developed by Rhino Security Labs. You may have noticed so far in this book that Rhino Security Labs also develops some of the other pentesting tools that I've mentioned, such as Pacu and CloudScraper.

GCPBucketBrute is a script to enumerate Google Storage buckets, see which components and entities have access to them, and whether or not they can be privilege escalated. It's very dangerous if cybercriminals have access to your organization's buckets, especially if they can privilege escalate to do whatever they want. So, it's a good idea for pentesters to run this tool to find these vulnerabilities and attack paths before the bad guys find them.

According to the README file (`https://github.com/RhinoSecurityLabs/GCPBucketBrute/blob/master/README.md`), these are the steps that the script takes to find security problems:

1. *Given a keyword, this script enumerates Google Storage buckets based on a number of permutations generated from the keyword.*
2. *Then, any discovered bucket will be output.*
3. *Then, any permissions that you are granted (if any) to any discovered bucket will be output.*
4. *Then the script will check those privileges for privilege escalation (storage.buckets.setIamPolicy) and will output anything interesting (such as publicly listable, publicly writable, authenticated listable, privilege escalation, etc).*

Scout Suite

I've mentioned nccgroup's Scout Suite (`https://github.com/nccgroup/ScoutSuite`) before. It also works great with GCP, so I'll mention it again. As the README says:

"ScoutSuite is an open source multi-cloud security-auditing tool, which enables security posture assessment of cloud environments. Using the APIs exposed by cloud providers, Scout Suite gathers configuration data for manual inspection and highlights risk areas. Rather than going through dozens of pages on the web consoles, Scout Suite presents a clear view of the attack surface automatically."

As with many of the tools that I mentioned, you can run ScoutSuite directly from the CLI that you use on each cloud platform.

Hayat

Hayat (`https://github.com/DenizParlak/hayat`) was developed by Deniz Parlak. Hayat means "life" in Turkish, and the developer also named his script after his niece. How sweet!

Hayat is a script that can audit Cloud SQL instances, IAM, Cloud Storage, networking configurations, VMs, logging and monitoring systems, and Kubernetes clusters.

Parlak says that's it *for now*, which seems to imply that more features will be added in the future. I can't wait!

gcp_firewall_enum

Chris Moberly's **gcp_firewall_enum** (`https://gitlab.com/gitlab-com/gl-security/threatmanagement/redteam/redteam-public/gcp_firewall_enum`) parses your GCP data output to enumerate compute instances that are exposed to the internet through their network ports! Too much of that is definitely a bad thing.

Then, gcp_firewall_enum generates Nmap scripts based on the results. Nmap is one of the most commonly used network security testing tools; it's a network mapper that can be used to map a network. I love these descriptive names—they're very convenient.

Gcploit

Gcploit (`https://github.com/dxa4481/gcploit`) is a collection of pentesting tools that are designed to find security vulnerabilities in GCP.

Let's take a look at them!

- **BFS Search** is a threat modeling tool. It can help you figure out how threat actors could attack your GCP applications.
- **Mock Graph** can also be used for threat modeling.

- Then, the main Gcploit component executes two particular exploits, **actAs** and **dataproc**. The Dataproc API is used for provisioning data resources and actAs is an exploit that can be used for malicious access.

Gcploit is based on Dylan Ayrey and Allison D's presentation at Black Hat 2020. In Gcploit's README, they mention that there are other exploits they'd like to add, but they haven't yet.

gcp-iam-role-permissions

Brad Geesaman and Josh Larsen's **gcp-iam-role-permissions** (`https://github.com/darkbitio/gcp-iam-role-permissions`) is a script that looks for primitive and predefined GCP IAM roles and their permissions.

You need to be very careful when you set up user accounts in GCP, and leaving default settings is usually a very bad idea because attackers may try exploits based on those settings. User accounts and their access should be customized for some of the same reasons why default passwords should be changed, too.

Geesaman and Larsen's tool helps pentesters to detect those sorts of vulnerabilities before the bad guys do.

GCP Scanner

GCP Scanner (`https://github.com/google/gcp_scanner`) has a bunch of different contributors, and it's released under Google's official GitHub account. But the README starts with this disclaimer:

"This project is not an official Google project. It is not supported by Google and Google specifically disclaims all warranties as to its quality, merchantability, or fitness for a particular purpose."

That must have something to do with Google's lawyers. It's like Google's saying "Here's this cool pentesting tool for you folks, but don't blame us if it doesn't work properly." I think you should try it anyway, especially if you want to give it a run in the GCP deployment you can make for your own educational purposes.

GCP Scanner can help you to determine the level of access of certain credentials you have within your GCP network and applications. You can use GCP Scanner's findings in a pentest report, and also to security harden how your organization has configured IAM.

GCP Scanner works with these sorts of credentials:

- GCP VM instance metadata
- User credentials stored in Google Cloud (`gcloud`) profiles
- OAuth2 refresh token with cloud-platform scope granted
- GCP service account key in JSON format

GCP Scanner can test Compute Engine, App Engine, Cloud Storage, GKE, Bigtable, BigQuery, and Cloud Functions.

We will definitely run GCP Scanner at the CLI in *Chapter 11*; it should be fun!

Summary

GCP's roots stem from when Google released App Engine in 2008, a way for businesses and other entities to launch their own web applications within Google's platform. App Engine proved to be very popular. So, in the years since, Google has released a large number of additional cloud services that enterprises and organizations can use for their production networks and networking applications.

GCP is how Google competes with Amazon's AWS and Microsoft Azure. However, many organizations deploy multi-cloud networks that use all of those cloud platforms and more.

The two most important GCP components that are used in IaaS (but can also be used in SaaS and PaaS) are Compute Engine and Cloud Storage. Compute Engine is like the CPU, and Cloud Storage is your disks.

Google also provides a lot of very useful security controls that your organization really ought to use to harden their security against cyber attacks. They include Cloud Firewall, IAM, Secret Manager, Cloud IDS, and some other applications. Administrators can use the integrated interface in Security Command Center for a comprehensive live view of your organization's security posture, security events, and vulnerabilities.

There are a number of third-party tools that you can use to pentest GCP. They include Scout Suite, GCPBucketBrute, Hayat, GCP Scanner, Gcploit, and gcp_firewall_enum.

Now that we've explored pentesting GCP in general, in the next chapter, we will be pentesting Docker and Kubernetes clusters in GCP.

Further reading

To learn more on the topics covered in this chapter, you can visit the following links:

- *GCP Free Tier*: `https://cloud.google.com/free`

- *Google Cloud products*: `https://cloud.google.com/products`

- *Google Cloud Platform Terms of Service*: `https://cloud.google.com/terms/`

11

Pentesting GCP Features through Serverless Applications and Tools

Now that we've learned a bit about the various services that **Google Cloud Platform** (**GCP**) has to offer, it's time to start our own GCP deployment and learn about some GCP pentesting tools through hands-on practice.

We will install and execute some pentesting tools in the GCP virtual machine we set up in *Chapter 10*. They include Prowler, GCPBucketBrute, and GCP Scanner. We'll also look at the security tools that Google provides for us in Security Command Center.

This chapter will cover the following topics:

- GCP free tier
- Launching a GCP network
- Using GCP Cloud Shell
- GCP native security tools
- GCP pentesting tools
- Exploiting GCP applications

Let's get started!

Technical requirements

We will be working with Google's infrastructure. Massive GCP data centers will be doing the bulk of the computer processing work for the exercises in this chapter. So, fortunately, you don't need to have a top-of-the-line workstation. You will need the following:

- A web browser

- A desktop or laptop PC

- An Android phone or iPhone

- A good reliable internet connection

Check out the following video to view the Code in Action: `https://bit.ly/4093wMk`

GCP free tier

I strongly recommend setting up your own GCP network to test out the exercises in this chapter and *Chapter 12*.

There are several GCP products and services that you can enjoy in the free tier without incurring charges to your account. Do keep in mind though that you will need to give GCP your credit card number when you sign up. Your credit card will be charged if you go over the free tier limits, so you must check your usage and billing very carefully. When I signed up, I was given a 300 USD free credit for service fees in the first 90 days of my subscription. Depending on when you sign up, where in the world you sign up from, and the specifics of your situation, you may or may not receive a similar credit. Later in this chapter, I will show you where you can check your billing status so that you can make sure you don't incur service charges that you can't afford or otherwise wouldn't want to pay for.

As of this writing in 2023, here are the services that are available in GCP's free tier, as well as their limits (`https://cloud.google.com/free/docs/free-cloud-features`):

- **Compute Engine** is the service that powers virtual machines on GCP. The free tier includes one e2-micro instance per month. That means "*1 non-preemptible e2-micro VM instance per month in one of the following US regions: us-west1, us-central1, us-east1. 30 GB-months standard persistent disk. 1 GB network egress from North America to all region destinations (excluding China and Australia) per month*" (`https://cloud.google.com/free/docs/free-cloud-features?hl=en#compute`). Remember that the regions are where GCP's data centers are. *You* don't have to physically be in the United States. You and your laptop can be in Brazil, India, Ethiopia, or any country that can connect to GCP services. So long as the GCP data center you're using is in `us-west1, us-central1,` or `us-east1`, you're covered.

- **Cloud Storage** is the main service for storing your data. 5 GB per month is included in the free tier. What does 5 GB per month mean? "*5,000 Class A Operations per month, 50,000 Class B Operations per month, 100 GB network egress from North America to all region destinations* *(excluding China and Australia) per month."* (`https://cloud.google.com/free/docs/free-cloud-features#storage`). If you use your GCP network the way I demonstrate in this book, you should be fine.

- **BigQuery** is a serverless data analytics platform. We won't be using it in this book, but in the free tier, you get 1 TB of BigQuery queries per month.

- **App Engine** is a platform for deploying web applications and mobile apps. You get 28 instance hours per day in the free tier. We won't be using App Engine in this book, but if you deploy an App Engine app with lots of users, you will definitely be charged for it.

- **Cloud Run** is a service for deploying stateless containers. The free tier limit is 2 million requests per month, so you should be fine.

- **Cloud Build** can import builds from source code from Cloud Storage, Cloud Source Repositories, GitHub, or Bitbucket to create Docker containers or other sorts of software artifacts. You get 120 build minutes per day in the free tier. We won't be using this service in this book; we will just be using standard default Docker and Kubernetes container images. You'll be fine.

- With **Google Kubernetes Engine**, you get one Autopilot or Zonal cluster per month. We'll just deploy one cluster in *Chapter 12*.

  In the free tier, you get some Cloud Logging, Cloud Monitoring, and Cloud Trace allotments in the operations suite (formerly known as Stackdriver). Those are functions that you can use to analyze your cloud activity in GCP. The free allotments are a bit complicated, but it's unlikely that you will go over them by following the instructions in this book. Read more about the free allotments just to be safe (`https://cloud.google.com/stackdriver/pricing`).

- **Firestore** is a NoSQL document database service. You get 1 GB of storage in the free tier, but I won't be using it here. It's for application development.

- You get 2 million invocations per month in the free tier for **Cloud Functions**. It's a serverless environment to build and connect cloud services. We probably won't be using it anyway.

- **Workflows** facilitates service calls between GCP and external HTTP APIs. You get 5,000 free internal steps per month, which should be more than enough.

- The free tier includes free access for five users in **Cloud Source Repositories**, a service for hosting private Git repositories for application development. We won't be using that service anyway.

- We will be using **Secret Manager**, which stores passwords, certificates, API keys, and the like. The six secret versions we get per month in the free tier should be plenty.

Alright! Now that we know what we're getting, let's deploy a GCP network together. We'll need our own GCP deployment to test our pentesting skills in this book. Just like when we deployed instances in AWS and Azure, I'll walk you through the process step by step.

Launching a GCP network

As with AWS and Azure, all you need is a modern laptop or desktop PC running Windows, macOS, or a Linux distribution to launch and manage a GCP network. Google's computers and infrastructure do all of the heavy lifting as far as computing resources are concerned.

I would also recommend using Google Authenticator on your Android phone (`https://play.google.com/store/apps/details?id=com.google.android.apps.authenticator2&pli=1`) or iPhone (`https://apps.apple.com/us/app/google-authenticator/id388497605`) so that you can use **multi-factor authentication** (**MFA**) with your GCP services. I would not recommend using your phone to do most of your GCP work as a PC screen and a physical keyboard are ideal for those purposes. But you may install the Google Cloud app (`https://cloud.google.com/app`) on your phone if you want to check the status of your GCP services. It's especially great for checking your billing on the go to make sure you're not doing anything expensive!

A PC or a MacBook made in the past 10 years and a reliable internet connection are all you need on your end, wherever in the world you are, to deploy GCP and do pentesting on GCP.

All the work to start your own GCP deployment is done in your web browser. Let's get started:

1. The first step to setting up your own GCP network is to visit the Google Cloud free tier page (`https://cloud.google.com/free`) in your web browser and click the blue **Get started for free** button in the middle of your screen:

Solve real business challenges on Google Cloud

Figure 11.1 – Google Cloud signup page

2. On the next screen, make sure your Gmail or Google account is logged in. Set up an account if you don't already have one, or sign in to the one you already have. In the drop-down box, select your country and answer the **What best describes your organization or needs?** question. I

chose **Other**. Make sure you select that you've read the **Terms of Service** details, and click on the blue button that says **CONTINUE**:

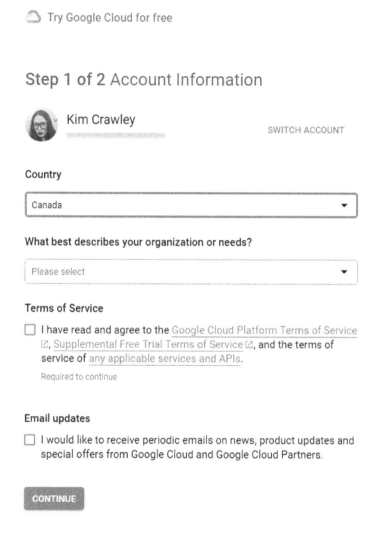

Figure 11.2 – Google Cloud signup screen

3. The next screen requires you to select your **Payments** profile. Google needs to have a way to charge you in case you incur GCP service charges, even if you manage to stay within the free tier's limits. I already have a **Payments** profile because I've paid for Google Play applications and services, I'm a YouTube Premium subscriber, and I've used Google Pay. If you don't have a **Payments** profile, you may need to enter your credit card number or link your Google Pay account (`https://payments.google.com/`).

4. Under **Account type**, I've entered **Individual**. Unless you're setting up GCP on behalf of a business or organization, I would recommend **Individual** for you.

5. Under **Name and address,** make sure your name and street address match what's on your credit card or Google Pay account.

6. Underneath, click on the blue **Start my free trial** button. Any time limits for bonus services and credits, such as my 90-day $300 services credit, start now!

If you scroll down a little bit, you'll see buttons to launch GCP projects. First, there are pre-built solution templates:

- **Deploy load balanced managed VMs**
- **Create a secure CI/CD pipeline**
- **Deploy a Java application using Compute Engine**

There are also buttons for launching a product without a template:

- **Create a VM**
- **Create a containerized app**
- **Run containerized apps**
- **Modernize and run apps**
- **Execute your builds**
- **Get started with containers**

This is what the project launch page looks like:

Figure 11.3 – Google Cloud project launch page

7. For now, let's click on **Create a VM** to deploy a simple VM on GCP with Compute Engine that we can use for the pentesting we'll do in this chapter.

8. The next screen says **Compute Engine API** and the overview says **Creates and runs virtual machines on Google Cloud Platform**. Click on the blue **Enable** button.

9. You'll be directed to the VM instances dashboard, which looks like this. Click on the blue **CREATE INSTANCE** button:

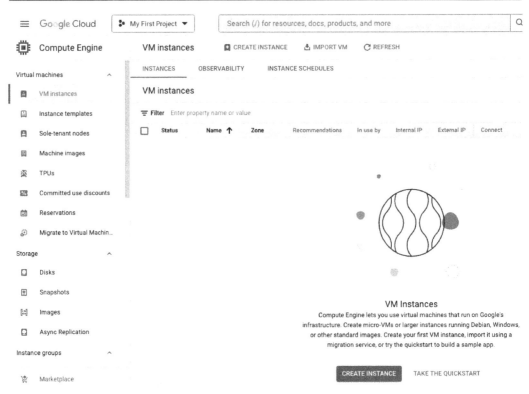

Figure 11.4 – GCP Compute Engine screen

10. On the next screen, we can name our instance and choose its region and zone, as well as its machine configuration. I will walk you through a configuration that will be the least likely to incur service charges:

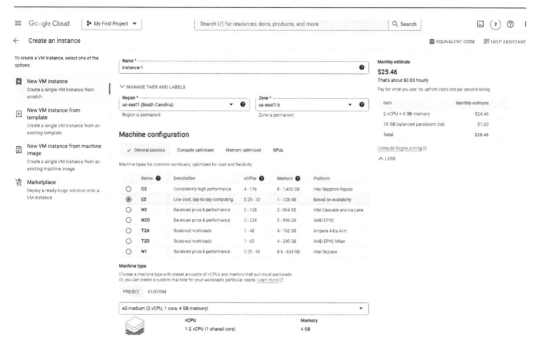

Figure 11.5 – Machine configuration for a VM instance

- In the **name** field, name your instance whatever you want. I named mine `crowgirl-1`.

- In the free tier, our usage of Compute Engine is limited to "*1 non-preemptible e2-micro VM instance per month in one of the following US regions: us-west1, us-central1, us-east1.*" So, I chose **us-east1** as my region. You can select **us-west1**, **us-central1**, or **us-east1** regardless of where in the world you are.

- Under **Machine configuration**, to save money, I chose **General purpose**, **E2 under Series**, the **e2-micro** machine type (the only machine type that's covered under the free tier), and the Standard VM provisioning model. At the bottom, click on the blue **Create** button.

In a few seconds to a minute, our very basic VM in Compute Engine will be ready! You'll see a screen that looks something like this:

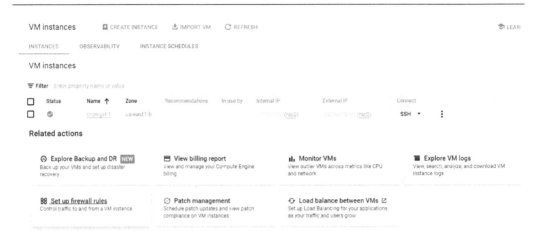

Figure 11.6 – List of VM instances in a project

The default Debian Linux image will be installed. We have a Linux VM that can use the Bash CLI!

I always prefer to use the CLI that's built into the cloud platform's web interface. So, let's launch GCP Cloud Shell.

Using GCP Cloud Shell

To launch GCP Cloud Shell, look at the menu bar at the top and click on the icon that looks like >_ to the immediate right of the search bar. Do you notice how similar GCP's web interface is to the web interfaces in AWS and Azure?

Figure 11.7 – Top menu bar in the GCP console

All of the Bash commands we used in *Chapter 5* for AWS and *Chapter 8* for Azure will work here. Our Linux VM in GCP is functionally just like any other Linux-based computer; a Bash CLI is standard. If you want, you can review some Bash commands from *Chapter 5*.

The Cloud Shell screen looks like this:

Figure 11.8 – The Cloud Shell screen

Next, let's check out some of the tools Google provides that will help us when we work as GCP pentesters.

GCP native security tools

Security Command Center is your starting point for all of the security tools that are built into GCP. It integrates various first-party GCP security tools that I mentioned in *Chapter 10*. This means you can see data from these applications and services within your **Security Command Center (SCC)** panel:

- **Identity and Access Management** (https://cloud.google.com/iam), which manages all of the user identities and machine identities (such as a TLS certificate for a web server) in your GCP network with robust logging that's integrated into SCC and can also be integrated into an organization's third-party security monitoring services. *"Identity and Access Management (IAM) lets administrators authorize who can take action on specific resources, giving you full control and visibility to manage Google Cloud resources centrally."*

- **Cloud IDS** (https://cloud.google.com/intrusion-detection-system), which serves the same functions as most network-based IDSs. It reads your network logs in real time and notifies security administrators of when there may be indications of network threats. It can observe and generate alerts for both ingress (east-west, from one internal server or application to another) and egress (north-south, between your cloud network and the public internet or other external networks) traffic. This is a central concept of zero-trust network security – malicious traffic can come from anywhere. The days of a firm network security perimeter between the internal network and external networks are in the past. Possible threats that Cloud IDS can detect include malware and command and control center-driven attacks.

- **Cloud Firewall** (https://cloud.google.com/firewall), which has functions similar to most other stateful inspection-based network firewalls. There are global network firewall policies that can be applied to permit or forbid traffic according to general GCP security baselines. IAM-governed tags can be used to permit or forbid traffic according to how user and machine identity accounts are marked with tags. Google Cloud Threat Intelligence lists can also be applied so that when Google learns of new cyber threats, your firewall is updated accordingly. Of course, security and network administrators can also block or permit specific users and machines manually.

- **Cloud DLP** (`https://cloud.google.com/dlp`), a tool for **data loss prevention (DLP)**. It tracks how data travels through your GCP network and how it exits your GCP network to ensure that sensitive data isn't breached by your network. Sensitive data can be prevented from being uploaded to your network to an external destination, or it can be tokenized or masked according to the situation (for example, writing a credit card number as *45xx-xxxx-xxxx-xxx*).

While testing SCC, I learned that I had to set up Cloud Identity to access the application. There is a service called Cloud Identity Premium, which is a paid service with extra features. I chose **Cloud Identity Free** because we're keeping costs low to practice pentesting GCP:

1. Go to `https://workspace.google.com/gcpidentity/signup?sku =identitybasic` to set up Cloud Identity Free once you've established a GCP account. The following screenshot shows what the first step in setting up **Cloud Identity Free** looks like:

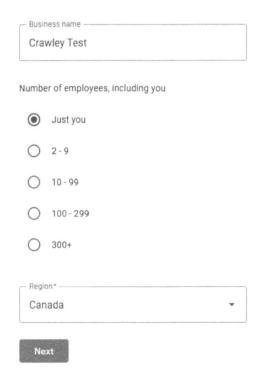

Figure 11.9 – Setting up a Cloud Identity account

2. On the next screen, you will need to enter your first and last name and contact email address. Click **Next**. Then, you'll need to enter a domain name (such as `packtpub.com`, but not `packtpub.com` because that domain belongs to the publisher of this book) that you have access to. Fortunately, I already had a domain name that I used for another project. If you don't have your own domain name that you have administrative access to, I recommend getting one through `namecheap.com`. Depending on the top-level domain (such as `.com`, `.net`, or `.io`) that you choose, it may only cost you 5.00 USD per year.

3. Once you've given Cloud Identity Free a domain name that *you own and have administrative access to*, the final step is to enter a username and password for your new Cloud Identity/ Google Workspace account:

How you'll sign in

You'll use your username to sign into your Google Workspace account and create your business email address. ⑦

Username

0 / 64

Password

0 / 100

☐ Show Password

We know you're probably not a robot, but we just have to ask: Are you a robot?

☐ I'm not a robot

reCAPTCHA
Privacy · Terms

By clicking **Agree and continue**, you agree to the Cloud Identity Agreement.

Agree and continue

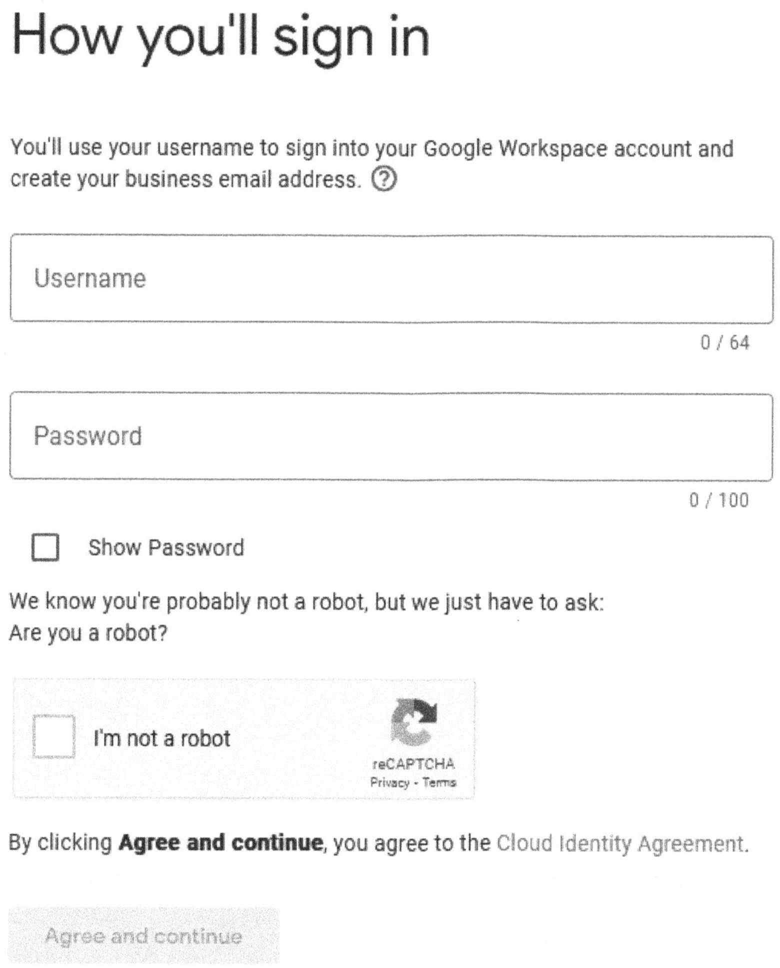

Figure 11.10 – Cloud Identity credentials creation screen

4. Next, the Cloud Identity wizard will direct you to add a DNS verification record to your domain so that Cloud Identity can protect it. The application knew that I used Namecheap to register my domain, and directed me in the process of adding a verification record, like so:

1 **Find your DNS records or settings**

> **ⓘ** **Make sure no one else can use your domain to sign up for Google Workspace**
> We'll show you how to prove that you own this domain. Learn more

(a) Sign in to your account at Namecheap. ☑

(b) Click the **Manage** button next to the domain you're setting up today.
     Click **Advanced DNS**.

     Then **come back here** and click Next: Go to Step 2 to add a verification record.

What to look for on Namecheap's Dashboard:

Recently Active in Your Account

All	Products	Expiration	
⊠ ...xyz 🐾 ADD CATEGORY	🏠	Jul 23, 2021 Domain	MANAGE

🏠 ....**.xyz**
🐾

🏠 **Domain**	🎁 Products	🏃→ Sharing & Transfer	🗄 Advanced DNS

Figure 11.11 – How to connect your Cloud Identity account with your DNS provider

Once you've followed the steps in the wizard, you may need to wait a few minutes for the DNS verification process to complete.

5. Then, you'll see a screen like this, where you can click on the blue **CONTINUE** button:

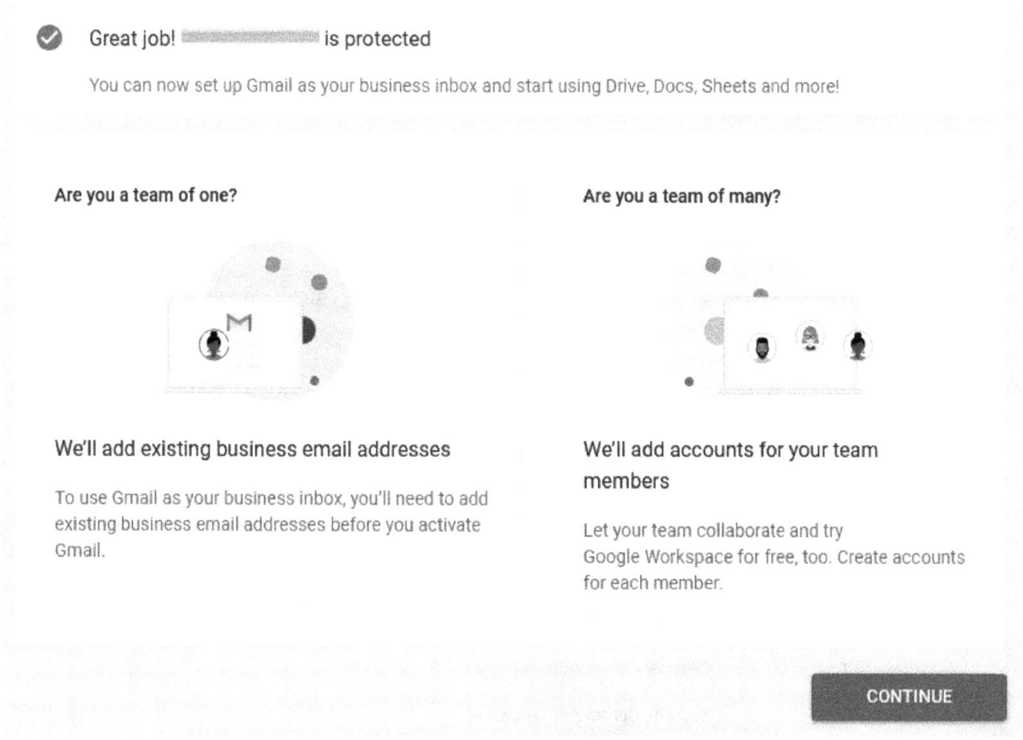

Great job! ▓▓▓▓▓▓▓▓▓ is protected

You can now set up Gmail as your business inbox and start using Drive, Docs, Sheets and more!

Are you a team of one?

We'll add existing business email addresses

To use Gmail as your business inbox, you'll need to add existing business email addresses before you activate Gmail.

Are you a team of many?

We'll add accounts for your team members

Let your team collaborate and try Google Workspace for free, too. Create accounts for each member.

CONTINUE

Figure 11.12 – Cloud Identity user setup screen

Once Cloud Identity has been established, Google won't let you access SCC yet. Follow the instructions on the *Creating and managing organization resources* (`https://cloud.google.com/resource-manager/docs/creating-managing-organization`) page in the Google Cloud documentation to add your Cloud Identity to an organization with SCC access. I found TechTrapture's YouTube video *How to create Organization,Folder and projects in GCP* (`https://www.youtube.com/watch?v=QvpedBNZqvA`) to be helpful to make sure my Cloud Identity account was an organization I could add a project to so that I could access SCC.

In the IAM section of my Google Cloud console (`console.cloud.google.com`), I had to make sure that my owner account had Security Center Admin access, like so:

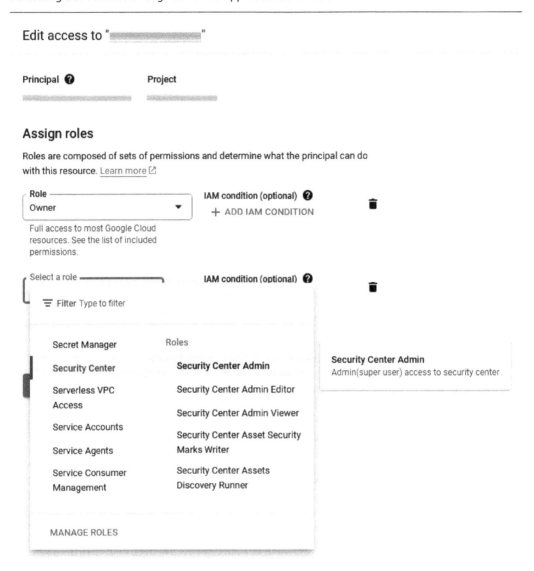

Figure 11.13 – Assigning roles to user accounts in GCP

Exploring the GCP console

Once you're in, you'll see a menu on the left-hand side that consists of the following panels:

- **Overview**
- **Threats**
- **Vulnerabilities**

- **Compliance**

- **Assets**

- **Findings**

- **Sources**

Now that we've had a look at SCC, we know how to access it while we're conducting pentests to access important security posture information.

Once you've set everything up with your administrative Cloud Identity account and your organization, you can access SCC at any time from the web application at `console.cloud.google.com`. The way I always find it is by going to the search bar in the menu bar at the top of the console screen and searching for `Security Command Center`.

You can use this data in your pentest report. The **Compliance** panel is especially important for your organization's blue team. There are many data protection regulations that your organization may need to be compliant with, including PCI DSS, Sarbanes Oxley, HIPAA, GDPR, and many others. Which ones apply to your organization will depend on your industry, where in the world you are, and which foreign countries your company manages the data of. For instance, your company may be in India, but if some of your customers are in the European Union, the GDPR will apply to how your organization handles their data.

Make sure you look through **Security Command Center** before you pentest GCP, and before you write your pentest report. The **Vulnerabilities**, **Assets**, and **Findings** panels are especially useful for your report.

Now, let's run some vulnerability scans and pentests in GCP!

Installing GCP pentesting tools

There are a few different third-party tools that we'll use to conduct security scans in our GCP instance. First, we'll install them.

Prowler

I mentioned Prowler for AWS in *Chapter 5* and for Azure in *Chapter 8*. You can also use Prowler to find vulnerabilities in GCP. I'll briefly walk you through this process as Prowler has already been covered quite a bit in this book.

Everything we'll be doing will be in Cloud Shell. From the GCP console web application, click on the icon that looks like >_ on the right-hand side of the search bar in the top menu bar to open Cloud Shell. The default CLI is a terminal, which is Bash. All of the Linux Bash commands we used in the AWS and Azure chapters will work here.

First, I verified that I had `pip` installed and which version it was with this command:

```
pip -V
```

This was the response I got at the command line:

```
pip 20.3.4 from /usr/lib/python3/dist-packages/pip (python 3.9)
```

So, `pip` with Python 3.9 was already installed in my GCP-based Linux VM without me having to do anything. `pip` is a program that's used to install Python applications. Prowler is based on Python. So, you can use these commands to install Prowler in GCP:

```
sudo apt-get install python3-distutils
```

```
pip install prowler
```

Alternatively, you can use GitHub to install Prowler with these commands, and then verify the installation after:

```
git clone https://github.com/prowler-cloud/prowler
cd prowler
python prowler.py -v
```

Next, let's install GCPBucketBrute, which I introduced in *Chapter 10*.

GCPBucketBrute

GCPBucketBrute is specifically designed to scan Google Storage buckets, determine what access you have to them, and whether or not they can be privilege escalated. This can be very useful data for your pentest report because if GCPBucketBrute can access your buckets easily, so can malicious cyber attackers!

We can use `git` to install GCPBucketBrute from Cloud Shell (if you're still in the Prowler directory, return to your main directory with the `cd` command first):

```
git clone https://github.com/RhinoSecurityLabs/GCPBucketBrute.git
cd GCPBucketBrute/
pip3 install -r requirements.txt
```

Now, let's install GCP Scanner.

GCP Scanner

GCP Scanner is a GCP pentesting application that's developed by people at Google but they state this in the README file (`https://github.com/google/gcp_scanner`):

"This project is not an official Google project. It is not supported by Google and Google specifically disclaims all warranties as to its quality, merchantability, or fitness for a particular purpose."

I found that installing GCP Scanner with `git` worked best:

```
git clone https://github.com/google/gcp_scanner
cd gcp_scanner
pip install .
```

Next, let's run the applications we've just installed!

Exploiting GCP applications

Now that we've installed a few third-party scanning tools, it's time to use them.

Prowler

Let's go through the basics of scanning GCP with Prowler first.

By default, Prowler will use the credentials of whichever account you used to log in to GCP for your VM. If you need to change your account, verify your accounts in IAM in the GCP web console. Verify your account credentials. You can change accounts in GCP with this command:

```
gcloud config set account <account>
```

Now, we can run a default Prowler scan in GCP with this command. Make sure you're in the Prowler directory first, then run a scan:

```
cd prowler
prowler gcp
```

If you used GitHub to install Prowler, use `prowler.py` instead of `prowler` in your commands.

I recommend executing the `help` file first so that you can see all of the commands and options you can use in Prowler. As in previous chapters, you can get Prowler to list services and checks, and run specific service scans and checks in particular locations with particular logging options. All of that information can be printed on your screen the Cloud Shell CLI with this command:

```
prowler -h
```

Alternatively, you can use the following command:

```
python prowler.py -h
```

Scan results can be printed both on screen and in CSV, JSON, or HTML files in your Prowler directory. You can use those logs when you write your pentest report.

GCPBucketBrute

Next, let's scan with GCPBucketBrute. So long as you're logged into a user account instead of a service account, you can get effective results with an unauthenticated scan. You may need to go to your GCP web console first to make sure you're logged in to a user account.

Next, enter this command:

```
python3 gcpbucketbrute.py -k <enter your keyword here> -u
```

In the CiA video, I used the test keyword, like this:

```
python3 gcpbucketbrute.py -k test -u
```

I would also suggest trying other keywords that may appear in the files of your buckets, such as file or print.

When I ran a scan with test, this was the beginning of my results. The printout at my CLI was much longer than this though:

```
EXISTS: test-pubsub
EXISTS: project_test
EXISTS: dl_test
EXISTS: test_6
EXISTS: test-export
EXISTS: gcplogs-test
EXISTS: teamcity-test
EXISTS: testproject
EXISTS: appenginetest
EXISTS: test-artifacts
EXISTS: estest
EXISTS: ops_test
EXISTS: staging_test
EXISTS: testtemp
EXISTS: templates-test
EXISTS: bucket_test
EXISTS: testservices
```

```
     EXISTS: syslog-test
     EXISTS: test-sitemaps
     EXISTS: cloudtest
     EXISTS: trace-test
     EXISTS: audit_test
     EXISTS: test_ml
     EXISTS: gcp-logs-test
     EXISTS: test-videos
     EXISTS: ux_test
     EXISTS: test_tasks
     EXISTS: tmp_test
     EXISTS: dockertest
     EXISTS: testassets
     EXISTS: testops
     EXISTS: test_support

UNAUTHENTICATED ACCESS ALLOWED: pictures-test
     - UNAUTHENTICATED LISTABLE (storage.objects.list)
     - UNAUTHENTICATED READABLE (storage.objects.get)
     - ALL PERMISSIONS:
         [
             "storage.objects.get",
             "storage.objects.list"
         ]
```

GCP Scanner

Now, let's give GCP Scanner a try. First, make sure you're in the directory that GCP Scanner is in:

```
cd gcp_scanner
```

Create a folder to save your scan results in:

```
mkdir <folder name of your choice here>
```

If you enter this command, you will get a handy help guide printed at the command line:

```
python3 scanner.py -h
```

I ran a simple metadata scan with this command. This checks the metadata in your GCP VM's files to see whether sensitive credentials are exposed in them:

```
python3 scanner.py -o <folder name you used in mkdir command here> -ls
-m
```

Feel free to play around with all of the options and arguments that are shown in GCP Scanner's help guide:

```
GCP Scanner

optional arguments:
  -h, --help              show this help message and exit
  -ls, --light-scan       Return only the most important GCP resource
fields in the output.
  -k KEY_PATH, --sa-key-path KEY_PATH
                          Path to directory with SA keys in json format
  -g GCLOUD_PROFILE_PATH, --gcloud-profile-path GCLOUD_PROFILE_PATH
                          Path to directory with gcloud profile. Specify
- to search for credentials in default gcloud config path
  -m, --use-metadata      Extract credentials from GCE instance metadata
  -at ACCESS_TOKEN_FILES, --access-token-files ACCESS_TOKEN_FILES
                          A list of comma separated files with access
token and OAuth scopes.TTL limited. A token and scopes should be
stored in JSON format.
  -rt REFRESH_TOKEN_FILES, --refresh-token-files REFRESH_TOKEN_FILES
                          A list of comma separated files with refresh_
token, client_id,token_uri and client_secret stored in JSON format.
  -s KEY_NAME, --service-account KEY_NAME
                          Name of individual SA to scan
  -p TARGET_PROJECT, --project TARGET_PROJECT
                          Name of individual project to scan
  -f FORCE_PROJECTS, --force-projects FORCE_PROJECTS
                          Comma separated list of project names to
include in the scan
  -c CONFIG_PATH, --config CONFIG_PATH
                          A path to config file with a set of specific
resources to scan.
  -l {DEBUG,INFO,WARNING,ERROR,CRITICAL}, --logging
{DEBUG,INFO,WARNING,ERROR,CRITICAL}
                          Set logging level (INFO, WARNING, ERROR)
  -lf LOG_FILE, --log-file LOG_FILE
                          Save logs to the path specified rather than
displaying in console
```

Congratulations, you've just produced a bunch of GCP pentest scanning logs that you can reference in your pentest report!

In the next chapter, we'll conduct pentesting scans within Docker and Kubernetes containers in GCP.

Summary

Everything you need to create a GCP network to practice pentesting can be done with the services in the GCP free tier. Just make sure you check your billing in the GCP web console to make sure you aren't incurring charges.

You may need to set up a Google Workspace or Cloud Identity account to get the most out of GCP. That includes using SCC. SCC is your starting point for all of the security tools that are built into GCP. It integrates various first-party GCP security tools. You can use SCC to check for some threats, vulnerabilities, and security recommendations based on Google's threat intelligence. As with running third-party pentesting tools, SCC may provide you with useful information that you can use in your pentest report.

Just like with AWS and Azure, Prowler can be used to scan for vulnerabilities and regulatory compliance in GCP. We ran a Prowler vulnerability scan at the command line in Cloud Shell.

GCPBucketBrute checks whether attackers can access your GCP buckets and whether they can be privilege escalated. Because we just set up a simple GCP deployment with a VM without much on it, it's surprising that GCPBucketBrute was still able to find somewhere with unauthenticated access!

GCP Scanner can be used to determine what level of access particular credentials have in your GCP deployment.

In the next chapter, we will deploy Docker and Kubernetes clusters in GCP and run some vulnerability scans in them.

Further reading

To learn more about the topics that were covered in this chapter, take a look at the following resources:

- *List of free services in GCP*: `https://cloud.google.com/free?hl=en`
- *TechTrapture's YouTube video How to create Organization,Folder and projects in GCP*: `https://www.youtube.com/watch?v=QvpedBNZqvA`
- *Prowler in GCP*: `https://docs.prowler.cloud/en/latest/#google-cloud`
- *GCPBucketBrute*: `https://github.com/RhinoSecurityLabs/GCPBucketBrute`
- *GCP Scanner*: `https://github.com/google/gcp_scanner`

12

Pentesting Containerized Applications in GCP

If the organization you work for engages in DevOps or CI/CD application development, there's an excellent chance that they have Docker or Kubernetes clusters in GCP. Let's learn how to pentest them.

In this chapter, I will explain what containerization is, why containerization is used, and how containerization works in general. We'll learn how Docker and Kubernetes work in GCP and how to use Trivy with Docker- and Kubernetes-based applications in GCP.

In this chapter, we'll cover the following topics:

- How containerization works
- How Docker works in GCP
- How Kubernetes works in GCP
- Docker and Kubernetes pentesting techniques in GCP

So, let's explore containerization in GCP!

Technical requirements

We will work with Microsoft's infrastructure. Massive Azure data centers will do the bulk of the computer processing work for the exercises in this chapter. So, fortunately, you don't need to have a top-of-the-line workstation. You will need the following:

- A web browser
- A desktop or laptop PC
- An Android or iPhone mobile
- A good, reliable internet connection

Check out the following video to view the Code in Action: `https://bit.ly/404CEg8`

How containerization works

Virtualization in computing is all about software simulating the functions of hardware. For example, my laptop is one computer. But on my computer, I can run software that pretends to be several different computers at the same time. (Thank goodness I expanded the RAM in my laptop to 64 GB, because each of those simulated computers could need 4 GB of memory!) The CPU, RAM, disk drive, and I/O device interfaces for each of those computers are simulated in the software. The software uses my laptop's real CPU, RAM, disk drive, and I/O interfaces and allocates their capacity to make several imaginary computers. When operating systems and applications are installed in those imaginary computers, as far as the operating systems and applications know, they are each running on their own physical computer.

There are two common ways to deploy virtualization on cloud networks—VMs and containers.

VMs

VMs are simulated computers, as I described in my example. Instead of directly running on PC or server machine hardware, a VM imitates all of the hardware components that are needed to run an operating system. In this model, my laptop runs a hypervisor that acts as a layer between the VMs and my physical computer.

You can use an application on your own PC, such as Oracle VirtualBox or VMware Workstation Player, to work as a hypervisor for your VMs. All you need is a disk image file of an operating system you'd like to run in your VM, and then to configure it in your hypervisor. The operating systems don't have to match your host operating system, and very often they don't. I could run a Kali Linux VM on my Windows 11 PC. You could run a Windows 11 VM on your MacBook. And I could run a macOS VM on my Kubuntu Linux desktop.

VMs can also be run on cloud platforms such as GCP. Then, the virtualized computer is running on one of Google's computers, not on a computer you can physically touch on your own premises. VMs are a common use case for GCP, and they're a good solution when a company wants to run single computers on GCP for a long time, such as to use as a web server or an email server. A lot of the websites you visit every day are hosted on VMs run on cloud platforms such as GCP!

But VMs aren't the best option when companies deploy massive dynamic applications, such as with DevOps or CI/CD methodologies that require them to be very scalable and responsive. The amount of computer processing power, memory, and network bandwidth a DevOps or CI/CD application requires could halve one day and double the next, whereas you can't grow or shrink a VM's hardware capacity as quickly or to the same extent. The hardware resources allocated to a VM are relatively static.

Enter containerization.

Containers

Docker and Kubernetes are two containerization orchestration platforms commonly used by companies today. A containerization orchestration platform will automatically launch and kill containers without needing direct human interaction. These platforms manage how containers are deployed, and also handle the load balancing within the virtualized hardware, allocating hardware resources such as CPU and memory only as much as is needed.

Cloud platforms have made containerized applications possible for companies and other sorts of enterprises. Google has massive computer networks and computer hardware resources in its various data centers around the world, a lot of which is dedicated to deploying GCP to its business customers all over the world.

How Docker works in GCP

Docker isn't the first containerization technology to exist, but it's probably the first to be widely used by companies and organizations around the world. It also serves as the foundation for Kubernetes, the other popular way to deploy containers. Docker and Kubernetes aren't competitors like Coca-Cola and Pepsi. Rather, Kubernetes is kind of a fork of Docker, like comparing Debian Linux to Ubuntu Linux (which is based on Debian).

Here's the basic architecture of a Docker containerization orchestration system (you can refer to *Chapter 6* for the architecture diagram).

The Docker host runs directly on your computer or on the computer you manage on a cloud service (such as **Google Compute Engine**, or **GCE**). In the Docker host, the Docker daemon stores Docker images and makes and manages containers based on those images. Docker images are very much like disk image ISO files for operating systems that you can use to make VMs. In fact, many Docker images are made with ordinary operating systems such as Ubuntu Linux. However, the images and their containers may not have all of the operating system components, but only as much as is needed to run your containerized application.

The Docker host connects to a registry, which is usually (but not always) hosted on an external network that's most often the internet. The registry makes Docker images available for your Docker host to download. The registry also maintains those images and updates them like any other internet-hosted software, kind of like a Git repository.

Finally, a Docker client running in a place such as your GCP console or on your endpoint in Docker Desktop is where you can execute commands to your Docker daemon (under the umbrella of your Docker host) in order to manage it. That's how you send instructions to your Docker containerization orchestration system. We will be executing commands that way to a Docker system in this chapter.

The default way to deploy a Docker containerization system in GCP uses Cloud Build to simplify the Docker build steps, and Cloud Run to help run containerized apps, all while your Docker host runs in GCE.

Here's Google's description of Cloud Build (`https://cloud.google.com/build`):

> *"Cloud Build scales up and down with no infrastructure to set up, upgrade,*
> *or scale. Run builds in a fully managed environment in Google Cloud with*
> *connectivity to your own private network."*

Cloud Build is a system that runs in the background when you deploy Docker containerization in GCP in the usual way. It spares developers the tedium of having to manage the servers that run your Docker containers.

And here's Google's description of Cloud Run (`https://cloud.google.com/run/docs/overview/what-is-cloud-run`):

> *"Cloud Run allows developers to spend their time writing their code, and very little*
> *time operating, configuring, and scaling their Cloud Run service. You don't have*
> *to create a cluster or manage infrastructure in order to be productive with Cloud*
> *Run."*

Cloud Run is another system that runs in the background when you deploy Docker containerization in the usual way in GCP. It spares developers from having to tweak the computer processing configurations that execute their Docker containers.

Now that we've looked at Docker in GCP, it's time to learn about how Kubernetes works in GCP.

How Kubernetes works in GCP

Kubernetes can be used to deploy containerized applications in AWS and Azure. In *Chapters 6* and *9*, I walked you through deploying Kubernetes on those platforms, and we pentested them. But GCP is arguably the home of Kubernetes. Here's why.

Kubernetes was originally developed by a team at Google. The Kubernetes project was announced by Google cloud computing specialist Eric Brewer in 2014 (`https://web.archive.org/web/20150910171929/http:/www.wired.com/2014/06/google-kubernetes`). Kubernetes was inspired by some of the containerization innovations pioneered by Docker. But Kubernetes was mainly influenced by Borg (`https://web.archive.org/web/20160701040235/http:/www.wired.com/2015/06/google-kubernetes-says-future-cloud-computing/`), which was proprietary in-house cloud computing middleware that Google wanted to keep for its own purposes. Borg helps to run the backend for Gmail, Google Search, Google Maps, and a number of other popular Google services.

Google's Joe Beda, Brendan Burns, Brian Grant, Tim Hockin, and Craig McLuckie conceived of Kubernetes as being an open source platform that could be used for many of the same use cases Google deployed for Borg internally. By July 2015, the first version of Kubernetes was publicly released. By 2017, big tech companies and software developers including Red Hat (IBM), VMware, Docker, Inc., Microsoft Azure, and AWS all announced support for it. That's the beauty of **open source software** (**OSS**) and open standards! And just as some organizations have multi-cloud networks that integrate services from AWS, Azure, and GCP, some organizations have both Docker and Kubernetes containerized applications.

Here's the basic architecture of a Kubernetes containerization orchestration system (you can refer to *Chapter 6* for the architecture diagram).

The control plane supports the entire containerization system and works as the vector between your Kubernetes-based network and the cloud platform, such as **Google Kubernetes Engine** (**GKE**) in GCP. The control plane contains a handful of components, including those listed here:

- `etcd` is a key-value store. It maintains data about all of your clusters.

- Pods run with the support of nodes, and `kube-scheduler` assigns nodes to newly created Pods.

- `kube-apiserver` manages the Kubernetes API. So, it helps your Kubernetes-based application integrate with external applications. It's also where `kubectl` (**ctl** stands for **command-line tool**) connects to in order to send commands to your Kubernetes system.

- `kube-controller-manager` runs controller processes. There are controllers for maintaining nodes, controllers for executing scheduled jobs (such as "back up these files every day at 6 p.m."), controllers to generate links between services and Pods, and controllers to create service accounts. Pods and nodes will be explained later in this section.

- `cloud-controller-manager` connects your Kubernetes network to your cloud provider's APIs. In GCP, `cloud-controller-manager` usually interfaces with GKE.

- *Nodes* are the control plane's children. There could be 2 nodes, 20 nodes, or many different numbers of nodes according to what your application needs at any given time. Each node contains a kubelet. The kubelet is a node agent that registers the node with the API server using a hostname or another sort of identifier specific to the cloud provider.

- *Pods* are the children of nodes, which also makes Pods the grandchildren of the control plane. The kubelet in each node defines the nodes according to a PodSpec, which is written as a YAML or JSON file. It helps to know that YAML is similar in some ways to HTML, and JSON was created for use with JavaScript—two technologies that were developed for the web. YAML and JSON files can be viewed in a text editor, and sometimes they only have a few lines of code. The vulnerability scans you'll be running as a pentester and in your red team engagements will sometimes scan YAML and JSON files depending on the situation. But you don't need to know how to write your own YAML or JSON files for the purposes of this book.

Each Pod has a container runtime in which your containers run. Containers are made from container images that are like the ISO disk images of operating systems that are used in VMs. But a Kubernetes container image will have just the operating system components that are needed to execute the code that it'll process. There are many default container images that can be used, and also, container images are sometimes custom-made for a particular company and its application.

Finally, the nodes (which contain Pods) interface with a load balancer, which helps manage the hardware and network resources that are needed at any given time. The load balancer also provides an interface between your Kubernetes-based application and your end users.

As a cloud pentester, it helps to know that both the load balancer and the API servers can be vectors for cyber attacks on your Kubernetes application! The load balancer is most often subject to cyber attacks from an Ingress, north-south direction between your cloud and external networks, and the API servers are more often subject to attacks from an east-west direction between components within your cloud network. Sometimes, cyber attacks enter from the public internet through the ingress route and then travel between parts of a cloud network using lateral movement that may involve privilege escalation. That's kind of like a burglar breaking into a department store's jewelry department and then moving on to the fragrances and cosmetics.

The entire Kubernetes containerization system is called a cluster. Some organizations may deploy multiple clusters. But no matter how many clusters an organization uses, each cluster is composed of a control plane, nodes, and Pods, in the order of bottom to top.

GKE (`https://cloud.google.com/kubernetes-engine`) is a GCP service that's specially designed to run Kubernetes-based applications. It automates cluster and node management and how hardware resources are provisioned through the load balancer. The vast majority of the time, organizations both large and small will prefer to run Kubernetes applications in GCP through GKE.

The beauty of cloud computing and containerization is that applications can be made to be very scalable, dynamic, and efficient with hardware resources. A lot of the drudgery of application deployment and network management can be automated. So, it's natural that organizations will prefer to use GKE so that they aren't burdened with server management tasks. A containerized application in the cloud can literally double and halve within days. There should always be just as much computing power and bandwidth as is needed at any given time, and containers sometimes only have a lifespan of hours.

It's no wonder that cloud computing has revolutionized how all kinds of organizations of all sizes and in all industries deploy applications through the internet. However, the containerized applications that organizations deploy through the cloud can be just as attractive targets to cyber attackers as VMs deployed through the cloud. They interface with the internet, which provides an access route for attackers. And they can contain sensitive information that can make cyber criminals a lot of money, such as sensitive financial data.

Your job as a cloud pentester is to make sure you discover how an attacker could harm your client's cloud networks before an attacker tries to do it. That way, the company you work for can improve its security accordingly.

So, in the final set of hands-on pentesting exercises in this book, let's get into pentesting Docker and Kubernetes in GCP!

Docker and Kubernetes pentesting techniques in GCP

Now that we understand Docker and Kubernetes, let's deploy them in GCP. Then, we'll pentest them. First, let's deploy the Docker and Kubernetes clusters that we'll practice pentesting in.

Deploying Docker

We will use basic default Docker container images in our Docker deployment because we're not doing anything fancy with it; we're just trying out our pentesting tools! Follow these steps:

1. The simplest way for us to deploy a Docker cluster in GCP is to start with Cloud Run. Use your web browser to log in to the Google Cloud account we set up in *Chapter 11*. Once you're in the GCP web console, go to `https://console.cloud.google.com/run` to use Cloud Run.

    The Cloud Run screen should look something like this:

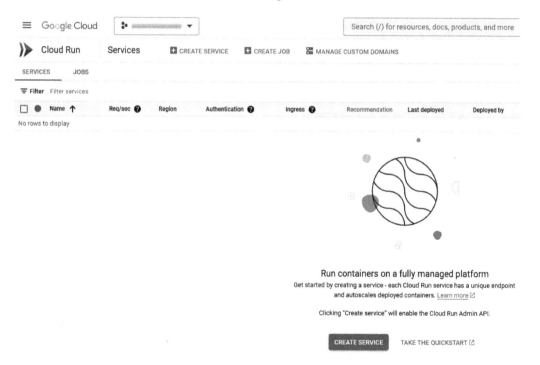

Figure 12.1 – Cloud Run panel in the GCP console

2. Click on **+CREATE SERVICE** at the top, just underneath the top menu bar. You'll see a screen that looks like this:

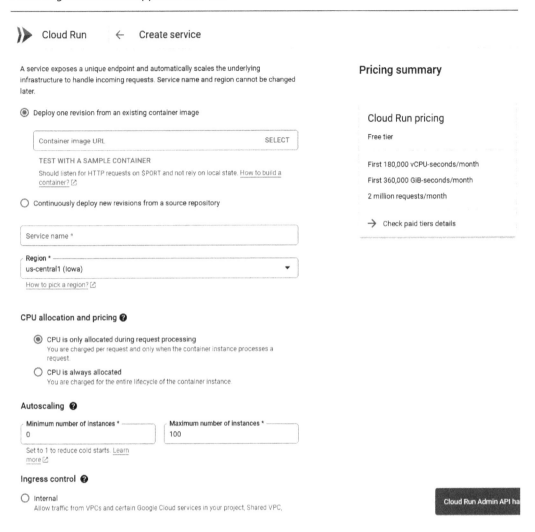

Figure 12.2 – Creating a Cloud Run service in GCP to run Docker

We will be using as many defaults as possible just to create a basic Docker environment to try our pentesting tools in. In situations where you may want to deploy a particular type of application with Docker containers, you may have to use different settings in Cloud Run.

To keep it simple, these are the options I chose for my Docker deployment in Cloud Run:

- At the top where it provides the **Deploy one revision from an existing container image** and **Continuously deploy new revisions from a source repository options**, I chose the first option.

- Next, instead of entering a container image URL, I clicked on **TEST WITH A SAMPLE CONTAINER**.

On this screen, I clicked on the **CONTAINER REGISTRY** tab and chose the `hello` demo container. Then, I clicked on **SELECT** next to the container image URL:

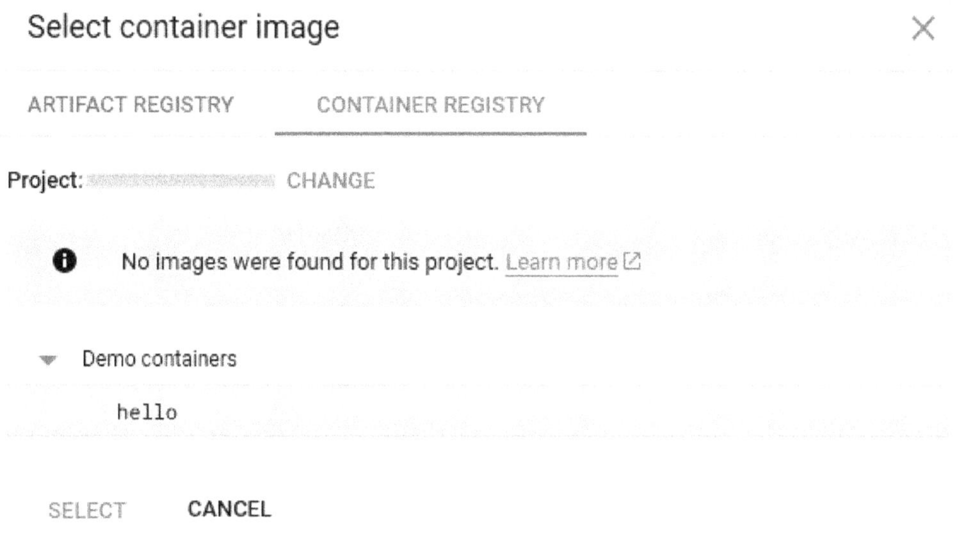

Select container image   ✕

ARTIFACT REGISTRY   CONTAINER REGISTRY

Project: ▒▒▒▒▒▒▒▒▒▒▒▒▒▒▒▒ CHANGE

   ⓘ   No images were found for this project. Learn more ☒

▼   Demo containers

       hello

SELECT   CANCEL

Figure 12.3 – Choosing a Docker image for our Docker instance

- In the **Service name** field, I entered `crawleydockertest`. I left my default region, which in my case is **us-central1 (Iowa)**. Your default region might be something else. Each region represents a particular Google data center, and it may not even be in your country.

- To save money, under **CPU allocation and pricing**, I chose **CPU is only allocated during request processing**.

- I left the **Autoscaling** option alone. By default, **0** is the minimum number of instances and **100** is the maximum. This sort of setting reflects the scalable nature of cloud applications. New instances can be automatically generated according to your application's needs.

- Under **Ingress control**, I selected **All**, which will allow direct access to your service from the internet.

- Under **Authentication**, I chose **Allow unauthenticated invocations**. These options may not be the best practices for cybersecurity, but they make trying out pentesting tools in our Docker application a lot easier.

3. Finally, I clicked on the blue **CREATE** button at the bottom.

Your web console screen will look like this as your service is created. The creation process took about 30 seconds for me; I wasn't waiting very long:

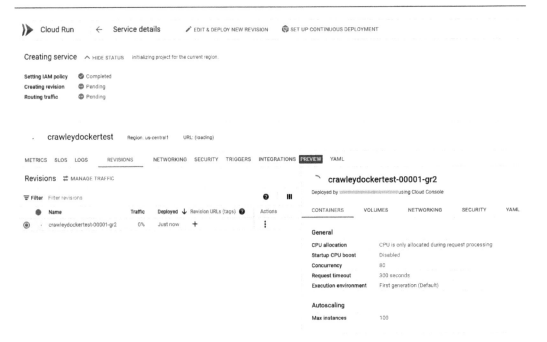

Figure 12.4 – Creating a service for our Docker instance

Now that our Docker environment has been created in GCP, it's time to make a Kubernetes environment!

Deploying Kubernetes

It's possible to deploy Kubernetes in Cloud Shell or in some other CLI. But I prefer to use the web console for deploying services and to use the CLI for pentesting tools. Follow the next steps to deploy Kubernetes:

1. While logged in to GCP from the web and in the web console, go to `https://console.cloud.google.com/projectselector2/home/dashboard`.

2. For the time being, leave the project selector you just opened in one web browser tab. Open **Enable access to APIs** in another tab while using this link: `https://console.cloud.google.com/flows/enableapi?apiid=artifactregistry.googleapis.com`.

You will see a screen like this:

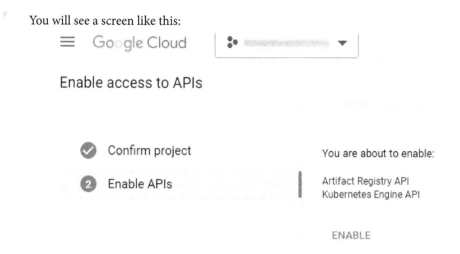

Figure 12.5 – Enabling the required API access for Kubernetes

3. Click on **Confirm project**. **Enable APIs** will transition and say that you're about to enable **Artifact Registry API** and **Kubernetes Engine API**. That's exactly what we want to do. Click on **ENABLE**.

4. You may have to wait a few moments for your enabling of those APIs to process. I was surprised that this took more time than creating my Docker test container. But when that's done, go back to your web browser tab with the project selector dashboard. That'll look something like this:

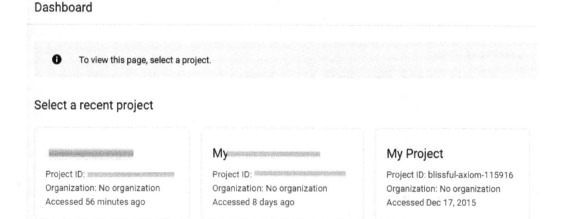

Figure 12.6 – Selecting a project in GCP for our Kubernetes instance

5. Click on a project. Make note of your project ID; it should be something similar to `blissful-axiom-115916`, as in the preceding screenshot.

6. Now, we will do the rest of the work in Cloud Shell in the CLI. Click on the icon that looks like this in the top menu bar on the right-hand side: `>_`.

7. First, we'll make sure that our selected project is the default by entering this at the command line:

    ```
    gcloud config set project <your project ID goes here>
    ```

8. Next, we'll create a default autopilot Kubernetes cluster with this command. If the region you set up earlier isn't `us-central1`, then change it to the name of your region:

    ```
    gcloud container clusters create-auto hello-cluster \
        --location=us-central1
    ```

    As you can see in the *Code in Action* video of this exercise, it may take a few minutes for your cluster to be created. Be patient! Thankfully the command line in Cloud Shell will show you what's going on while you wait.

9. After the several-minute process of creating your Kubernetes cluster is done, you next need to create authentication credentials for your cluster. This will make `kubectl` (the program you use to manage your Kubernetes cluster at the command line) ready to use your new cluster. Just be sure to change `us-central1` to the name of your region if it's different:

    ```
    gcloud container clusters get-credentials hello-cluster \
        --location us-central1
    ```

10. Next, we're going to create an application deployment in our new Kubernetes cluster with the following command. The directory path after `image=` is our default `hello` Kubernetes container image for testing purposes. If you want to do something specific with Kubernetes in GCP at some point after reading this book, you can modify the command to use a different container image:

    ```
    kubectl create deployment hello-server \
        --image=us-docker.pkg.dev/google-samples/containers/gke/
    hello-app:1.0
    ```

11. Now, we need to set up the load balancer so that we can expose our deployment to the internet. We will be accessing our Kubernetes deployment through the internet in order to pentest it, so this step is absolutely necessary:

    ```
    kubectl expose deployment hello-server \
        --type LoadBalancer \
        --port 80 \
        --target-port 8080
    ```

12. Finally, we need to run some checks to make sure our new Kubernetes Deployment is ready to use. First, let's inspect the Pods:

    ```
    kubectl get pods
    ```

    The command line should show a `hello-server` Pod.

13. Now, we'll inspect `hello-server`:

    ```
    kubectl get service hello-server
    ```

14. Copy the external IP that prints at the command line.

15. In a new web browser tab, enter `http://<your external IP here>` in the address bar and hit *Enter*.

16. My external connection to my Kubernetes Deployment was slow. But it eventually worked. I got an error in Firefox that warned me that the destination was HTTP and not HTTPS. I clicked the button to go to the HTTP site, and my screen showed this. It worked!

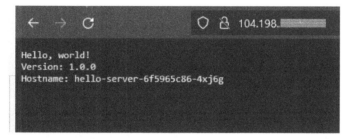

Figure 12.7 – Viewing the IP address for our Kubernetes Deployment in a web browser

Now that we have both a working Docker environment and a working Kubernetes environment in GCP, it's time to use those environments to try out some pentesting tools.

Trivy

Trivy (`https://github.com/aquasecurity/trivy`) is a pentesting tool that's developed by Aqua Security and available on GitHub. It's a security scanner that can find vulnerabilities in filesystems, VM images, and AWS. But it can also be used to scan Docker and Kubernetes images.

Trivy can be run from Red Hat and CentOS, Arch Linux, and macOS. The installation instructions for all supported platforms can be found here: `https://aquasecurity.github.io/trivy/ v0.44/getting-started/installation/`. The Linux VM I have running in my GCP deployment is based on Debian, so I'll use the Debian installation instructions:

```
wget https://github.com/aquasecurity/trivy/releases/download/v0.44.1/
trivy_0.44.1_Linux-64bit.deb
sudo dpkg -i trivy_0.44.1_Linux-64bit.deb
```

Now that we have Trivy installed on our Linux VM in GCP, let's try a couple of basic container scanning exercises. Trivy users and developers have a wide range of container pentesting tutorials on their website (`https://aquasecurity.github.io/trivy/v0.45/tutorials/overview/`) if you'd like to try some others.

Let's try looking for misconfigurations in how I configured my Docker image. Remember—misconfigurations are security vulnerabilities that can be exploited by cyber attackers! Follow the next steps:

1. I used GCP's default `hello` test Docker image to build my Docker containers. This is its name and address:

    ```
    us-docker.pkg.dev/cloudrun/container/hello
    ```

2. You will need to verify the name and address of the image you used. In your GCP console, search for `Cloud Run`. You will then see a screen like this:

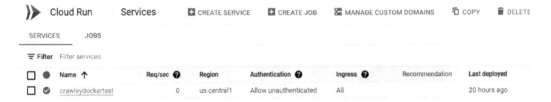

Figure 12.8 – Viewing our Docker instance in the Cloud Run interface

3. I clicked on the name of my Docker cluster, which in my case is `crawleydockertest`.

    Then, I clicked on the **YAML** tab to see the YAML file that was used to build my Docker cluster. Where it says `image:` is where I found the name and address of the Docker image that I used. You can find yours the same way:

```
1   apiVersion: serving.knative.dev/v1
2   kind: Service
3   metadata:
4     name: crawleydockertest
5     namespace: '                    '
6     selfLink: /api                                                    rvices/crawleydockertest
7     uid: e0
8     resourceVersion:
9     generation: 1
10    creationTimestamp: '2023-08-
11    labels:
12      cloud.googleapis.com/location: us-central1
13    annotations:
14      run.googleapis.com/client-name: cloud-console
15      serving.knative.dev/creator:
16      serving.knative.dev/lastModifier:
17      run.googleapis.com/operation-id:
18      run.googleapis.com/ingress: all
19      run.googleapis.com/ingress-status: all
20  spec:
21    template:
22      metadata:
23        labels:
24          run.googleapis.com/startupProbeType: Default
25        annotations:
26          run.googleapis.com/client-name: cloud-console
27          autoscaling.knative.dev/maxScale: '100'
28      spec:
29        containerConcurrency: 80
30        timeoutSeconds: 300
31        serviceAccountName: 4
32        containers:
33        - image: us-docker.pkg.dev/cloudrun/container/hello
34          ports:
35          - name: http1
36            containerPort: 8080
37          resources:
38            limits:
39              cpu: 1000m
```

Figure 12.9 – Viewing the YAML file that was used to create my Docker cluster

4.   Now, let's run the scan:

```
trivy image --image-config-scanners config <insert image
location and name here>
```

My Docker image was found, and it was very misconfigured! Here are the results I got:

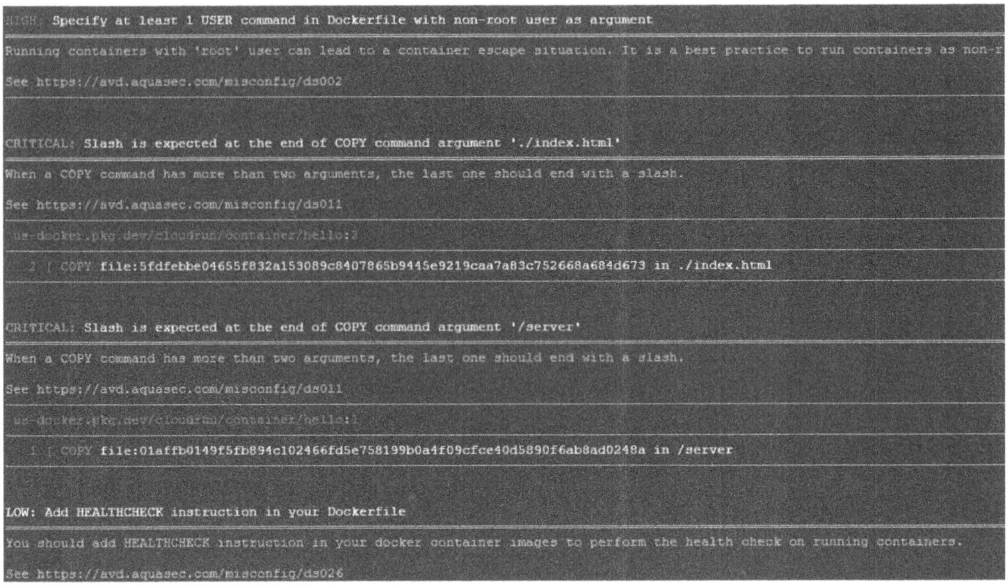

```
HIGH: Specify at least 1 USER command in Dockerfile with non-root user as argument

Running containers with 'root' user can lead to a container escape situation. It is a best practice to run containers as non-r

See https://avd.aquasec.com/misconfig/ds002


CRITICAL: Slash is expected at the end of COPY command argument './index.html'

When a COPY command has more than two arguments, the last one should end with a slash.

See https://avd.aquasec.com/misconfig/ds011

 us-docker.pkg.dev/cloudrun/container/hello:2

    2 [ COPY file:5fdfebbe04655f832a153089c8407865b9445e9219caa7a83c752668a684d673 in ./index.html


CRITICAL: Slash is expected at the end of COPY command argument '/server'

When a COPY command has more than two arguments, the last one should end with a slash.

See https://avd.aquasec.com/misconfig/ds011

 us-docker.pkg.dev/cloudrun/container/hello:1

    1 [ COPY file:01affb0149f5fb894c102466fd5e758199b0a4f09cfce40d5890f6ab8ad0248a in /server


LOW: Add HEALTHCHECK instruction in your Dockerfile

You should add HEALTHCHECK instruction in your docker container images to perform the health check on running containers.

See https://avd.aquasec.com/misconfig/ds026
```

Figure 12.10 – Trivy scan output

You could use this sort of data in your pentest report if you were conducting a real pentest.

Now, let's try Trivy to conduct a pentest against my Kubernetes cluster in GCP:

1. First, I found that I had to expose my Kubernetes cluster again in order for Trivy to be able to scan it:

    ```
    kubectl expose deployment hello-server \
        --type LoadBalancer \
        --port 80 \
        --target-port 8080
    ```

2. Then, I inspected the Pods:

    ```
    kubectl get pods
    ```

3. Now, here's a Trivy command that conducted a very thorough scan of my Kubernetes cluster:

    ```
    trivy k8s -n kube-system --report summary all -timeout 1500s
    ```

After a few minutes in the Cloud Shell CLI, I got a very detailed summary that I could use in a pentest report:

Namespace	Resource	Vulnerabilities					Misconfigurations					Secrets				
		C	H	M	L	U	C	H	M	L	U	C	H	M	L	U
kube-system	ServiceAccount/pod-garbage-collector															
kube-system	ConfigMap/cilium-hubble-config															
kube-system	ConfigMap/ingress-uid															
kube-system	ServiceAccount/expand-controller															
kube-system	ServiceAccount/namespace-controller															
kube-system	DaemonSet/pdcsi-node-windows			4	11				7							
kube-system	Deployment/l7-default-backend								2	6						
kube-system	DaemonSet/gke-metrics-agent							1	2	4						
kube-system	ServiceAccount/default															
kube-system	ServiceAccount/node-local-dns															
kube-system	ConfigMap/netd-config															
kube-system	DaemonSet/kube-proxy		1	4				2	4	10						
kube-system	DaemonSet/nvidia-gpu-device-plugin-large-ubuntu	1	17	29				8	10							
kube-system	ServiceAccount/netd															
kube-system	ConfigMap/fluentbit-gke-config-v1.4.0															
kube-system	ResourceQuota/gcp-critical-pods															
kube-system	DaemonSet/anetd-win								3							
kube-system	DaemonSet/tpu-device-plugin		5	6				2	4							
kube-system	ServiceAccount/filestorecsi-node-sa															
kube-system	ServiceAccount/konnectivity-agent-cpha															
kube-system	ServiceAccount/pkgextract-cleanup-service															
kube-system	ConfigMap/core-metrics-exporter-conf															
kube-system	ConfigMap/gke-common-webhook-heartbeat															
kube-system	DaemonSet/anetd			28				8	15							
kube-system	DaemonSet/gke-metrics-agent-scaling-10							1	2							
kube-system	DaemonSet/nvidia-gpu-device-plugin-medium-ubuntu	1	17	29				8	10							
kube-system	DaemonSet/nvidia-gpu-device-plugin-small-cos	1	17	29				8	10							
kube-system	Service/kube-dns															
kube-system	Deployment/metrics-server-v0.5.2								2	6						
kube-system	DaemonSet/gke-metrics-agent-scaling-100							1	2							
kube-system	DaemonSet/fluentbit-gke-small			4	11			7	11							
kube-system	DaemonSet/fluentbit-gke-big			4				7	11							
kube-system	ServiceAccount/clusterrole-aggregation-controller															

Figure 12.11 – Trivy scan vulnerability report

Trivy is a lot of fun to explore!

Summary

In this chapter, we learned which services manage containerization in GCP. We deployed our own Docker and Kubernetes clusters. Then, we conducted a security assessment with Trivy.

The default way to deploy a Docker containerization system in GCP uses Cloud Build to simplify the Docker build steps and Cloud Run to help run containerized apps, all while your Docker host runs in GCE.

The simplest way to deploy Kubernetes in GCP is to use GKE.

Trivy is a third-party pentesting application that has lots of great features for vulnerability scanning both Docker and Kubernetes deployments.

In the next and final chapter, I'll quiz you on what we've learned in the previous 12 chapters. Plus, I'll give you tips for writing and signing pentesting contracts, more tips for writing pentest reports, and introduce you to cloud and pentesting-related certifications that may make you more employable as a cloud pentester.

Further reading

To learn more about the topics covered in this chapter, you can visit the following links:

- *Google Cloud Run*: `https://cloud.google.com/run`

- *Google Cloud Build*: `https://cloud.google.com/build`

- *GKE*: `https://cloud.google.com/kubernetes-engine`

- *Google Cloud documentation on deploying containers to Cloud Run*: `https://cloud.google.com/run/docs/deploying`

- *Google Cloud documentation on deploying Kubernetes applications in GKE*: `https://cloud.google.com/kubernetes-engine/docs/deploy-app-cluster`

- *Trivy*: `https://github.com/aquasecurity/trivy`

Best Practices and Summary

So, we've learned about the most popular cloud platforms—AWS, Azure, and GCP. We've also tried out a bunch of vulnerability scanning and pentesting exercises in our own test AWS, Azure, and GCP deployments.

Now, let's review what we've learned. We'll also give you useful information about professional certifications, pentesting contracts, and pentest reports. In this chapter, we'll cover a content review with questions and answers based on the material that appeared earlier in this book, what you should have in your cloud pentesting toolkit, and useful cloud and pentesting certifications that you can pursue.

We will also discuss what should be included in a pentesting contract and how to write an effective pentest report.

We'll cover the following main topics:

- Content review
- Your cloud pentesting toolkit
- Cloud and pentester certifications
- Pentesting contracts
- Pentesting reports

Let's jump right in!

Content review

You have learned so much from reading this book! We've covered not just one cloud platform, but the three most used cloud platforms around—AWS, Azure, and GCP. Plus, you've read a lot about the basic principles and concepts in penetration testing and red teaming, and how to share your security vulnerability discoveries with defensive cybersecurity specialists and corporate leadership.

That's a lot of information to absorb. You will probably read bits of this book again from time to time during your first few years working as a cloud pentester. However, in order to prepare for your professional journey, it's important to see whether you can remember what you've learned. The human brain is more likely to remember information when it thinks in more than one way. So far, you've absorbed information, and then put your learning into practice by trying out the many pentesting tutorials in this book. Now, it's time to recall what you've learned so that you can track your progress and be more likely to remember.

Fortunately, this isn't a formal examination. It's just an exercise for your own benefit. Don't be hard on yourself if you answer some of these questions incorrectly. You'll discover areas that you need to focus on in order to improve. The learning process always involves learning from mistakes!

Okay—let's get into it!

Questions

Here are a few questions to help you understand your progress:

1. What is a multi-cloud network?
2. What is a hybrid cloud network?
3. When it comes to security responsibility in the cloud, what is the cloud provider responsible for and what is your organization (the cloud provider's customer) responsible for?
4. Are there any circumstances in which Amazon permits you to simulate DDoS attacks in AWS?
5. What's the difference between SaaS, PaaS, and IaaS?
6. What's the difference between external cyber attacks and internal cyber attacks?
7. What's the MITRE ATT&CK database?
8. What does the CIA triad stand for, and what does it mean?
9. What is a zero-trust network?
10. Why should cloud pentesters look for exposed services?
11. What's a vulnerability assessment?
12. What is IAM?
13. What is RBAC?
14. What's the CVE database?
15. What is CVSS?
16. What is EPSS?
17. What's the difference between a red team and a blue team?
18. What's purple teaming?

19. What's a pentest report?

20. What is AWS Security Hub?

21. What is Amazon Inspector?

22. What is Prowler used for?

23. What is Pacu used for?

24. What is a VM?

25. What is containerization?

26. What is Docker?

27. What is Kubernetes?

28. What is a control plane?

29. What's a container image?

30. Name some of the pentesting tools mentioned in this book that can be used on all three cloud computing platforms—AWS, Azure, and GCP. (This excludes tools that can only be used in one of the cloud platforms, such as MFASweep for Microsoft Azure or Pacu for AWS.)

Answers

Here are the answers to the preceding questions:

1. A multi-cloud network is a cloud network that uses more than one cloud platform. A multi-cloud network could have AWS and GCP, Azure and AWS, AWS, Azure, and GCP, and it could also entail cloud platforms that aren't covered in this book, such as DigitalOcean, Salesforce, IBM Cloud, Oracle Cloud, Rackspace Cloud, and many others. A company's cloud network with any combination of two or more cloud providers is a multi-cloud network. Organizations often deploy multi-cloud networks because they may want to have functionality or applications that are only provided by one cloud platform. For instance, a company may use Microsoft Azure for its native Active Directory support for its Windows Server machines on its premises, and GCP for its native support for Google Maps and other Google service APIs. AWS, Azure, and GCP all have the ability to be integrated with each other in one big corporate cloud network.

2. A hybrid cloud network combines a cloud network with a network on an organization's own premises. There has been a huge trend of companies all over the world and in all industries migrating the functions of their on-premises networks to the cloud in the past 10-15 years. But sometimes, organizations find that at least some of their network has to stay on their own servers in their own facilities for a multitude of reasons. AWS, Azure, and GCP are all able to be integrated with a company's own on-premises network. Hybrid cloud networks may use just one cloud platform, or they can also be multi-cloud networks. Pentesting and red teaming a multi-cloud hybrid network can be especially challenging for pentesters!

3.   An easy way to remember what security responsibilities a cloud provider has and what security responsibilities your organization has is to remember this—the cloud provider is responsible for the security *of* the cloud and your organization is responsible for security *in* the cloud.

For example, Amazon has very strong physical security for its various data centers around the world. There are very few people who are allowed inside of one. Even if your company spends $100,000 USD per month on AWS services, it won't let you inside one of its data centers. The cloud provider is fully responsible for the physical security of its data centers. It is also responsible for securing its networking infrastructure and all of its physical hardware. If a disk drive physically fails, it's up to the cloud provider to replace it. The cloud provider is also responsible for the software code that it develops and maintains.

Your organization is responsible for the security of the software code that you put into cloud infrastructure. Your organization is also responsible for the network traffic you move through it. SaaS, PaaS, and IaaS are categorizations that are all about how much of the code is developed by your organization (or acquired from third-party developers) and how much of it is developed by the cloud provider. So, from that foundation, it's easy to understand how the shared security responsibility model applies a bit differently to each type of cloud service.

4.   Most of the time, you're forbidden from simulating DDoS attacks in any cloud platform because they may be disruptive to the cloud provider's other customers. However, AWS will permit DDoS simulation testing in certain circumstances. As per the AWS *DDoS Simulation Testing Policy* (https://aws.amazon.com/security/ddos-simulation-testing/). Some DDoS testing is permitted if the bit volume of the test doesn't exceed 20 GB per second. If the packet volume doesn't exceed 5 million packets per second when testing CloudFrunt or 50,000 packets per second when testing other types of AWS resources, the DDoS simulation may not originate from another AWS resource, and AWS may tell your organization to terminate the simulation testing at any time. AWS may make exceptions to these rules *if* your organization applies for an exception request *and AWS expressively approves it*! If these criteria are too complicated for your red team or pentesters, or if you're even slightly concerned that your DDoS simulation may be forbidden by a cloud provider, just don't try it in the first place. It's not worth it to risk violating a cloud provider's policies.

5.   **SaaS** means **Software-as-a-Service**, **PaaS** means **Platform-as-a-Service**, and **IaaS** means **Infrastructure-as-a-Service**. SaaS means that the cloud provider has most of the software code and most of the security responsibility—for example, Gmail in the Google ecosystem. PaaS means the provider develops a software foundation for some of your organization's own code (or code you acquire from a third-party developer). Amazon **Elastic Kubernetes Service (EKS)** is an example of PaaS. Amazon is responsible for its own Amazon EKS code, but your own container images, third-party container images, your containers, and how your organization uses your Kubernetes cluster in Amazon EKS is your organization's security responsibility. IaaS is when a cloud provider basically just provides the cloud infrastructure. An example of IaaS is Azure VMs, where Microsoft just provides the physical servers and the hypervisor for your organization's VMs. If a cyber attacker exploits a vulnerability in an operating system in your VM, that's on your organization, not Microsoft.

6. External cyber attacks originate from outside of your company's network, whereas internal cyber attacks originate from inside of your company's network. External cyber attacks include the classic kinds of cyber attacks most people think of. A bad person hacks into your company's servers through the internet and deploys ransomware. Stuff like that. What's sometimes forgotten are internal cyber attacks. They come from people and entities that already have privileged access from within your company's network. They're often employees, contractors, executives, or trusted supply chain entities. For instance, an employee may suspect that they're going to be fired soon, so they get revenge by breaching your company's sensitive data on a public website. Internal cyber attacks can be easier to conduct and more destructive because they don't have to hack their way into your company's network; they're already inside because they're supposed to be there. However, they may conduct privilege escalation attacks and lateral movement to access parts of the internal network that they're not allowed to access.

7. The MITRE ATT&CK database (`https://attack.mitre.org/`) is a useful and freely available resource online to learn about cyber exploitation techniques that attackers often use. Most cyber attacks involve more than one exploitation technique as they progress along the attack chain. The database is maintained by the MITRE Corporation, and it's occasionally updated to include newly discovered cyber exploitation techniques.

8. The **CIA** triad stands for **Confidentiality, Integrity, and Availability**. Those are the properties of data that cyber attacks harm. All cyber attacks impact one or more of those three components. Confidentiality is all about making sure that data is only accessible to the entities that are permitted access to it. For instance, if an attacker could read my email inbox, that's an attack on my confidentiality. Integrity is all about making sure only authorized entities can alter data. So, if an attacker used my email to send emails as me, or altered the contents of the emails in my inbox or the emails I'm receiving through the IMAP protocol, that's an attack on the integrity of my email. Availability is all about making sure that data and data services are usable and accessible when they're supposed to be. If an attacker DDoS attacks my email server and I can't receive or send new emails, that's an attack on the availability of my email. Some attacks impact more than one part of the CIA triad. For instance, enterprise ransomware these days often doesn't just maliciously encrypt data away from its rightful owners; it also threatens to breach sensitive data to the public if a ransom isn't paid.

9. In a zero-trust network, no machine, device, or user is automatically trusted, regardless of its origin. Zero-trust networks exist in contrast with the old traditional perimeter security model. In the perimeter security model, there is a security perimeter between the internal network and external networks (such as the internet). Entities originating from external networks need to be authenticated and authorized at the security perimeter in order to be allowed into the internal network, but all data traveling around the internal network and all entities originating from the internal network is automatically trusted. That security model may have worked in the 1990s before cloud computing was a thing, organizations had completely on-premises networks, and the cyber threat landscape was less sophisticated. But with the advent of the cloud and other 21st-century computing technologies, only the zero-trust model is effective for good network security, within the cloud and beyond the cloud. Given the way cloud networks

operate, only the zero-trust model can properly be applied anyway. Plus, it obviously works better for detecting and preventing internal cyber attacks as well. In a zero-trust network, your device is being authenticated at every possible authentication point.

10. Exposed services are internet services and ports in your organization's cloud network that an attacker can use to cyber-attack your network through the internet. It's absolutely crucial that the organization you work for makes sure that it has zero exposed services. The cloud networks that companies operate are constantly changing, so you could have no exposed services today but 20 exposed services next week. Some of the pentesting tools I've demonstrated in this book, such as Pacu, have modules that can find exposed services that you can mention in your pentest report. Some of the security tools that the cloud providers make available for their customers, such as Amazon Inspector, can also find exposed services.

11. A vulnerability assessment is when a checklist is used to identify common security weaknesses, misconfigurations, and other vulnerabilities pertaining to a type of computer system. Most of the third-party pentesting tools in this book can be used to perform vulnerability assessments. Some of the checklists that form the basis of a vulnerability assessment include CIS security benchmarks for particular services and applications and security standards such as the **Payment Card Industry Data Security Standard** (**PCI DSS**) regulations for **point-of-sale** (**PoS**) computer payment systems.

12. **IAM** stands for **Identity and Access Management**. It's a specialization in cybersecurity that has to do with maintaining user accounts and machine identities (such as TLS certificates for encryption), authentication methods such as passwords and biometrics, access control systems such as RBAC, user account permissions, and making sure that users and machines can only access data and systems that they're authorized to access. It's an area of cybersecurity expertise that predates cloud networks. However, AWS, Azure, and GCP all have their own IAM systems. Securing IAM is absolutely crucial for the security of your network, applications, and data as a whole!

13. **RBAC** stands for **role-based access control**. There are many different access control methodologies, such as **mandatory access control** (**MAC**), **rule-based access control**, and **discretionary access control** (**DAC**). But RBAC is the methodology that's used in cloud networks the most often. It's also the access control methodology that's native to Kubernetes. In RBAC, users are put into user groups based on their roles within the organization, and then privileges are assigned to the user groups. For instance, only users in the administrative group may be able to create new user accounts, and only users in the payroll group have access to the payroll server. Users should only be put into particular user groups if they absolutely must have that access for the sake of their jobs; that's the **principle of least privilege** (**PoLP**).

14. The CVE database (`https://www.cve.org/`) is another freely accessible database that's maintained by the MITRE Corporation. **CVE** stands for **Common Vulnerabilities and Exposures**. It's intended to be as comprehensive of a database of known security vulnerabilities as possible. There may be a delay of a few months between an organization discovering a vulnerability in one of its products and it appearing as a record in the CVE database in order to give the organization

time to patch the vulnerability before it becomes public knowledge, accessible to potential attackers. CVE records are numbered with this format—CVE-YYYY-NNNN. An example is CVE-2023-1234 (`https://www.cve.org/CVERecord?id=CVE-2023-1234`). The year (YYYY) indicates when the number was reserved; it may or may not be the year the vulnerability was discovered or published in the database. NNNN is just a random four-digit number unique to the year, from what I can tell. If the rate at which vulnerabilities enter the database increases, they may have to add a digit. Published vulnerabilities often have patches available, but not always! That's a scary thought. In my work and for the sake of pragmatism, I generally define known vulnerabilities as those that have CVE records. Some of the pentesting and vulnerability scanning tools in this book will identify the vulnerabilities they find by CVE records.

15. **CVSS** is the **Common Vulnerability Scoring System** (maintained by FIRST) that's used to classify vulnerabilities in the CVE database according to their severity. The CVSS Score Qualitative Rating uses the following categorizations. 0.0 means the vulnerability is no problem at all (I've never seen a 0.0 rating), 0.1 to 3.9 is low, 4.0 to 6.9 is medium, 7.0 to 8.9 is high, and 9.0 to 10.0 is critical. The higher the number, the more dangerous it is for a computer system to be exploited by that vulnerability.

16. The **Exploit Prediction Scoring System (EPSS)** is FIRST's system to describe the likelihood or probability that a vulnerability will be exploited by cyber attackers. EPSS scores are given according to a percentage likelihood that a vulnerability will be exploited. A vulnerability may have a CVSS score of 9.5, but if its EPSS score is 5%, it may be a lower priority on your pentest report than a vulnerability with a CVSS score of 5.7 but an EPSS score of 95%.

17. A red team simulates cyber attacks in its company's network according to new and emerging cyber threats. A pentesting engagement might only be done once and be conducted over the course of a week or two. Red teaming entails constant and continuous red teaming campaigns to simulate ever-evolving cyber threats over time in order to discover vulnerabilities. They're a type of offensive security specialty. Blue teaming is the defensive security equivalent. The blue team consists of defensive security specialists who conduct blue team engagements to simulate strategies to protect their network from cyber attacks.

18. When you mix red and blue, you get purple. Purple teaming is when the red team and the blue team come together to conduct purple team exercises together. The red team simulates cyber attacks while the blue team simulates cyber defense. Purple teaming can be a great way for offensive and defensive security specialists to come together to learn about their organization's security posture in order to improve it.

19. A pentest report is the product of your pentesting. It's an extensive guide to the vulnerabilities you found over the course of your pentest, how the vulnerabilities can be exploited to harm your organization's network, and how the vulnerabilities should be triaged and mitigated. All of your hard work as a pentester won't do any good if you can't communicate your security findings effectively to the defensive security team and corporate executives so that they know what to do with your information and security harden accordingly.

20. AWS Security Hub is where all of Amazon's native AWS security services come together. Data is aggregated from AWS IAM, Amazon Macie, AWS Health, AWS Systems Manager, Amazon Inspector, AWS Firewall Manager, Amazon GuardDuty, and AWS Config. You can see live information about your company's security posture in AWS, so it can be helpful to pentesters as well as security administrators.

21. Amazon Inspector is a first-party tool that's built into AWS that not only provides dynamic security data to be shown in AWS Security Hub but can also be used to conduct vulnerability scans when a security administrator or pentester decides to conduct one. It has some of the functionality of some of the third-party pentesting tools in this book, including classifying vulnerabilities according to CVE records and CVSS scores.

22. Prowler is a third-party security testing tool for pentesters to run a variety of types of vulnerability scans with pre-programmed checks and services. It can be used in AWS, Azure, and GCP. As with all of the third-party tools in this book, Prowler can be run from the command line. Prowler might be the most essential third-party tool in this book.

23. Pacu is a third-party tool that's used for finding security vulnerabilities in AWS. It has a plethora of modules that can be used to simulate a variety of kinds of cyber attacks; it's no mere vulnerability scanner.

24. A VM is a virtualized computer that's just another application as far as your host operating system is concerned. It virtualizes hardware components such as memory, disk storage, and network connections. If my Windows OEM laptop is my computer, a VM is my "computer's pet computer." VMs can run from an application within a host operating system, such as a VMware client or Oracle VirtualBox. Or, a hypervisor with multiple VMs can run directly within a computer's hardware; no host operating system is required. Within a host operating system, a VMware client or Oracle VirtualBox also serves as a hypervisor. I can run multiple VMs on my Windows OEM laptop, and the VMs could use Linux or Mac operating systems if I wanted; the VMs' operating systems don't have to match the host operating system. VMs are also commonly used in the cloud. Many cloud providers' IaaS services are basically everything you need to run your own VMs on the provider's infrastructure and nothing more.

25. Containerization is another way to use virtualization. A VM runs an operating system with all of said operating system's components, whereas a container only runs the components that are necessary to execute the code that runs through it. A containerization cluster can contain dozens of containers or more at any given time, responsive to what a cloud application's needs are at any given moment. Individual containers may only have a lifespan of days. Cloud networks have the infrastructure that's necessary for organizations to truly benefit from the scalability that containerization makes possible.

26. Docker is one of the more popular containerization orchestration platforms. Here's how it works. The Docker host runs directly on your computer or on the computer you manage on a cloud service. In the Docker host, the Docker daemon stores Docker images and makes and manages containers based on those images. The Docker host connects to a registry, which is usually hosted on an external network that is most often the internet. A Docker client is where you can execute commands to your Docker daemon.

27. Kubernetes is another popular containerization platform that builds upon the foundation Docker created. Kubernetes clusters contain a control plane, nodes, and Pods. Nodes are supported by the control plane, nodes support Pods, and Pods generate and run containers.

28. The control plane supports the entire containerization system and works as the vector between your Kubernetes-based network and the cloud platform. The control plane contains a handful of components, including `etcd`, `kube-scheduler`, `kube-apiserver`, `kube-controller-manager`, `cloud`, and `controller-manager`.

29. A container image is similar conceptually to the ISO files (disk images) of operating systems that can be installed directly onto a computer or used to make VMs, except container images are specialized to be used to make containers. Container images don't contain an entire operating system, just the necessary components according to how the container is going to be used. Sometimes, organizations will create their own custom container images. Container images can be acquired by third parties for particular use cases, or you could also use container images that AWS, Azure, and GCP provide for you.

30. How many pentesting tools you can use on all three cloud platforms were you able to remember? Here are all of the ones that are mentioned in this book: Prowler, ScoutSuite, Vishnunair's `automated-pentest` (only in Docker), `kube-bench` (only in Kubernetes), `kube-hunter` (only in Kubernetes), `kdigger` (only in Kubernetes), and Trivy (in Docker and Kubernetes).

Now, let's look at the tools that you need to do your job while practicing the exercises in this book and while working as a cloud pentester.

Your cloud pentesting toolkit

Here are the tools you should have in your cloud pentesting toolkit. You can use those tools to follow the tutorials in this book, and also to conduct real-life cloud penetration testing:

- The majority of Windows and Mac laptop and desktop PCs produced in the past decade work great for your cloud pentesting toolkit. You don't need to have cutting-edge hardware specs because the cloud network's computing power does most of the work. If you need me to be more specific, look for a Windows or Mac PC with at least a quadcore 64-bit CPU that's Intel or AMD x86-64 architecture or Apple M1, and with at least 4 GB of RAM. Ethernet and Wi-Fi networking should also be supported by your computer's hardware. Windows 8, 10, or 11, macOS 11 Big Sur or later, or any currently supported Debian, Ubuntu, or Fedora Linux operating system work great. It's also nice to have at least 100 GB of internal disk storage space, but it's very unlikely that you'd have less with the rest of those hardware specs.

- A currently supported web browser is a must-have. That's what you'll use to open the web consoles for AWS, Azure, and GCP. It'll act as your interface with the cloud network that you're working with. Web browsers are very frequently updated as far as versions are concerned, but any currently supported version of Mozilla Firefox, Google Chrome, Apple Safari, Microsoft Edge, or Opera will do. If your web browser is out of date, your browser will probably remind you to update it.

- A currently supported iPhone or Android smartphone is a nice-to-have. You can use it to run Google Authenticator or Microsoft Authenticator to provide an additional factor of authentication for your AWS, Azure, and GCP accounts. The security benchmarks for those platforms strongly recommend implementing **multi-factor authentication** (**MFA**) on all of your accounts. Here's Google Authenticator for Android: `https://play.google.com/store/apps/details?id=com.google.android.apps.authenticator2`. Here's Google Authenticator for iPhone: `https://apps.apple.com/us/app/google-authenticator/id388497605`. Here's Microsoft Authenticator for Android: `https://play.google.com/store/apps/details?id=com.azure.authenticator`. And here's Microsoft Authenticator for iPhone: `https://apps.apple.com/us/app/microsoft-authenticator/id983156458`.

- GitHub isn't something that you need to install, but you'll find it to be a very useful service to open in your web browser in order to install third-party pentesting tools and scripts. Maybe you should keep `github.com` in its own web browser tab.

- The AWS web console at `console.aws.amazon.com`. You'll be logging in to it once you set up your own AWS deployment or when you have access to your organization's AWS network.

- The Azure web console at `azure.microsoft.com`. You'll be logging in to it once you set up your own Azure deployment or when you have access to your organization's Azure network.

- The GCP web console at `console.cloud.google.com`. You'll be logging in to it once you set up your own GCP deployment or when you have access to your organization's GCP network.

- Prowler (`https://github.com/prowler-cloud/prowler`) is one of the most useful pentesting tools in this book. You won't be installing it on your own computer; you will install it on your cloud provider's computer. (The same applies to all of the third-party pentesting tools here.)

- Pacu (`https://github.com/RhinoSecurityLabs/pacu`) is an exploitation framework specifically designed for AWS.

- Cred Scanner (`https://github.com/disruptops/cred_scanner`) is a pentesting tool for AWS that looks for exposed access points and secret keys in files.

- CloudFrunt (`https://github.com/MindPointGroup/cloudfrunt`) is a tool for identifying misconfigured CloudFront domains in AWS.

- MFASweep (`https://github.com/dafthack/MFASweep`) is a tool that can be used in Microsoft Azure and 365 to check whether MFA is enabled. It's very important to enable MFA on user accounts because providing more factors of authentication makes a user account more secure.

- ScoutSuite (`https://github.com/nccgroup/ScoutSuite`) is a security auditing tool that works for AWS, Azure, and GCP.

- GCPBucketBrute (`https://github.com/RhinoSecurityLabs/GCPBucketBrute`) is a script that enumerates Google Storage buckets, checks whether they can be accessed and how, and determines whether they can be privilege escalated. Google Storage buckets are exclusive to GCP.

- GCP Scanner (`https://github.com/google/gcp_scanner`) is not an official Google project, but it's maintained by a team at Google. It's a GCP resource scanner that can help determine what level of access certain credentials possess on GCP.

- Docker Desktop (`https://www.docker.com/products/docker-desktop/`) isn't essential, but it can be useful for you to install on your local computer if you're pentesting a Docker cluster. It can be installed locally on Windows, Mac, or Linux.

- Vishnunair's automated-pentest (`https://hub.docker.com/r/vishnunair/pentest`) is a Docker container image based on Parrot OS that can be used to pentest Docker deployments. You'll actually be installing this in Docker, not directly in your cloud platform!

- kube-bench (`https://github.com/aquasecurity/kube-bench`) runs vulnerability assessments in Kubernetes to make sure they comply with the CIS Kubernetes Benchmark, which is a standard for configuring Kubernetes securely. It runs directly in your Kubernetes cluster, and it can be run within Kubernetes as a scheduled job.

- kube-hunter (`https://aquasecurity.github.io/kube-hunter/`) hunts for security vulnerabilities in Kubernetes clusters. It can be run from both a Pod within your Kubernetes cluster and from another machine. I used a VM in Azure to scan my Kubernetes cluster in Azure.

- kdigger (`https://github.com/quarkslab/kdigger`) is a Kubernetes-focused container assessment and context discovery tool for penetration testing. It's recommended to run it in Pods instead of on your host machine.

- Trivy (`https://github.com/aquasecurity/trivy`) is a comprehensive and versatile security scanner that can work with both Docker and Kubernetes.

- This one last part of your toolkit is absolutely essential but easy to overlook—a reliable internet connection! All of your actions with your cloud networks will need to go through the internet. Hopefully, you have a reliable internet connection at home or in your workplace. If not, an internet cafe or public library will do. But be extra careful to use a VPN if you're using public Wi-Fi for your work. Using a VPN at home is probably a good idea too.

Next, we'll look at some cloud- and pentesting-related certifications that you can choose to pursue that may help you acquire cloud pentesting jobs.

Cloud and pentester certifications

There are a number of certifications that may make you more employable as a cloud pentester. Some are from vendors; some are vendor-neutral. Some pertain to cloud networking, and some are general pentesting certifications.

Cloud

Amazon offers a dozen AWS cloud certifications (`https://aws.amazon.com/certification/exams/`). Here are the ones that are the most useful for cloud pentesters:

- The entry-level Foundation certification is Cloud Practitioner (`https://aws.amazon.com/certification/certified-cloud-practitioner/`). It covers the basics of cloud computing; no prior experience is required.

- SysOps Administrator (`https://aws.amazon.com/certification/certified-sysops-admin-associate/`) is the Associate-level certification that I recommend for cloud pentesters. When studying for the exam, you'll learn the following:

  - How to deploy, manage, and operate workloads on AWS

  - How to implement security controls and meet compliance requirements

  - The AWS Management Console and the AWS CLI

  - The AWS Well-Architected Framework and AWS networking and security services

- Solutions Architect (`https://aws.amazon.com/certification/certified-solutions-architect-professional/`) is the Professional-level certification that I recommend for cloud pentesters. You'll learn the following:

  - How to optimize security in AWS

  - How to automate manual processes

  - How to provide complex solutions to complex problems

  There are two certifications that I recommend at the AWS Specialty level. That's the highest level of AWS certification:

  - Advanced Networking (`https://aws.amazon.com/certification/certified-advanced-networking-specialty/`) can come in handy if you ever become able to develop your own cloud pentesting tools! It covers advanced network architecture skills.

  - Security (`https://aws.amazon.com/certification/certified-security-specialty/`) is the other AWS Specialty-level certification that I recommend. The certification validates your expertise in creating and implementing security solutions in AWS.

Microsoft has its own Azure security certifications (`https://learn.microsoft.com/en-us/certifications/browse/?roles=security-engineer&products=azure`). None of them are entry-level; they're at the Intermediate and Advanced levels.

- Microsoft Azure Security Technologies (`https://learn.microsoft.com/en-us/certifications/exams/az-500/`) is at the Intermediate level. The certification covers securing identity and access, data, applications, and networks through the Azure platform. It also shows you how to secure multi-cloud and hybrid-cloud networks.

- Microsoft Security Operations Analyst (`https://learn.microsoft.com/en-us/certifications/exams/sc-200/`) is another Intermediate-level certification. It's focused more on security incident triage, **incident response** (**IR**), threat hunting, **threat intelligence** (**TI**) analysis, and vulnerability management. All of these certifications are very defensive, including this one, but understanding the defensive side can help you improve your cyber offense.

- Azure Security Engineer Associate (`https://learn.microsoft.com/en-us/certifications/azure-security-engineer/`) is another Intermediate-level certification. It covers threat modeling, threat protection, vulnerability management, and managing your organization's security posture.

- Microsoft Identity and Access Administrator Associate (`https://learn.microsoft.com/en-us/certifications/identity-and-access-administrator/`) is also Intermediate. It covers the design, implementation, and operation of IAM in Azure Active Directory.

- Microsoft Identity and Access Administrator (`https://learn.microsoft.com/en-us/certifications/identity-and-access-administrator/`) is the next level up from the previous certification. It's at the Advanced level.

Altered Security (`https://www.alteredsecurity.com/`) is a third-party organization that's independent of Microsoft and offers a couple of Azure-related certifications that could be useful to you:

- Altered Security offers a free introduction to Azure penetration testing course at `https://azure.enterprisesecurity.io/`.

- **Certified Azure Web Application Security Professional** (**CAWASP**) (`https://www.alteredsecurity.com/azureappsec`) is a certification based on hands-on skills that you will develop in the labs that are provided in its training program. Some of the areas that are included are enterprise apps, app services, functions, OAuth permissions, API security, storage accounts, key vaults, and databases. (This isn't a free program.)

- **Certified Azure Red Team Professional** (**CARTP**) (`https://www.alteredsecurity.com/azureadlab`) demonstrates your ability to conduct red team exercises in Azure. The training program is full of hands-on labs on red teaming skills and techniques. The 24-hour-long examination is also hands-on in Altered Security's labs. (This certification also isn't free.)

Google, the company that owns and develops GCP, has a few cloud certifications (`https://cloud.google.com/learn/certification#why-get-google-cloud-certified`) for you to consider, as follows:

- Cloud Digital Leader (`https://cloud.google.com/learn/certification/cloud-digital-leader`) is Google's entry-level cloud certification. It's the Foundational level of the Google Cloud certification chain. The four areas it covers are set out here:

  - Digital transformation with Google Cloud

  - Innovating with data and Google Cloud

  - Infrastructure and application modernization

  - Google Cloud security and operations

- Cloud Engineer (`https://cloud.google.com/learn/certification/cloud-engineer`) is the next level up. It's the Associate level of the Google Cloud certification chain. The exam tests your ability to do the following:

  - Configure access and security in the cloud

  - Set up, plan, configure, deploy, and implement cloud solutions

  - Ensure the successful operation of cloud solutions

There are nine certifications so far at the Professional level of the Google Cloud certification chain, so I'll just point out the certifications that are more relevant to cloud pentesters:

- Cloud Security Engineer (`https://cloud.google.com/learn/certification/cloud-engineer`) covers the following areas:

  - Configuring access in cloud solutions

  - Configuring network security

  - Data protection

  - Managing cloud operations

  - Ensuring regulatory compliance

That's all very much on the defensive security side, but understanding cyber defense better can make you better at cyber offense!

- Cloud Network Engineer (`https://cloud.google.com/learn/certification/cloud-network-engineer`) gets a bit more technical into computer networking. It covers the following areas:

  - Network service configuration

  - Managing, monitoring, and optimizing network operations

- • Implementing hybrid interconnectivity

- • Implementing **Virtual Private Clouds (VPCs)**

- • Designing and planning Google Cloud networks

- One of the vendor-neutral cloud certifications that I most strongly recommend is Cloud Security Alliance's Certificate of Cloud Security Knowledge (CCSK) (`https://cloudsecurityalliance.org/education/ccsk/`). It covers the following areas:

  - • IAM best practices

  - • Cloud IR

  - • **Security-as-a-Service (SECaaS)**

  - • Application security

  - • Data encryption

The last cloud certification I will recommend is ISC2's Certified Cloud Security Professional (**CSSP**) (`https://www.isc2.org/Certifications/CCSP`).

The certification shows that you have the technical skills to secure data and applications in the cloud using best practices, policies, and procedures.

Pentesting

Now, here are some pentesting certifications that I recommend:

EC-Council's **Certified Ethical Hacker (CEH)** (`https://www.eccouncil.org/train-certify/certified-ethical-hacker-ceh-v12/`) is a certification that you'll hear about a lot. The learning program for the CEH includes over 200 hands-on pentesting labs, over 500 attack techniques, and many hacking tools.

The other pentesting certification you'll hear about most often is the OSCP, (`https://www.offsec.com/courses/pen-200/`), the OffSec (formerly Offensive Security) Certified Professional. Make sure you have a good understanding of TCP/IP networking, Bash and Python scripting, and Windows and Linux administration experience before you start working toward your OSCP.

Finally, CompTIA's PenTest+ (`https://www.comptia.org/certifications/pentest`) certification should not be overlooked. It covers the following areas:

- Planning and scoping pentesting engagements

- Information gathering and vulnerability scanning

- Attacks and exploits

- Reporting and communication

- Tools and code analysis

Now, let's look at what you should expect from pentesting contracts.

Pentesting contracts

The key difference between a pentest and a real cyber attack is that a pentest is conducted with the full legal consent of the owner of the computer system that you're pentesting.

Full legal consent shouldn't be merely a verbal agreement or a "gentleman's agreement" signed with a handshake. You absolutely must have written legal documentation signed by both a representative of the computer system's owner and you. Not having signed legal documentation before a pentest is a recipe for disaster because conducting the actions of a pentester without legal consent often constitutes digital crime in most countries around the world. There can be severe legal repercussions both in a civil court *and possibly a criminal court*. A signed legal contract is proof of what both parties consented to, whereas verbal agreements and other sorts of informal agreements absolutely will not hold up in court! You want to protect yourself legally, especially if there's a dispute at some point in the future.

It doesn't matter whether you're an employee of the organization you're pentesting, a third-party contractor, or working in any other circumstances. Nor does it matter whether or not you ever meet the members of your organization offline. Even a simple vulnerability scan without written verifiable mutual consent can get you into a lot of trouble. If you want proper legal advice, I strongly recommend speaking with a lawyer. A qualified lawyer will confirm what I've written here, plus may be able to advise you on whether or not the pentesting contract your client or organization presents to you to sign is in your legal best interests. Getting a lawyer to look at your contracts before you sign them is a good idea if you can afford the service.

PentestUSA has an example generic pentesting contract (`https://www.pentestusa.com/pdfs/PentestUSAPentestContractTemplate.pdf`) that I encourage you to look at so that you know what to expect.

Cure53 has a collection of pentest contract templates (`https://github.com/cure53/Contracts`) on GitHub that may be useful for you.

A good pentesting contract worthy of your signature will define the full scope of what you're expected to pentest. The defined scope may include specified IP addresses, network segments, and domain names. Make sure the defined scope is specific! You should never in any circumstances ever conduct any pentesting activity outside of the scope that's defined in your contract, even if you think it's in your organization's best interests.

You should also make sure that your pentesting contract doesn't expect you to do anything that's forbidden under Amazon, Microsoft, and Google's pentesting policies. Feel free to review those policies as often as you need to; they're listed here. Remember—you'll be pentesting in Amazon, Microsoft, and Google's infrastructure, so their rules trump what your organization wants you to do:

- AWS Customer Support Policy for Penetration Testing: `https://aws.amazon.com/security/penetration-testing/`

- Amazon EC2 Testing Policy: `https://aws.amazon.com/ec2/testing/`

- AWS DDoS Simulation Testing Policy: `https://aws.amazon.com/security/ddos-simulation-testing/`

- Microsoft Online Subscription Agreement: `https://azure.microsoft.com/en-us/support/legal/subscription-agreement/`

- Microsoft Cloud Penetration Testing Rules of Engagement: `https://www.microsoft.com/en-us/msrc/pentest-rules-of-engagement`

- Google Cloud Platform Terms of Service: `https://cloud.google.com/terms/`

- Google Cloud Platform Acceptable Use Policy: `https://cloud.google.com/terms/aup`

Now, let's take one last look at the product of your pentesting, the pentest report.

Pentest reports

The pentest report is the fruit of your pentesting labor. All of that hard work you put in over days or weeks running various vulnerability scans and simulated exploits is all for nothing if you don't communicate your vulnerability findings to your organization's defensive security team and corporate leadership in an effective way. They need to have all of the possible information you've found about your network's security posture communicated in a way that's easy to understand. If your pentest report is effective, then your organization will be able to use your security findings to security harden its network and applications.

Pentest reports can be anywhere from just a few pages to over 100 pages; it all depends on how many pentesting exercises and scans you've conducted. 50 pages is close to the average based on what I've experienced. But don't set a goal of making your report approximately 50 pages; the length will vary according to how much information you have to share. Your report can be in PDF or Word DOCX format. You should probably have your report available in both formats, just in case.

These are the sections your pentest report should have:

- An *executive summary*, at the beginning. It should only be a page or two long. This is literally what the executives look at. You should concisely describe the theme of what your pentest found. "The cryptographic keys are stored well, but too many accounts with privileged access lack multi-factor authentication, making those accounts susceptible to cyber attackers." "Our virtual machines hosted on Azure are fortunately difficult for external attackers to find. But there are way too many exposed services connected to our Google Cloud buckets." Make sure to mention that if the vulnerabilities you've found aren't mitigated, a successful cyber attack could cost your organization a lot of money. Money is what motivates corporate executives. If the vulnerabilities you've found could make your organization susceptible to a data breach, it's useful to cite monetary figures from IBM's Cost of a Data Breach Report (`https://www.ibm.com/reports/data-breach`).

- In the next section, explain the scope of your pentest and what kinds of vulnerabilities you looked for. You could call this section "*Audit Scope*" or "*Penetration Test Scope.*"

- The next section can be called "*Vulnerability Findings.*" A lot of the tools in this book will generate scan results with discovered vulnerabilities mentioned according to CVE records and, sometimes, CVSS scores. EPSS ratings are also very important. If you know a vulnerability's CVE record number but don't know its CVSS score or EPSS rating, I recommend looking them up from CVEDetails.com (`https://www.cvedetails.com/`). Sort the vulnerabilities in order of EPSS rating, followed by CVSS score. For instance, vulnerabilities with an EPSS rating of 90% should be near the top. If more than one vulnerability has an EPSS rating of 90%, mention the vulnerability with the higher CVSS score first. Be sure to include descriptions of each vulnerability from the CVE database, and communicate in your own words how an attacker may be able to exploit the vulnerability.

- If you have security findings that don't correspond to CVE records, you can mention them in another section titled "*Other Findings*" or "*Additional Findings.*" Here, you can mention things such as "these user accounts lack multi-factor authentication" or "web forms don't sanitize pop-up window output, possibly giving attackers information they can use to conduct cyber attacks."

- The following section can be titled "*Remediation Advice.*" You can mention how the vulnerabilities can be patched or otherwise mitigated. The vulnerability findings section should give the defensive security team a clue as to how to triage the vulnerabilities if you follow my guidance and order vulnerabilities from most critical to least critical (based on EPSS and CVSS). But you can still explain here in your own words how you'd advise the defensive security team to prioritize the vulnerabilities. They can't remediate all the vulnerabilities at the same time, and occasionally a vulnerability can't be remediated and a security analyst or CISO may need to choose risk acceptance or risk transference (which is usually cybersecurity insurance).

- At the end, you can add a "*Conclusion*" or a "*Summary*" that, as with the executive summary, generalizes the theme of your findings. But you can use more technical language here.

- If you have any references to cite, including things such as CVE records or explanations of exploits that other cybersecurity specialists have written about online; they get listed and hyperlinked at the very end.

Here are a few handy resources to help you with pentest reports.

I gave a presentation at *SANS PenTest HackFest Summit 2021*, titled "*Writing Reports: The Overlooked Pen Testing Skill.*" You can watch it on YouTube! (`https://www.youtube.com/watch?v=r-6LBjlM14Y`.)

Juliocesarfort keeps a very large collection of real-life pentest reports on his GitHub (`https://github.com/juliocesarfort/public-pentesting-reports`) that I recommend you look through.

Summary

Congratulations! You're ready to start your journey as a cloud pentester.

The tools you need for your work are an ordinary PC, an updated web browser, and a good reliable internet connection. You can conduct most of your work through web applications. Isn't the internet wonderful?

Amazon, Microsoft, Google, the Cloud Security Alliance, OffSec, ISC2, and CompTIA offer certifications in cloud networking and pentesting that may make you more employable.

All proper pentests begin with a well-written legal pentesting contract and end with a well-written pentest report.

Further reading

To learn more on the topics covered in this chapter, you can visit the following links:

- *MITRE ATT&CK database*: https://attack.mitre.org/
- *MITRE CVE database*: https://www.cve.org/
- *Common Vulnerability Scoring System*: https://www.first.org/cvss/
- *The Exploit Prediction Scoring System*: https://www.first.org/epss/

Index

Packtpub.com

Subscribe to our online digital library for full access to over 7,000 books and videos, as well as industry leading tools to help you plan your personal development and advance your career. For more information, please visit our website.

Why subscribe?

- Spend less time learning and more time coding with practical eBooks and Videos from over 4,000 industry professionals

- Improve your learning with Skill Plans built especially for you

- Get a free eBook or video every month

- Fully searchable for easy access to vital information

- Copy and paste, print, and bookmark content

Did you know that Packt offers eBook versions of every book published, with PDF and ePub files available? You can upgrade to the eBook version at packtpub.com and as a print book customer, you are entitled to a discount on the eBook copy. Get in touch with us at customercare@packtpub.com for more details.

At www.packtpub.com, you can also read a collection of free technical articles, sign up for a range of free newsletters, and receive exclusive discounts and offers on Packt books and eBooks.

Other Books You May Enjoy

If you enjoyed this book, you may be interested in these other books by Packt:

Practical Threat Detection Engineering

Megan Roddie, Jason Deyalsingh, Gary J. Katz

ISBN: 978-1-80107-671-5

- Understand the detection engineering process
- Build a detection engineering test lab
- Learn how to maintain detections as code
- Understand how threat intelligence can be used to drive detection development
- Prove the effectiveness of detection capabilities to business leadership
- Learn how to limit attackers' ability to inflict damage by detecting any malicious activity early

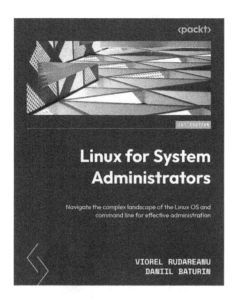

Linux for System Administrators

Viorel Rudareanu, Daniil Baturin

ISBN: 978-1-80324-794-6

- Master the use of the command line and adeptly manage software packages
- Manage users and groups locally or by using centralized authentication
- Set up, diagnose, and troubleshoot Linux networks
- Understand how to choose and manage storage devices and filesystems
- Implement enterprise features such as high availability and automation tools
- Pick up the skills to keep your Linux system secure

Packt is searching for authors like you

If you're interested in becoming an author for Packt, please visit `authors.packtpub.com` and apply today. We have worked with thousands of developers and tech professionals, just like you, to help them share their insight with the global tech community. You can make a general application, apply for a specific hot topic that we are recruiting an author for, or submit your own idea.

Share your thoughts

Now you've finished *Cloud Penetration Testing*, we'd love to hear your thoughts! Scan the QR code below to go straight to the Amazon review page for this book and share your feedback or leave a review on the site that you purchased it from.

`https://packt.link/r/1803248483`

Your review is important to us and the tech community and will help us make sure we're delivering excellent quality content.

Download a free PDF copy of this book

Thanks for purchasing this book!

Do you like to read on the go but are unable to carry your print books everywhere?

Is your eBook purchase not compatible with the device of your choice?

Don't worry, now with every Packt book you get a DRM-free PDF version of that book at no cost.

Read anywhere, any place, on any device. Search, copy, and paste code from your favorite technical books directly into your application.

The perks don't stop there, you can get exclusive access to discounts, newsletters, and great free content in your inbox daily

Follow these simple steps to get the benefits:

1. Scan the QR code or visit the link below

https://packt.link/free-ebook/9781803248486

2. Submit your proof of purchase
3. That's it! We'll send your free PDF and other benefits to your email directly

www.ingramcontent.com/pod-product-compliance
Lightning Source LLC
Chambersburg PA
CBHW080628060326
40690CB00021B/4853